Exploring
Oxfordshire
Surnames

People, Places and Lives

Richard Merry Sue Honoré Simon Draper
Charles Eldridge Christopher Farrand Tony Hadland
Simon Townley Jessica Feinstein

Matador
Unit E2 Airfield Business Park,
Harrison Road, Market Harborough,
Leicestershire. LE16 7UL
Tel: 0116 2792299
Email: books@troubador.co.uk
Web: www.troubador.co.uk/matador
Twitter: @matadorbooks

ISBN 978 1803132 037

British Library Cataloguing in Publication Data.
A catalogue record for this book is available from the British Library.

Printed and bound by CPI Group (UK) Ltd, Croydon, CR0 4YY
Typeset in 11pt Minion Pro by Troubador Publishing Ltd, Leicester, UK

Matador is an imprint of Troubador Publishing Ltd

This book is dedicated to all those people in Oxfordshire Family History Society and beyond who have contributed to research into Oxfordshire ancestors.

Contents

Foreword

Malcolm Graham

This book is a key outcome of the Oxfordshire Surnames research project launched in 2017 by the Oxfordshire Family History Society (OFHS). The project was built on foundations laid by the Oxfordshire DNA Project launched in 2013, and it set out to examine surnames recorded in Oxfordshire parish registers and other sources between 1300 and 1899 in order to build a comprehensive database of Oxfordshire surnames. The aim was to trace the whereabouts of these names in different parishes over time, their origins, hotspots, DNA connections and many other facets of Oxfordshire surnames.

Thanks to a small army of over 700 contributors, including 482 members of the Oxfordshire DNA group and around twenty transcribers of documents – not to mention all the local heroes who originally transcribed Oxfordshire's parish registers – OFHS now has a database containing over 100,000 incidences of individuals recorded in Oxfordshire with a given surname, including all spelling variants and close-sounding names, which will be available to OFHS members. Individual surname reports are gradually becoming available, describing the occurrence of a surname in Oxfordshire over time, noting family groups, and containing references to many other places where individuals with that surname in Oxfordshire can be found. The Society has a large pool of parish register transcripts, enabling project coordinators Sue Honoré and Richard Merry to map Oxfordshire surnames, although they are still keen to hear from people with a good pre-1900 Oxfordshire ancestry.

It was never going to be possible to distil all the above evidence into a single volume providing a comprehensive guide to Oxfordshire surnames. The editors Jessica Feinstein, Sue Honoré and Richard Merry have therefore compiled or gathered in a fascinating and diverse collection of chapters which provide family historians with an introduction to Oxfordshire and its surnames. Some of this information will almost certainly be relevant to their surnames of interest or to the lives their ancestors led, and it will act as a catalyst for further research into their family histories. This point, which is always a priority for OFHS, is emphasised in the final chapter by Jessica Feinstein who summarises the content of each preceding chapter and considers the implications for family historians.

Anyone who studies the history of Oxfordshire soon becomes aware of surnames that seem to have been associated with the county for a very long time. Richard Merry warns us, however, that surnames were rarely confined to one county, and the wasp-waisted shape of pre-1974 Oxfordshire meant that county boundaries were never far away. Sue Honoré stresses also that Oxfordshire has long been a 'through county' for people on a migratory route towards London and further afield, thus providing a major reason for the coming and going of surnames. The Oxfordshire Surnames Project does in fact include surnames from former North Berkshire parishes, and Sue Honoré rather charmingly admitted to an enquirer that 'we do count areas of Bucks, Berks, Glos, Northants, Warwicks close to the Oxfordshire borders as "ours" if families were fairly settled'. The top ten of Oxfordshire surnames in 1881 – Smith, Harris, Cox, Taylor, Green, King, White, Stevens, Butler and Gardner – does not feature typical Oxfordshire surnames such as Drewett, Quarterman, Mace and Shayler, but these are among the top 408 names that the project coordinators chose to investigate in depth for this book and for individual surname reports.

Surname research inevitably leads to queries about variant spellings and the origins of the name. The OFHS Family Migration Map features a dropdown index of popular Oxfordshire surnames from baptism records which notes, for example, twenty-five variants of the name Harris without even considering the dropping of the initial H. Richard Merry stresses the need for imaginative searching of old records, where the surname Eustace can appear as Yewstis! In another chapter, he discusses the Oxfordshire surnames derived from place names and, while cautioning against the presumption that such names represent places of origin, he concludes that they do imply movement from elsewhere. As ever, the family historian needs to carry out detailed research to confirm when and why an ancestor settled in the county. Simon Townley and Simon Draper, from the Oxfordshire Victoria County History, take the fascinating origin of surnames back into the medieval period, revealing the adoption of names based on places, topographical features, occupations, status, relationships, personal appearance and nicknames. William le riche was clearly the man to know in Ramsden in 1316!

Family history research can lead you into many new and unexpected areas, and other contributors to the book offer valuable guidance about plotting a way through them. Ancestors who seem to have 'disappeared' from official sources may be found in Catholic, Nonconformist or Quaker records, and those working in a specific trade such as coopering may be traceable through apprenticeship records and other trade documentation. DNA testing for genetic genealogy must be the newest avenue for further research, and will provide greater insight into the relatedness of people with Oxfordshire connections as the technology is refined and more people come forward to take the tests. For anyone who is looking to extend their research, or perhaps fondly imagines that they have completed their family tree, this book offers a plethora of interesting ideas and suggestions.

Figure 1. View from St Michael at the Northgate Church looking south-east towards Radcliffe Camera.

Introduction

The inspiration for the production of this volume came from projects of the Oxfordshire Family History Society: the Oxfordshire DNA Project, managed through FamilyTreeDNA, and the Oxfordshire Surnames Project. These projects gathered information from many individuals on their Oxfordshire ancestry as well as transcriptions of Oxfordshire surname lists going back to medieval times from a variety of sources. With Y-DNA testing came the opportunity to obtain DNA 'fingerprints' for Oxfordshire surnames. In addition, the projects generated many questions about Oxfordshire surnames and ancestry. This led to a need to connect good family tree information with DNA confirmation and to try to provide background on Oxfordshire surnames to a wider audience.

Most family historians diligently set about collecting documentary records relating to their families of interest. Increasingly, the descendants of families that have left the county in earlier times for elsewhere in the UK or other parts of the world want to know more of their origins and the lives and times of their ancestors.

Oxfordshire has a wealth of sources for information about life in the county over the period when surnames came into general use. The Victoria County Histories, now mostly available online, are a great example of sources of information about village, town and industrial life that may have been part of the lives of our ancestors. However, for most of us 'ordinary' people whose ancestors led unremarkable lives it may be more difficult to obtain background and some overview of how they came to acquire their surname, why they lived where they did, why they moved, and so on, though since 1841 the censuses have helped us trace people over the decades and learn of their occupations. Parish records since 1538 have also helped us trace our families, but may not tell us much more than names, parishes and dates. Surname dictionaries attempt to locate surname origins and may give some very general guidelines to the beginnings of a family, but do not provide detail and may be inaccurate when there are actually several origins to a surname, some of which arose in Oxfordshire as well as in more distant locations. Spelling of surnames varied enormously, especially when few people were literate, and it is often difficult to link or separate different lines. The broad Oxfordshire accent was certainly responsible for the early spelling of many of the names in the county.

It is therefore an almost impossible task to create a comprehensive guide to Oxfordshire surnames and this book does not attempt to do that. What we have attempted in this volume is to gather together a number of chapters covering what are perhaps disparate topics, but all of which relate in some way to Oxfordshire and its surnames, and could be viewed as an introduction to what is possible or new for family historians. We hope that readers will find information relevant to their surnames of interest or to the lives their ancestors led, and that it will act as a catalyst to conduct further research into their family histories. We are also producing individual Oxfordshire surname sheets which will provide information at a surname level, but that work will take many years to complete. A comprehensive database of Oxfordshire surname records based on our research and transcription work will be available in time.

There are so many people who have contributed in some way to the Surnames and DNA projects and to this book and we would like to thank them all. Each contribution has been valuable, given generously, added to our knowledge and often been just plain fascinating. The number of contributors now exceeds 700 people, so we can't name everyone, but thank you all.

No one person could pull together a book such as this, and we would like to thank the authors of chapters on specialist subjects – Simon Townley and Simon Draper, Charles Eldridge, Tony Hadland and Christopher Farrand. Several people reviewed chapters, including John Lenton, Simon Draper, Malcolm Graham, Susan Mattheus, Angie Trueman and Ellie Reid. Thanks are also due to Stella Bristow for providing information on Methodists, Helen Drury of the Oxfordshire History Centre for her enthusiastic help with images and Alan Simpson for his support with the OFHS Search Services.

Greg Rinder in South Australia has done wonderful work with the graphics for the book. It has been a true team effort by many people.

We could not complete transcription of records without permission from generous authors of original sources. They include, but are not limited to: the EurekA Partnership (Eileen and John Bartlett); Black Sheep Publications (Carol Richmond); the Oxfordshire History Centre; the Victoria County History for Oxfordshire (Simon Townley); Oxfordshire Record Society; Oxford Historical Society; Oxfordshire Family History Society (for the works of Howard Fuller and others); Jeremy Gibson; Joan Howard-Drake; Bill Seary; Derek Lester and John Hampden's Regiment of Foote; and Roy Edward Hurst.

We had nearly twenty transcribers, who worked through many volumes between them. A special mention is given to those who did a considerable amount of work: Peter Evans, Gerry Bolton, Sally Abbey and Jacques Honoré.

Finally, many thanks to Oxfordshire Family History Society – the Executive Committee and members – for supporting our projects.

Figure 2. Maud Reeves née Hewer with Reeves ice cream trolley.

About the Authors

Richard Merry

Richard is a retired soil and environmental scientist and a graduate of the universities of Tasmania and Adelaide. He was always interested in family history and began more serious researching about thirty years ago – his paternal great-grandfather was born in Eynsham. He has been active in his local genealogy society in Adelaide for some time, administers or co-administers four DNA group projects and the Oxfordshire Surnames Project, and is a member of the Guild of One-Name Studies.

Sue Honoré

Sue has spent her career as a manager in various international business and academic roles but has wider interests and has accumulated degrees in biology, business, networked learning and local history. She has been researching her own family history since the early 1980s and has been volunteering with the Oxfordshire Family History Society for nine years as the journal editor and joint administrator of the DNA and surname projects.

Simon Draper

Simon is Assistant Editor of the Oxfordshire Victoria County History (VCH). A landscape archaeologist by training, he worked as a local historian first for the Gloucestershire VCH before joining the Oxfordshire project in 2012. For two years from 2010 he was part of a small team at the University of the West of England which compiled a dictionary of over 40,000 current UK surnames published in 2016 as the *Oxford Dictionary of Family Names in Britain and Ireland*.

Charles Eldridge

Charles is a retired chemical engineer who worked in the oil and gas industry. His interest in family history was stoked by his paternal grandmother with two family myths that he later proved to be incorrect. His main interests are now linked to the use of DNA in genealogy which he has used to break down many brick walls that could not be solved with conventional records.

Christopher Farrand

Christopher is a retired union officer living in Ohio. He is a member of the Religious Society of Friends, and current editor of the Quaker Family History Society's journal *Quaker Connections*. He has been researching his Farrand ancestors from Kingham, Oxfordshire as well as early Quaker ancestors from the Banbury area.

Tony Hadland

Tony Hadland has been a member of the Oxfordshire Family History Society for more than forty years, at various times being vice chairman, journal editor and radio voice of the society. He has also been chair of the Oxfordshire Local History Association and administrator of the Vale and Downland Museum. For the Oxfordshire Record Society he has transcribed, translated and tabulated the eighteenth- and nineteenth-century registers of the Oxford Catholic Mission. He was one of the first OFHS members to use DNA testing.

Simon Townley

Simon has been County Editor of the Victoria County History of Oxfordshire (VCH) since 1996, and has a particular interest in medieval landscape, society and religion. In that context he has long worked with medieval bynames, which in the period before they became fully hereditary can shed important light on settlement, farming, trade, migration and social status.

Jessica Feinstein

Jessica has had a career in academic publishing and is a qualified genealogist. In addition to teaching family history, Jessica edits a family history journal and is the Education Coordinator for the Oxfordshire Family History Society.

Figure 3. The county of Oxfordshire split into parishes, based on an original map by Howard Fuller.

One

What is an Oxfordshire Surname?

Richard Merry

For many reasons this might be considered a silly question, but not to those interested in family history. The increased mobility of people over the past few centuries makes giving a simple geographical answer to such a question more difficult. In western society, surnames are a patriarchal thing and mostly have followed Y chromosomes. Recent advances in Y-DNA testing have given added impetus and a new way to establish origins, even when the family tree might be lacking.

So, what do we mean by an Oxfordshire surname, and is there such a thing? This idea may be approached in many ways. There will always be problems with such a task. These include the availability or lack of documentary records over time, the geographic shape of the county, migration into or from the county, common or rare surnames, whether family trees support the idea, and whether the surname was present in very early times. With respect to migration into or out of the county, can the presence of the university in Oxford be ignored? We can probably mostly ignore it as the proportion of students relative to the population of the county as a whole has always been quite small. Most students were likely to have originated from elsewhere or moved away from the county after completing their studies, though some may have remained, such as parsons or teachers. University support services, commercial people and many of the people of Oxford would have regular interaction with university staff and students. Surnames which were not usually recorded in Oxfordshire and arrived in the county from elsewhere through association with the university or for other reasons (such as land purchase, business or industrial development) may be identified by their first record appearing in Oxford or the other large towns and be distinct from cross-border spread. Other, rarer surnames disappeared over time through genetic drift or 'daughtering out', while many have prospered over the centuries.

Family historians attempt, with varying success, to assemble family trees and trace their line back in time to a town or village in or near Oxfordshire. Places of interest might be close to the county boundary and require tracking of families backwards and forwards across it over time. The modern county is bordered by six counties, with several more close by. During the nineteenth century, many Oxfordshire families had branches that were established in larger urban centres a little further distant – London and Birmingham – or in the industrial midlands and north-east of England, and perhaps south Wales where previously their surnames did not exist.

There is no doubt that many surnames have been associated with Oxfordshire over long periods of time. This may be easier to investigate if the surname is rare, but sometimes the surnames are not so rare or may be a particular variant spelling of a more widespread surname. One way of assessing this could be to compare the frequencies of a surname in Oxfordshire with Britain as a whole in the 1881 census. However, there are problems with this as families with male children to pass on the surname will increase and decrease over time, or may relocate into or out of Oxfordshire, or may have left before 1881. In Table 1 it is apparent that the ranking of baptisms for common names from parish register records in Oxfordshire over time (1538–1899) differs considerably from the ranking in the country as a whole from the 1881 census for many surnames. Although this is a crude approach, it does not mean that the other surnames are not Oxfordshire names but indicates that the apparently overrepresented surnames may be more significant within the county. Common surnames such as Cox and Gardner are in the top ten among baptisms in Oxfordshire, but much less frequent in Britain in 1881.

Using this way of comparing, other surnames apparently turn out to be much more highly represented in Oxfordshire than the country as a whole: names such as Wheeler, Simmons, Townsend, Coles, Haines, Howse, Castle, Busby, French and Wiggins, all of which are in the top 50 frequency rank of Oxfordshire surnames recorded in parish baptisms but rank between 200 and 1450 in the 1881 census. There are many more surnames that are

Surname	Number of Baptisms 1538–1899	Oxfordshire Baptism Rank	Oxfordshire Banwell Ratio 1881[2]	Whole Census Rank in 1881
Smith	13547	1	1.17	1
Harris	6093	2	3.96	27
Cox	5409	3	4.03	65
Taylor	4961	4	0.99	5
Green	4366	5	2.71	20
King	4347	6	2.02	37
White	4265	7	1.43	13
Stevens	4103	8	2.90	103
Butler	3753	9	4.43	109
Gardner	3715	10	6.19	184

Table 1. A comparison of the rank of common surnames among Oxfordshire parish register baptisms between 1538 and 1899 and the rank of the same surname in the 1881 census of England, Wales and Scotland.

less common which are also mainly found in Oxfordshire and adjacent counties.

Another approach could be to use Banwell Ratios.[1,2] This number is calculated *at a point in time* as the ratio of the frequency of a surname in a defined geographical area (Poor Law union, county, telephone district) to the frequency in a larger area (usually the country as a whole). Because of skewed distributions of county frequencies, the ratio is difficult to deal with in a simple way statistically, but higher values are meaningful and are usually a reasonable guide to relative frequency in the county. The use of Banwell Ratios is usually with relatively modern data (since 1881) because it is difficult to assemble the suitable records, at least prior to 1841. In Table 1 these common surnames with Banwell Ratios greater than about 4 indicate that their relative frequency in Oxfordshire is likely to be significantly greater than that of Britain as a whole. The Busby surname has a Banwell Ratio of nearly 33 and rarer surnames can be much higher (for example, Sturch with a ratio of 53, Goodgame 71 and Tustain 110).

Surnames are rarely confined to one county. As mentioned above, at some time in the past, Oxfordshire shared or was close to variable borders

Figure 4. A strong representation of Oxfordshire surnames in the police force in 1920. Group portrait of Police Supt. James Smith and colleagues, probably taken outside the County Police Station, New Road, Oxford. Featuring, left to right, back row: P.C. Higgs M.M., P.C. Wharton, P.C. Purrett, P.C. Cox; third row: P.C. Bond, P.C. Merriman, P.C. Lock, P.C. Rouse, P.C. Stevens, P.C. Jacobs; second row: P.C. Green, P.C. Hermon D.C.M., P.C. Harris D.C.M., P.C. Peachy, P.C. Panting, P.C. Holland, P.C. Allnutt, P.C. Cleaver, P.C. Dunn; front row: A/P.S. Jordon M.S.M., Det. Insp. Hedges, Supt. James Smith D.C.C., Major D. Roberts (Chief Constable), Supt. Charles Fernsey (Chief Clerk), Sgt. Hawtin, A/P.S. Hitchcock.

with Gloucestershire, Worcestershire, Warwickshire, Northamptonshire, Buckinghamshire, Berkshire and Wiltshire. The geographic shape of the county, with extended 'arms' towards Banbury in the north and Henley in the south-east and the many neighbouring counties, means that families frequently crossed borders so surnames are mostly shared with these neighbouring counties. Maps of Oxfordshire made in the eighteenth century indicate the complexity of borders of hundreds and counties at that time, and they were more complex in previous centuries. However, lines on maps mostly did not prevent people moving across them for accommodation or work. For administrative reasons we have the legacy of many records of interest to family historians being kept within counties. Guppy,[3] who worked on the distribution of English surnames in the second half of the nineteenth century, attempted to classify the surnames that he investigated into a class that he called 'Peculiar to Oxfordshire', found in three or four counties including Oxfordshire, but he and others did not have the modern advantages of indexed censuses, wills, parish records and DNA. His classification of Peculiar to Oxfordshire was not always correct and, as might be expected, did not identify many surnames that we can identify today.

Oxfordshire, aside from those academics attending or associated with the university, was historically a mainly rural county with a relatively low population. Sustained population growth did not occur until after about 1921, as explained in Chapter 3. Many families resided in a village or local area for generations, often not moving great distances beyond neighbouring parishes, although some shepherds and farm workers migrated twenty miles at a time, circulating among four to eight farms through their working lifetime, as shown in Chapter 4. Over time, individuals or families relocated within the county to the larger population centres such as Oxford, Banbury, Henley and Thame. With industrialisation, families began increasingly to move to the very large population centres of London and Birmingham, or to industrial and mining areas for employment, or to undertake emigration overseas. These movements were more likely to involve a greater number of people than movement to Oxford or Banbury or to other larger population centres in neighbouring counties. The momentum for movement increased in the twentieth century as travel became easier.

In investigating Oxfordshire surnames we have been guided by the expectation that the holders of a surname were resident in the county over a significant period of time, at least five or six generations (about 150 to 180 years), and therefore interacted in a significant way with the county's resident gene pool. Indexing of baptism and burial records by the Oxfordshire Family History Society has enabled a much more detailed examination of a large number of Oxfordshire surnames at a finer geographical scale. Some surnames among the parish records are clearly Welsh or from other parts of Britain but have been present in the county for a long time, including from at least the mid 1500s. These almost certainly require Y-DNA matching to identify their geographic origins but should be thought of as Oxfordshire surnames for reasons of longevity. Many of the surnames that have been considered in detail were recorded for periods much longer than six generations and since about the time that the parish register system began in 1538 or earlier,[4] until about 1900. In some instances surname records from as early as the thirteenth century can be found in other sources but it is usually difficult to demonstrate

Figure 5. The St Giles Fair in Oxford 1905/6. The boy on the left by the bicycle is Frederick William Merry, born in 1893 in Oxford.

a definite connection to later records. McKinley[5] analysed Oxfordshire surnames and noted the existence of many present-day surnames that were also present in the thirteenth century, usually from Hundred Rolls and often remaining in similar locations. It is uncommon that a modern, researched family tree will extend with confidence to earlier than about 1700, though many Oxfordshire trees have been extended to earlier centuries, and may be assisted if there is a relevant one-name study for the surname.[6]

In trying to answer the question posed, defining an Oxfordshire surname involves a number of considerations by which it could be judged. Some are listed below:

- a long and well-documented presence of the surname and variants among records such as wills, civil registration, tax documents, early rolls, deeds, muster rolls, censuses and parish registers for places within the modern borders of the county;
- published accounts associating surnames with the county over an extended period of time;
- nineteenth-century census returns indicating relative concentration of a surname in Oxfordshire;

- surnames that have confirmed association with the county through Y-DNA information, surname projects or the Oxfordshire DNA Project; and
- well-researched family histories.

Any or all of these could define an Oxfordshire surname.

Notes

1. Rogers, C. D. 1995. *The surname detective*. Manchester: Manchester University Press.
2. Archer, S. 2017. *The British 19th century surname atlas*. Archer Software CD-ROM.
3. Guppy, H. B. 1890. *Homes of family names in Great Britain*. London: Harrison & Sons.
4. Fitzhugh, T. V. H. 1988. *The dictionary of genealogy*. Sherbourne, Dorset: Alphabooks.
5. MacKinley, Richard Alexander. 1977. *The surnames of Oxfordshire*. London: Leopard's Head Press.
6. Guild of One-Name Studies. https://one-name.org/.

Two

Oxfordshire Surname Variants

Richard Merry

Historians and others interested in surnames soon realise that difficulties may arise in tracing families over time because of variations in spelling. Is the person whose surname is spelled differently from the one being investigated really the one being sought? Few surnames have had consistent spelling over the past five centuries or so, though most have stabilised in the past 200 years. Sometimes the variants are obvious, but for many surnames they are less so and some imagination may be needed to make connections. For instance, in searching indexed records for the Eustace surname, would you look under the letter Y where some early records appear as Yewstis? An additional problem arises in deciding whether or not similarly spelled surnames are just variant spellings or different surnames. Deciding some of these questions may require well-researched family trees or Y-DNA testing to distinguish them.

Classifying variants

It is difficult to define or classify variant surnames as there are so many circumstances that lead to their appearance and use. Some people distinguish *true* variants from *deviant* variants. A true variant is a surname spelling recorded as being used by an individual or recorded in documents that differs from the usual (or modern) spelling. A deviant surname is one that appears in records but is never consistently used and may only occur in a single or few instances. Variants that occurred in the past that eventually settle to a single form are *transitional* variants. Both of these types of variants could be *transcriptional* in that they can arise from incorrect recording, such as in censuses or parish records, or other situations where the usual spelling is not used. Poor literacy may mean that the holder of the surname is unable to correct an incorrect record, or the person doing the recording spells the name in an alternative way, phonetically as interpreted from verbal communication or as known to be spelled in other places. True variants that are transitional tend to be corrected to the usual form after a short period of time or to develop into a more usual form as spellings normalised and literacy improved over more recent centuries. However, the usual spelling may differ regionally, even within counties. Foreign surnames, particularly those of French/Norman and Irish origin, are usually anglicised over time. Some less common variants may die out if a male line ceases, or may live on in the former British colonies.

The 1881 census: an illustration of surname variants entering the records

For this evaluation, the 1881 census of England, Wales and Scotland, the Channel Islands and the Isle of Man was used as presented in the *British 19th Century Surname Atlas*.[1] Although primarily aimed at mapping surname distributions, its presentation allows some analysis of surnames and their variant forms. The Atlas listed a total of 422,733 surnames. The 'real' number of surnames in Britain was probably less than one-tenth of that number. How can we reconcile this enormous difference? With a little thought, it is possible to account for most of the excess. At the time of this census not every person involved in recording was fully literate and able to ensure that spelling was accurate or even reasonable and may have required help, although children may have had more skill in this than their parents. Enumerators collected the census forms and copied the information into the enumerators' books, which is usually as we see them today. Enumerators may not have been familiar with local accents and recorded surnames (and place names) as they 'heard' them, interpreted them or thought they should be spelled, or offered some phonetic alternative. Then there were subsequent transcription errors, familiar to family historians, with transcribers being instructed to record 'what they see, not what they think'. Discussions of transcriber accuracy, such as that of Goose for the 1881 census,[2] make interesting reading. A few transcribers were completely accurate while others introduced many errors. Considering these possibilities, the opportunities for introduction of errors were large in number.

Figure 6 gives some idea of the extent of the introduction of errors in recording surnames in the 1881 census transcriptions. Recording and transcription errors (deviants) were mixed among 'real' surnames and their 'real' variants. About 40% of the more than 400,000 surnames were listed once only. As many as 88% of the individual surname or surname variant records in this census transcription occurred twenty or fewer times. There is very small likelihood that these were unique records of extremely rare surnames, though some may be a unique record of a foreign surname. About 12% were recorded only twice and thereafter the percentages decrease until about 2% were recorded ten times. Those recorded ten times still amount to about 8500 different surname spellings, as transcribed. These lower totals probably relate to couples and whole family units for which the spelling of the surname was unusual.

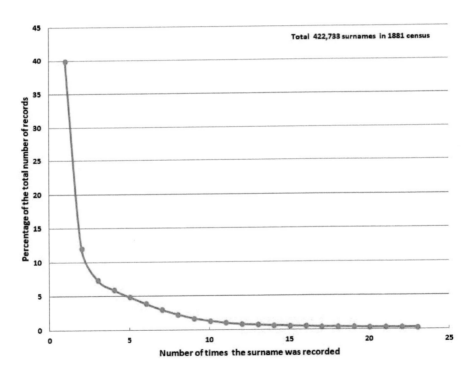

Figure 6. The number of times an individual surname (as recorded, including spellings arising by transcription error) was recorded amongst the total of 422,733 surnames and their variants recorded in the 1881 census plotted against the percentage of this total for single to 23 occurrences. Data from the 1881 British Surname Atlas.[3]

Variants in written and parish records

The surname variant occurrences in other written records are likely to show some features similar to the 1881 and other censuses, but perhaps with a greater likelihood that the rare, variant records for a surname were recorded in the earlier years of the registers, before they acquired more conventional and stable spelling. The spelling of the majority of surnames has varied over time and may not have settled down to a common spelling or a few main spellings until the later part of the nineteenth century. There are many reasons for these variations:

- In early times spelling was not standardised and it was not uncommon in these records, even those of the Royal Court, for the same surname to be spelled several ways in the same paragraph of a document.
- The common or regional spelling of a name may have become standardised nationally only in more recent centuries.
- Over time, some surnames could be shortened or lengthened.
- Illiterate people may not have been able to correct the spelling used by church officials or census enumerators even if they ever saw the version recorded or could decipher the handwriting.
- Some recorders had poor handwriting or indifferent spelling and later transcribers were left to interpret what they saw or faithfully transcribed a surname originally spelled in error.
- Church officials may be interpreting how a surname should be spelled (for example, by changing Filby to Philby) and were influenced by the local accent, their own accents and experience, or even what they thought the surname should be or how it sounded phonetically (this may include the addition or dropping of a leading H or N). In addition, although clergy may have trained in Oxford, many of them would have been from out of the county and probably unfamiliar with local spelling.

Some reasons for mistranscription among specific variant spellings could include:

- a flourish of the pen at the end of a surname resulting in deviant transcription with the addition of a trailing 'e' or 's' to a surname, or confusion in the transcription of these two letters;

- confusion of '-nam', '-num', '-ham', and '-man' at the end of a name;
- duplication of a letter, for example 'l' and 'll';
- addition or removal of a letter such as in '-e', '-y' or '-ey' endings;
- dropping a 'w' as in Benwell and Bennell, and possibly Bedwyn and Beddin(g);
- interchange of 'b' and 'p', usually as the first letter of a surname, that may be peculiar to parts of Oxfordshire, e.g. Banting/Panting;
- interchange of 'ea' and 'ee', 'ou' and 'ow', and similar sounding letter groups; and
- replacement of vowels, including 'y', with other vowels, e.g. Hiatt/ Hyatt, Couling/Coleing, Medcroft/Medcraft.

One of the consequences of earlier records changing the spelling of a surname was that the alternative spellings could be perpetuated. Today such surname relationships may only be connected or matched with some certainty by good documentary research or Y-DNA evidence. The range of spellings used for surnames can usually be found in surname dictionaries.

Many of these variants arise from sloppy writing or reading for transcription or indexing – the latter could readily be corrected by comparison with the original; something that doesn't happen often enough. However, for some variants, local accent and enunciation can be the cause, leaving the researcher to guess how a surname may be pronounced. Unusual spelling may give a clue to how a surname was pronounced locally. My grandfather was born in Oxford in 1879 and, many years ago, I spent some time trying to find his family in the 1881 census – the family certainly wasn't indexed under Merry. By already knowing the address at the time and following the enumerator's complicated path, the family was found at a known address, but was recorded as Murry (a transcriptional deviant). My recollections of my grandfather are dim, but I do recall that his pronunciation of our surname did sound a bit like Murry to my young Australian ear. As a researcher for this surname, I find the confusion of Merry with the Scottish Murray to be not uncommon. Searching back through Merry records, my family has been recorded (at Blockley in modern Gloucestershire and then Eynsham-Hanborough area from 1555) as Myrry and Myrrye (mostly sixteenth century) and very uncommonly Murrie before very definitely becoming Merry. In very early records a progression from Meri, Mery, Merey and even de Mereio to Merry can be demonstrated, sometimes with several different spellings appearing in the same paragraph of documents. During the sixteenth century a different Merry family at Lower Heyford usually had their surname spelled as Mery, in the seventeenth century as Merie and later Merry, in the eighteenth century as Myrry (even when a member of this family moved to a different parish) and later again as Merry. The pattern of these variant spellings would suggest that they were true variants that transformed over time and the Myrry forms may reflect local pronunciation at the time.

Figure 7. Fisher Row, Oxford, Oxfordshire. The waterman Abel Beesley on his punt full of bundles of rushes.

From the discussion above, it may be expected that, generally, the earlier a surname has been recorded in the parish registers, the greater the number of variants of all kinds that might be found, though there are reasons why this is not true for all surnames. That it is generally true is illustrated in Figure 9 for more than 400 Oxfordshire variant surnames where the recorded number from 1538 to 1899 is plotted against the year of first appearance in the baptismal records. A graph of burial records is very similar. Throughout the record there is great variation, especially from the 1540s. Even then, some surnames only had a few variants recorded while others had more than forty. After about the late 1500s the surnames recorded are likely to be mostly from new arrivals from

Figure 8. Fisher Row, Oxford, at Beesley's Rush Works. Osier peeling taking place in April alongside the river. The willow wands were made into a range of objects, such as the eel traps shown in the picture next to a foreman.

outside the county and if the recorder is unfamiliar with it he is probably more likely to ask how it should be spelled. In this discussion some surnames have been avoided as too difficult to distinguish. Good examples are the 'continuums' associated with Eyre, Ayres, Ayers, Ayris, Aris and Harris and the Basely, Beesley, Beisley and Bisley surnames, each with the more than seventy variants that have been recorded in Oxfordshire and thought to have multiple origins.

An example of the variations possible in the recorded spelling is that of the surname Druce, which is shown in Table 2 from the baptismal records for the parish of Marcham. This period of twenty-four years had four variants among nine records for what was likely to have been no more than two families. It is usually more common to have consistent spelling within a parish after about 1700 and not unusual to have consistent but different spelling in neighbouring parishes. Near to Marcham at Abingdon before and after the Marcham records and from Drayton from 1800, the Druce spelling for the surname is consistently used, though later at Abingdon the consistent spelling became Drew. At Witney, the spelling used was Druce in all but a few instances from 1637, when baptismal records of the surname appeared there.

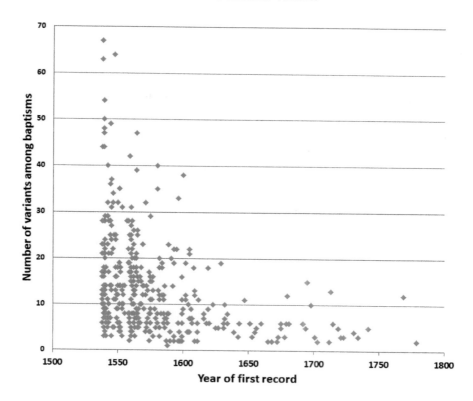

Figure 9. The number of variants of all kinds recorded for 406 Oxfordshire baptismal surnames plotted against the year of first record.

Figure 10. Druce & Co., drapers, London House, Sheep Street, Bicester, in the early twentieth century. The left part of the shop dates back to the seventeenth century.

Surname	First name	Parish	Year
Druce	Elizabeth	Marcham	1769
Drews	John	Marcham	1771
Drews	Samuel	Marcham	1774
Druse	Thomas	Marcham	1777
Druce	Richard	Marcham	1781
Drews	William	Marcham	1782
Drew	Richard	Marcham	1785
Druse	James	Marcham	1788
Druce	Jane	Marcham	1792

Table 2. Variation in spelling of the Druce surname in Marcham parish baptisms over 24 years.

Factors which influence the number of all variants recorded could include:

- the number of syllables;
- familiarity with the word(s);
- place names, local or further afield;
- from personal (first) names;
- surnames derived from occupations;
- removal to a parish where the surname was not generally known;
- the recorder's phonetic version of spelling;
- the recorder's version of how the surname was spelled elsewhere;
- later arrivals to the county; and
- names derived from foreign surnames.

To illustrate some of these points, Table 3 presents a selection of Oxfordshire surnames. Most of the surnames were present in Oxfordshire in the sixteenth century. There are always exceptions to what might be expected in the total number of variants, especially as transcriptional variants are included, and some of the post-1870 records are clearly transcriptional errors with the spelling occurring only once. The number of single records for a surname variant is an indicator of deviant records and is particularly high for Whicheloe, Lanchbury, Quarterman, Calcutt, Wakelin, Humphries, Wiggins and Fawdry.

Usually, the greater the complexity of the surname (i.e. more syllables), the greater the number of variants, exceptions being Drinkwater (where the components of the name were in common use) and some locally familiar place names used as surnames. These more complicated surnames usually carry more variants into modern times. Calcutt and variants are interesting because there are many places in Oxfordshire and nearby counties with similar names, which probably contributes to the high number of surviving variants. As might be expected, surnames with few syllables mostly have fewer variants recorded once.

Figure 11. St Leonards Church, Eynsham in 1906. Looking south from the medieval cross toward the mid 15th-century church and the Calcutt's shop next door.

Surname	First record*	Total baptisms	Total no. of baptism variants	No. recorded once	No. recorded after about 1870*	Recorded variants after about 1870
Single syllable						
Green	1538	5877	11	5	2	Green, Greene
Box	1539	344	3	1	1	Box
Cripps	1539	1234	14	3	1	Cripps
Cross	1539	1940	8	5	2	Cross, Crosse
Gomm	1558	791	20	5	3	Gomm, Gomme, Goom
Batts	1569	471	6	1	2	Batt, Batts
Biles	1594	209	4	2	2	Biles, Byles
Several syllables						
Quarterman	1538	1310	47	21	6	Quartermain, Quartermaine, Quarterman, Quarterman, Quartermaine, Quaterman
Lanchbury	1542	708	39	16	8	Lainchbury, Lainsbury#, Lamprey#, Lamprey, Lancebury, Lanchbury, Lansbury, Launchbury
Whicheloe	1547	514	64	28	7	Whichelo, Whichello, Whichelow, Whitchelo, Wichelo, Wichelow, Whicholle#
Drinkwater	1564	549	8	4	1	Drinkwater

Place name used as a surname – Oxfordshire

Place name						
Calcutt (OXF+)	1539	872	48	18	10	Calcott, Calcut, Calcutt, Calkett, Callcott, Colcut, Colcutt, Collcutt, Collicutt, Caulkett
Bloxham	1541	585	16	5	1	Bloxham
Enstone	1544	175	7	4	1	Enstone
Beckley	1553	395	9	5	2	Beckley, Beckly
Mullington	1557	130	5	2	1	Mullington
Clanfield	1569	324	23	9	1	Clanfield

Place name used as a surname – near Oxfordshire

Place name						
Padbury (BKM)	1539	220	13	8	1	Padbury
Clapton (GLS+)	1541	112	2	1	1	Clapton
Dumbleton (GLS)	1542	470	11	8	1	Dumbleton
Wing (BKM)	1545	490	5	0	2	Wing, Whing
Buckingham (BKM)	1546	1448	18	6	1	Buckingham
Kislingbury (NTH)	1605	148	22	10	1	Kislingbury

Place name used as a surname – distant

Place name						
Busby (NRY+)	1541	2063	25	10	3	Busbey, Busby, Bushby
Filbee (NFK)	1548	239	13	3	2	Filbee, Philbey, Philby (Filby about 1860)
Osbaldeston (LAN)	1558	108	16	7	0	Last recorded 1860
Blencowe (CUL)	1610	381	18	3	3	Blencoe, Blencow, Blencowe

From personal names

Surname						Variants
Humphries	1538	1777	63	23	8	Humfrey, Humphrey, Humphreys, Humphries, Humphris, Humphry, Humphrys, Humpreys
Wiggins	1538	1912	44	16	4	Wickens†, Wiggens, Wiggin, Wiggins
Hester	1543	946	10	5	1	Hester
Margetts	1544	481	29	8	5	Margett, Margetts, Margets, Margrett, Margretts
Wakelin	1575	670	35	12	4	Wakelin, Waklin, Walliken, Walkins

Later arrivals in the county

Surname						Variants
Gammage	1603	118	9	5	2	Gammage, Gamage
Mander	1611	314	7	3	3	Mander, Manders, Mender
Hounslow	1647	346	11	6	1	Hounslow
Juggins	1653	139	2	1	1	Juggins
Mobbs	1678	133	4	0	1	Mobbs
Grimsley	1723	131	3	1	1	Grimsley
Ilott	1742	144	5	2	1	Ilott

Occupational

Surname						Variants
Sadler	1539	804	7	2	2	Sadler, Saddler
Gardner	1544	4654	21	7	3	Gardener, Gardiner, Gardner

Occupational, cont.						
Hosier	1559	314	16	5	3	Hosher, Hosier, Hozier
Lardner	1562	1025	16	9	3	Lardner, Larnar*#, Larner†
Needle	1586	100	7	4	2	Needle, Needles
French origin						
Fawdry	1538	230	31	19	2	Fawdery, Fawdry
Havell	1540	89	8	2	1	Havell
Cambray	1540	99	9	4	2	Cambery, Cambray
Doyley	1542	269	23	8	2	Doily, Dolley
Neville	1543	978	11	5	4	Nevell, Nevil, Nevill, Neville
Florey	1564	272	14	7	2	Florey, Flory

* Note that the year of first record and the variants recorded after about 1870 applies to both baptismal and burial records.

† Also found in other counties.

These variants recorded only once.

† In Oxfordshire, Wickens was used interchangeably with Wiggins and Larner with Lardner.

Table 3. A selection of Oxfordshire surnames of various kinds and their recorded variants.

Surnames derived from first or personal names can have a great number of variants, many recorded only once, and more variants have survived to recent times. In contrast, those derived from biblical names may have fewer variants. Later arrivals also tend to have fewer variants while occupational surnames vary somewhat. Surnames of French origin show a range of variants, with Fawdry having many, including some starting with V.

In conclusion

The spelling of surnames can vary, so those searching for them should think broadly and may need to search much more widely than the obvious, common variants found in recent times, especially among early records. Careful searches of the records are needed, trees should be constructed and, for certainty, male-line Y-DNA matching may be required.

Notes

1. Archer, S. 2017. *The British 19th century surname atlas*. Archer Software CD-ROM.
2. Goose, Nigel. 2002. *Evaluating the 1881 census transcription: a pilot survey of Hertfordshire*. University of Hertfordshire. https://uhra.herts.ac.uk/bitstream/handle/2299/390/100251.pdf?sequence=1.
3. Archer, op. cit.

Three

Oxfordshire Population

Sue Honoré

Overall population

Oxfordshire was 44th in size out of 96 counties in Great Britain in the 1881 population statistics, with close to 180,000[1] people, on a par with other smaller counties such as Buckinghamshire and Cambridgeshire. Until recently it has been a mainly agricultural county with few large towns or cities.

Although population reconstruction prior to nineteenth-century censuses is fraught with danger, using good sources[2] and some consistent ratios to determine the data for the modern post-1974 county, a reasonable graph of Oxfordshire's population has been produced, as shown in Figure 12. Prior to 1900 the only significant increase in Oxfordshire population was between 1700 and 1850 when the population doubled in 150 years, with the biggest growth in the first half of the nineteenth century, when the county grew by just over 52%, but even that was below average for the country.[3] Otherwise, beyond the scope of this research, it is only from the twentieth century that Oxfordshire's population has grown significantly.

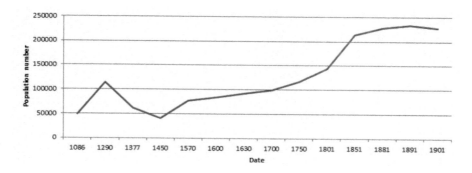

Figure 12. Oxfordshire (post-1974 county boundary) population reconstruction for 1086–1901 for key dates. Note graph dates not evenly spaced in time.

Even in nineteenth-century Oxfordshire, most parishes were stable or growing slowly. The main exception is Oxford city (see Figure 13). Of the city parishes, St Giles and St Thomas do increase sharply and St Ebbes grows strongly, at least until 1881; other city parishes decline. There is some growth in what would now be called Oxford suburbs such as Headington and Iffley. However, with few exceptions, namely Chipping Norton (with a large tweed mill) and Banbury (with strong commerce), most other county parishes show some growth in the first thirty years but, as agriculture struggled, the parish populations stabilised or declined. In fact, Oxfordshire as a percentage of the total England population had been in a steady decline from an estimated high of 2.3% in 1086 down to 0.6% in 1901, being less than 1% from 1841 onwards.

Implications and limitations in this surname study

What do these numbers mean for our study? Overall they are low, which can be a challenge statistically in terms of reaching conclusions about patterns and causes. Key indicators such as baptisms and burials are not high for many parishes and, in fact, may be relatively stable over the period of 1537 to 1899. Of the 408 surnames investigated in depth in this research, the ratio of baptisms to burials is 1.39 to 1 so indicating somewhat of a population increase but more likely an absence of people who had been baptised in

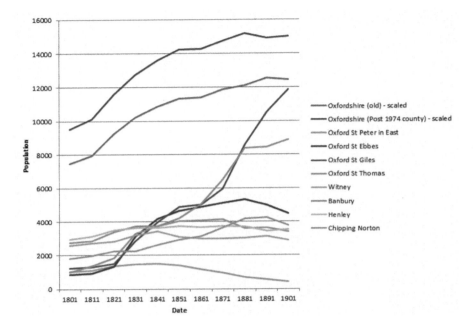

Figure 13. Nineteenth-century populations in Oxfordshire.[4] Note that similar flat graphs as in the Henley line can be drawn with values between 1500 and 4000 for Bicester, Burford, Deddington, Dorchester, Great Milton, Hook Norton, Stanton Harcourt, Thame, Woodstock and several inner Oxford city parishes.[5]

Oxfordshire but were buried elsewhere. Potentially this number reflects migration out of Oxfordshire and was influenced by Oxfordshire's position in England as a porous 'through county' – conveniently located as a place which acted as a stopping-off point for a short time.

The good news with smaller numbers is that in general, for surnames which were not ubiquitous in England and Wales (such as Smith and Jones), Oxfordshire provides the ability to trace distinct lines in the county and in some cases original immigrants. Unless a family encouraged other relatives to join them in Oxfordshire or were prolific, names may not have lasted long or in large numbers in Oxfordshire. Overall, researching Oxfordshire families may mean casting your net wider than this one county.

All the information in this chapter and Chapter 4 relates to our top 408 names selected as 'Oxfordshire' names and not to all names found in Oxfordshire. It also concerns the period 1537–1899 and is focused on baptism and burial data from Oxfordshire parish registers available in 2018. There are 398 parishes in Oxfordshire, which include some Nonconformist registers as separate parishes.[6]

Baptisms and burials

Comparing baptisms and burials

Some common patterns emerge from baptism and burial data for individual surnames as described below.

Smith, at the extreme as the most common surname in Oxfordshire, but not a distinctly Oxfordshire name, had a baptism to burial ratio of 1.3 to 1 and an average of forty-nine baptisms and thirty-six burials per parish where the surname occurred.

In the 408 Oxfordshire names studied, there was a much lower average of 8.19 baptisms per surname per parish in which they were found and 5.83 burials. Over the space of 363 years these are relatively small numbers.

Those names found in more than 200 parishes include Cox, Franklin, Gardner/Gardiner, Green, Harris, Hunt, Shepherd, Wells and Wheeler and these names also had relatively high total baptisms and burials (ranging from roughly 3900 to 12,500). Some of the names with the fewest parishes include A'Bear, Assendon, Beamsley, Buggins, Ell, Enser/Ensor, Harcourt, Pollicut, Rippendon, Stilgoe and Tugwood. In general, low numbers of parishes equates to low numbers of baptisms and burials, although some names such as Stilgoe, Buggins, Pitson, Wyton, Clisby, Coxhill and Pittaway are examples of surnames which simply stayed in a few parishes but had a moderate number of events.

Although across the county there are usually more baptisms than burials, there are some names where the reverse is true, including Aubery/Albury, Biggers, Blount, Colegrove, Fettiplace, Henley, Coppin, Gilkes, Lenthall, Lifolly/Lively, Minchin, Pangbourne, and Westcar where burials exceed baptisms by up to 22%. At the other end of the scale Pitson (with over 6.6 times the baptisms compared to burials), A'Bear, Assendon, Bitmead, Chown, Crapper, Ditton, Dunsby, Ebsworth, Pittaway, Pratley/Spratley, Putt, Quainton, Scarrott, Seacole, Skelcher, Swell, Towerton, Tutty and Witney have significantly more baptisms than burials with between two and three times the number of baptisms.

These ratios may help researchers to think about their own family structure and movement:

- More baptisms than burials – an increasing population in a given period; emigration; lack of male offspring (as females often change surname on marriage and are buried with a different surname).
- More burials than baptisms – a strong home Oxfordshire burial place which served even those who had moved away or alternatively families which arrived in Oxfordshire later in life.

Geographical spread of baptisms and burials

For this study the county was divided into six regions – North, South (includes Old Berkshire at 4% of the total), East, West, Central, and 'All', and individual surnames were classified as belonging to one of these regions based on baptisms and burials combined. 'All' meant the name was widely scattered across the county from at least 1537. The central region cuts across from west to east in a band in the middle of the county. The results are shown in a pie chart (Figure 14).

Even at this very crude level, although 22% of the surnames were widespread, the remainder had a core area where they could be found. The south, north and west were roughly equal in number of surnames, but the east had far fewer surnames associated with it. For whatever reason (the geography of the Chilterns, a more mobile population from Buckinghamshire, the strong draw of Oxford city and perhaps London, the surnames being outside our sample), eastern Oxfordshire did not produce as many 'Oxfordshire' names.

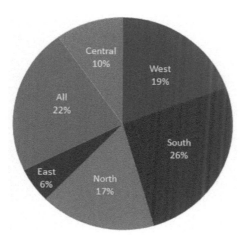

Figure 14. Geographic spread of 408 Oxfordshire surnames.

Introduction to case studies

The next step was to go into more detail, looking at individual surnames over time. The results in the following examples are in fifty-year blocks: a longer first one (1537–1599), then 1600–1649, and so on. Initial work was done on both baptisms and burials but in general they followed the same trend lines, often just at a slightly different time, so baptisms have been used in the examples.

To create a growing adult population, in the space of fifty years, there would need to be fifteen to twenty-five baptisms to show an active family of, say, a father, son and maybe grandson contributing to producing children – giving a child every two to three years.

The parish data are always going to be incomplete and there are many caveats impacting its analysis. Three are important here: the lack of parish records in the sixteenth century, missing records from the English Civil War and a potential lack of some Nonconformist records in the nineteenth century. However, the results are very interesting.

The typical surname profile

Most Oxfordshire surnames studied follow a common pattern of their frequency over time. In fact, 52% of the 408 names studied fit this pattern. In terms of baptisms the name grows slowly through to the end of the seventeenth century, accelerates upwards in the eighteenth century on a continuous fifty-year increase, and reaches a peak in the first half of the nineteenth century before declining (see Figure 15). When you compare it to the overall Oxfordshire population over this period (Figure 12), individual surnames form a different shape.

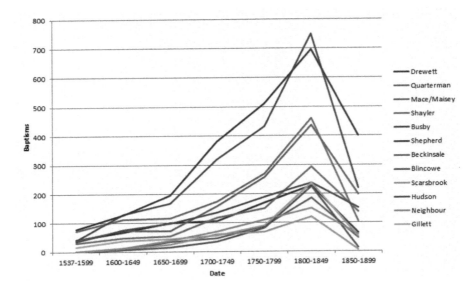

Figure 15. Typical surname profile for Oxfordshire surnames.

There are over 200 names in this group in total. Apart from the names on the graph, a selection of others showing the same shape includes Baughen, Bartlett, Beesley, Buckingham, Bunting, Calcutt, Couling, Collett, Cox, Crapper, Dumbleton, Gardner, Green, Gerring, Hadland, Harris, Howse, Luckett, Munday, Painting, Tombs and Wiggins.

For family history researchers this pattern may help to pinpoint time periods when there may be more (or fewer) records with that surname in the county. For some names it may mean it is worthwhile creating an Oxfordshire one-name study of that surname to trace all lineages.

There is an interesting variant on this pattern shown by 5% of the names, which shows a flattening of baptisms in the period 1750–1850 with only a marginal increase or decrease. Typical examples, apart from those drawn in Figure 16, include Cherrill, Cambray, Clinch and Pether. These families showed success up until 1750, but when the rest of the population was showing a large increase, appear to have maintained a relatively steady level of baptisms for up to one hundred years, before dropping back down in the late nineteenth century. These names may be those that were struggling in Oxfordshire more than most in this period, and for family historians this may be a hint worth investigating.

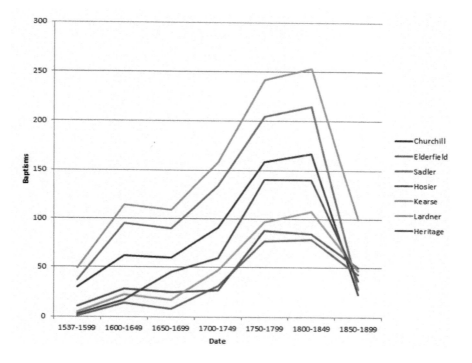

Figure 16. Surnames with a flat profile 1750–1850.

Variations in surname profile

Decline

There are some exceptions to the typical pattern of rise to 1850 then fall in the standard model above. The 'decline' profile is found in 11% of the surnames reviewed. There are two forms of decline for Oxfordshire surnames. In the first (Figure 17), a name will peak early and then decline from there on.

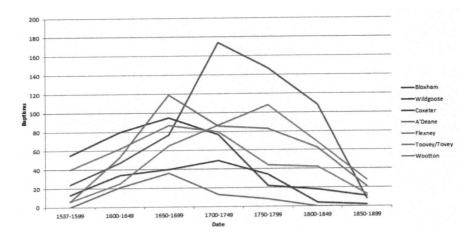

Figure 17. Early peak then decline profile.

Other examples include Fettiplace, Osbaldeston and Woodruffe (peaking 1600–1649); Slaymaker (1650–1699); Major/Maior, Blount, Sparrowhawk, Goodlake (1700–1749); and Fortnum, Lifoly and Souch (1750–1799).

Also there are names which may have peaked before 1537 and are in a fairly steady decline thereafter (Figure 18).

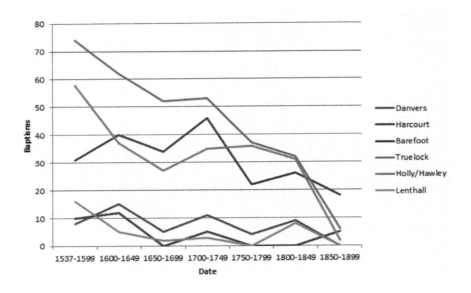

Figure 18. Surnames in decline 1537–1899.

Both these sets of declining names appear to be the more ancient names of the county – those that were more common in medieval and early modern times but which have since died out (or nearly died out) in Oxfordshire. Many of them appear to be the names attached to the wealthier people of the county who, by their nature, will have appeared in more records in earlier periods and who may have had many residences and hence were more likely to have baptised children elsewhere. One example is the Lenthall family who came from Hertfordshire in the fifteenth century and lived in Henley, Abingdon and Burford. Although present in low numbers in the eighteenth and nineteenth centuries in Oxfordshire, they had their heyday in the sixteenth and seventeenth centuries. The Knollys family of Rotherfield Greys had sixteenth-century prominence in royal circles. The Harcourt family were present in Oxfordshire in the twelfth century at Stanton Harcourt and Nuneham Courtenay but the lines 'daughtered out' in later centuries, and there is a large gap in baptisms from the early eighteenth century until the children of Augustus George Vernon Harcourt who worked at the university of Oxford in the nineteenth century. The Danvers family were in Epwell in the fourteenth century and well-known for living at Calthorpe near Banbury and Prescote, but registered their last few Oxfordshire baptisms in the 1770s–1830s in Claydon. Some of these families had Catholic connections and may not have recorded baptisms in conventional records.

Long-standing names

There are some names that, as in the declining variations above, seem to have been around in Oxfordshire for some time (at least since the sixteenth century), and manage to exist in a fairly steady state but, unlike the standard model, have one small early peak before 1700 and a second stronger peak in the early nineteenth century (Figure 17). These are classified as steady core Oxfordshire names for the period 1537–1899 and represent about 13% of the total. They provided enough male offspring to continue for a long period despite other pressures on the surname in the county (death, 'daughtering out', disease, emigration) and do thrive as the population increases, either through more children or immigration, but tend to fall between the standard names which increase continually and the names which decline.

Apart from those on the graph, other names include Aubrey/Albury, Brice, Ewers, Fidler, Kinch, Radband, Sabin, Seacole and Wing.

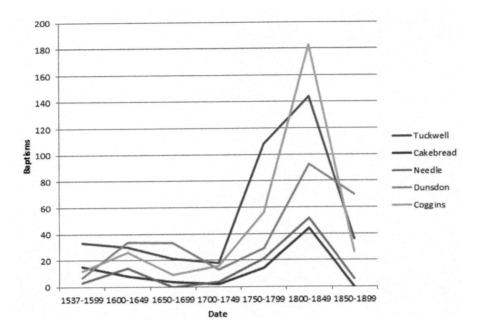

Figure 19. Core long-standing, but not prolific, Oxfordshire names.

There are other names that show an early rise but then continue in a stable state, usually between 1650 and 1849, before declining, as shown in Figure 20. This group makes up 8% of the total.

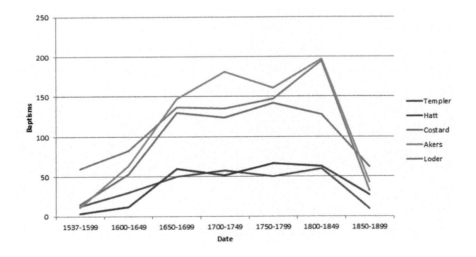

Figure 20. Stable baptism level especially 1650–1849.

Surnames that are close to this model include Coppin, Dore, D'Oyley, Ell, Jemmett, Lanchbury, Lindars, Piddington, Seary and Tredwell.

Two peaks

Yet another group of surnames has two (usually relatively even) peaks in their numbers at least fifty years apart, indicating either a new immigration or perhaps a family suddenly producing many more children after a couple of generations of relatively poor numbers. This shape represents about 12% of the total surnames reviewed (Figure 21).

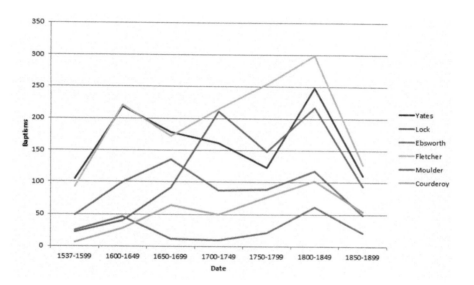

Figure 21. Two peaks of baptisms.

The second of the two peaks is consistently during the standard 1800–1849 period, but the first peak varies. Apart from Yates, Ebsworth and Fletcher (graphed), those that peak in the 1600–1649 period include Cross, Hitchman, Hyatt, Hedges, Messenger, Pulcher/Pulker, Salmon, and Sessions; those in 1650–99 include Parrott/Parrett, Box, Illsley/Hildesley, Warner and Blagrove; and those in 1700–1749 Gulliver, Towersey and Lovejoy. Amongst all the names that fit this pattern the most common period of 'dip' is 1750–99, a period of major changes in land management (enclosure, mechanisation) and changing job opportunities with young adults moving to London (in particular) and overseas.

Latecomers

Some surnames did not exist in Oxfordshire in sixteenth-century baptisms, but did appear later. They may have been latecomers to Oxfordshire, or in some cases their early records may no longer survive. They showed varied graphic profiles and success just as with the other names, although in general this group of surnames was more likely to thrive in Oxfordshire. Particular examples of latecomers were Beamsley, Coppock, Grimsley, Holyfield, Ilott, Putt and Westcar who all arrived from the late seventeenth century onwards. Other examples include Blincowe, Coppin, Costiff, Dore, Knipe, Lindars, Pollicut, Pether, Scarsbrook, Upstone and Wilsdon.

Surnames which increase

The vast majority of these 408 Oxfordshire surnames which have been around since at least the early seventeenth century declined in the second half of the nineteenth century, but there are a few exceptions (only 3% of the total) as shown in Figure 22. This group had obviously found a successful niche in Oxfordshire society in the nineteenth century, and were able to continue and flourish when others languished or left the county. Geographically they were spread across the county. Although all groups contained agricultural labourers in the nineteenth century, each of these families did have a large proportion of tradespeople, particularly the Coppock family, which may perhaps explain their success.

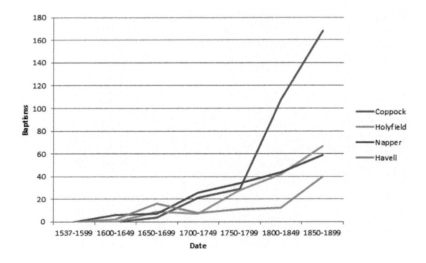

Figure 22. Names with rising late 19th-century baptisms.

Other examples of those that increase in the later nineteenth century include Clanfield, Wastie and Wiblin.

Witney – a case study

Figure 23. Eighteenth-century cottages in Corn Street, Witney, converted into shops.

Witney baptisms

Looking at the next level of detail, it is interesting to compare surnames in a specific parish to the county-level results. Witney is used as an example here, because of the availability of records over a long period and its size as a medium Oxfordshire town.

Names such as Beechey, Busby and Bartlett produce a standard graph of baptisms. Druce peaks early, then declines. Cox shows more of a core names profile. Akers had a stable middle period. Buckingham falls in the early nineteenth century when all other names rise, but then has a revival as others fall. So there is the full range of surname graphs in Witney.

What is driving these numbers at a local level? Each family has a different story. For example, names such as Buckingham and Akers were common in outlying villages for a long period, which may have fuelled influxes and declines as opportunities for work and social and religious communities changed over time in Witney.

A changing population

The research for this surname project shows that many surnames do not last for an extended period in Oxfordshire. The graphs indicate that often they seem to have a lifetime of one to two hundred years (or three to eight generations) and, as some names vanish, others appear. As an experiment to check this idea, names from six documents were pulled together for Witney. They were the Oxfordshire Hundred Rolls of 1279 published by Oxfordshire Record Society, the Hearth Tax of 1665, the *Victoria County History of Oxfordshire*, Volume 14 (Bampton Hundred part 2), the Protestation Returns of 1641, the EurekA Partnership *People of Witney Book 1* and names in Witney from the 1851 census. Surnames were grouped as for our original research into one master spelling for variants (e.g. Paintin, Panting, and Painting combined). The data was consolidated into 1126 surnames from these six sources and was then compared to baptism and burial records to ensure that the date range was accurate for that surname. Of course, this is not a full range of data for Witney and there may have been transcription errors and omissions in the sources. Also there is no guarantee that a surname at a later date indicates a solid pedigree back to the same surname line in earlier times; long term a more rigorous analysis could be completed. However, the results are summarised in Figure 24.

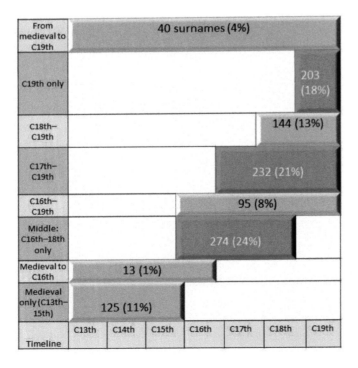

Figure 24. Distribution of surnames over time in Witney from 1279 to 1851.

Some of the key points from this analysis are:

- Very few surnames survive from medieval (4%) or even from the sixteenth to nineteenth centuries (8%).
- Most medieval names die out by 1500.
- Only a fifth of the names last 300 years from the seventeenth to nineteenth centuries inclusive.
- Most of the total names occur in the middle section – they arrive in the sixteenth century and die out by the end of the eighteenth (24%) – so follow the 'early decline' graph.
- What is surprisingly high is the 18% who seem to be present only in the nineteenth century – so newcomers to Witney.
- Chunks of roughly the same size (number of surnames) occur every hundred years.

These results mean that there was turnover or 'churn' in the population of Witney. It was not static, and names on the whole lasted about two centuries.

Only forty of the surnames can be found in Witney over the full range of time. They are mainly those medieval names that are derived from occupations, such as Collier, Dyer, Smith and Taylor and those from first names such as Godfrey and Martin. The names that occur in medieval times in Witney but never continue onwards in the records reviewed include surnames such as Babelake, Blewbury and Dukelintone (from place names), Cachepol (Catchpole) and others such as Bukpot, Water and Wellow. A small percentage of names extend out into the sixteenth century (and early seventeenth) in Witney from medieval times but then die out; for example, Fermor, Herring and Jope. The large group which exist in the middle period but die out before the nineteenth century in Witney include Aflett, Baseley, Barefoot, Ebsworth, Garlick, Gunn, Old, Peach, Perrott/Parrott, Priddey, Rainbow, Taunt, Vaisey, Whitehorn and Wilkes.

From then on there are names present in the nineteenth century but which first appear at different times: some start in the sixteenth century, some in the seventeenth, some in the eighteenth and some exist only in the nineteenth century. The pure nineteenth-century names are a mixture of common surnames such as Clarkson, East, Hardcastle, and Parr; 'Oxfordshire' names which may have been in the county for a long time, just not in Witney, who migrated into the town, such as Clack, Collis, Gillett and Mourby; and those names which are clearly rarer in Oxfordshire and are from elsewhere – such as Bumpus, Saltmarsh, Whittaker and Warrington. Given that 18% of the names fall into this nineteenth-century-only category, it indicates a strong influx of people into the town, probably driven by commercial trading opportunities and the textile industry. The names stretching from the sixteenth century include Ayres/Ayris, Beckinsale, Bishop, Brice, Buckingham, Hiatt, Humphreys, Kearse, Lardner and Yates. Those which start in the seventeenth century include Beechey, Druce, Hedges, Hitchman, Kite, Miles, Minchin, Munday, Paintin, Peisley, Shayler, Slaymaker, Tidmarsh, Turfrey, Verney and Willett. The eighteenth-century names include Archer, Bartlett, Batt(s), Burden, Coxeter, Early, Empson, Fowler, Knibbs, Lanchbury, Lankshear, Marriott, Nix, Ovenall, Phipps, Shuffrey, Tuckwell and Viner.

Again, this Witney example shows that there is a good level of surname churn in Oxfordshire over time.

Old vs. new names

Using the Witney data, two contrasting groups were extracted as a comparison – those names which were only in nineteenth-century Witney ('new' names), and those that had been present in the town from at least the sixteenth century, including those going back to medieval times ('old' names). There were 203 'new' names and 135 'old' ones; each name included all known spelling variants. These names were checked against the 1851 census for Witney to find households, ages, birthplaces and occupations. All adults (including spouses with no job or a status such a pauper or imbecile) and children over ten with a job were recorded. However, 29% of the old names and 39% of the new names had to be discarded. In most cases the name did not exist in the 1851 census – meaning that, although these people were present in the nineteenth century in Witney, they were not there in 1851 – which again indicates a good level of churn over the century. (A few exceptions were children present without parents and some naming/index errors.) The results are shown in Table 4.

	New	Old
Surnames	126	96
People	270	585
Households	159	319
Born in Witney	81 (30%)	330 (56%)
Born in Oxfordshire	179 (66%)	478 (85%)
Average households/name	1.26	3.32
Average qualifying people per household (adults/ jobholders over 10)	1.7	1.83

Table 4. New and old established surnames in Witney.

Even with a shorter list of surnames, there were many more 'old surname' individuals in Witney. Although the number of qualifying people per household is very similar, there were nearly three times as many households with the old names as the new. In most cases (from family trees, jobs and locations) these tended to be related people. Not only that, but the individuals with old surnames were also almost twice as likely to have been born in Witney and 85% of them had been born in Oxfordshire – usually in the surrounding villages, so a large number were local. Two-thirds of the new names were also local to Oxfordshire, so Witney did have a strong Oxfordshire population. The number of people in a household with named jobs was similar in both cases, showing a reliance on one or two people per household for income.

For all those who were foreign-born (i.e. not in Oxfordshire) the frequency of distribution of places was very similar for both groups (see Table 5). About half of the 'foreign' people came from the counties surrounding Oxfordshire (Berkshire, Buckinghamshire, Northamptonshire, Gloucestershire, Wiltshire and Warwickshire), with Gloucestershire being the largest source followed by Berkshire. Up to 20% came from the south-west of England and Wales, particularly Somerset which was known for its textile industry, and the next highest (15–16%) from the London area. Overseas places included the West Indies, Italy and India.

Place of birth	New names %	Old names %
Counties bordering Oxfordshire	49	52
South West & Wales	15	20
London & Home Counties	15	16
North	5	3
East	8	2
Scotland/Ireland/Channel Isles	3	5
Overseas	3	1

Table 5. Place of birth of 'foreign-born' Witney residents in 1851.

Looking at just the married couples, in the old group two-thirds had both partners born in Oxfordshire, whilst 38% were both Oxfordshire-bred in the new group, showing that a considerable number of couples had come from outside Oxfordshire to Witney in the recent years before 1851.

The new group had a foreign husband in 89% of foreign couples but the old group had a foreign husband only 48% of time. In both cases the older (working) children tended to be born in Witney. The likely scenario is that men came to Witney from elsewhere as young single men for work reasons, found local wives and then settled in the town. In the old surname group, however, in couples with one foreign partner, the opposite was true – it was the local men who more often found a foreign woman. It may have been that, although the men came from established local families and planned to stay in the locality, perhaps the large influx of young women coming to work in the factories and as servants from further afield caused the marriage situation to be reversed. Both groups had approximately a quarter of the foreign couples both being born outside Oxfordshire, so that was far rarer.

A similar result has been found in another study in Oxfordshire based on the 1881 census,[7] which showed 24% of Oxfordshire residents for the county had been born outside Oxfordshire.

Jobs in Witney

In terms of jobs, the new surname people were more likely to be at the wealthier end of the spectrum, involved in accountancy, banking or law, or to be independently wealthy people with no job (e.g. annuitant – 3% new vs. 1% old). At the other end of the scale, the old names contained more paupers in the community and people in the workhouse, often drawn from surrounding villages. The dominant industry in Witney at the time was textile manufacture, with mills employing 14% of the new sample and 16% of the old names. Not only were there textile mills but a strong presence of other jobs involving sewing, such as tailors, glovemakers, dressmakers, milliners, etc.; both groups had 11% of their totals in these trades.

The new surnames were more likely to be salesmen and work in shops. The old names were more involved in the more traditional areas of the building trade, ropemaking and metalwork (tin, smithing, brass). They were also more prominent in food production and selling (baker, confectioner, grocer, butcher, etc.) – 6% vs. 5% and in inns and the breweries (5% vs. 1%). The new names had more outdoor jobs involving farming or animal care, such as grooms or animal doctors (10% vs. 6%). General labourers were more likely to be in the old category but the servant level was equal (14%), mainly made up of young women who had come from nearby villages.

What does Witney reveal?

Certainly Witney supports the concept of an ever-changing population, with many surnames appearing each century, and often disappearing one to two centuries later. Christopher Dyer, in the annual British Association for Local History lecture in 2017,[8] said of changing English populations, 'This was not a new development consequent on advancing industrial employment and urban growth, as listings of villagers in the seventeenth and eighteenth centuries reveal a rapid turnover of population. In the fourteenth and fifteen centuries … it was not unusual to find that 80 or 90 per cent of names disappeared and were replaced in a hundred year period'.

Well-established Witney family surnames tended towards having individuals with more traditional jobs and had extended families living in the town. They tended to be at the poorer/middling rather than richer end of society. Recent nineteenth-century families came partially from the surrounding villages in Oxfordshire, but also from further afield, such as Gloucestershire, Berkshire and London. They tended to consist of fewer households, suggesting they were original immigrants to Witney.

Without further study it would be difficult to say if Witney were typical of the whole of Oxfordshire but it might give family historians a clue to the status and history of their own families in Oxfordshire towns.

Summary

There is no one model for the population of a surname in Oxfordshire over time, but the majority grow slowly until the eighteenth century, do well in the early nineteenth century, and then decline. The shape of a surname baptism graph may help to understand when and where a family thrived and if it had multiple immigrations or emigration from the county. There is a good level of churn in Oxfordshire surnames, with many lasting one to two hundred years in the county. Oxfordshire families tend to be local to the county but may have come from nearby counties, and some from further afield.

In terms of family history research:

- Look at surname graphs and use them to focus searches in different centuries or places.
- Consider a local Oxfordshire one-name study to better understand the wider surname group in the county. Ensure all variant spellings are included. Follow daughters as well as sons.
- Research local and social history to gain a better understanding of context of the family in Oxfordshire and why and when it may have flourished or declined.
- Look to see if it is possible to find the origins of the family, given where it first appeared in Oxfordshire and the time frame.
- Recognise that a family may not have stayed in Oxfordshire in any significant numbers for more than 200 years and may well have stayed in one location for only two to three generations.
- Look at family occupations to consider if they were likely to stay in one place or move, or if they were more likely to be in the country or urban locations.

Notes

1. Fransham, Mark. 2011. *200 years of the census in Oxford*. https://www.oxford.gov.uk/download/downloads/id/1046/two_hundred_years_of_the_census_in_oxford_march_2011.pdf.

2. Wrigley, Tony. 2007. *English county populations in the later eighteenth century*. https://www.campop.geog.cam.ac.uk/research/occupations/outputs/preliminary/paper9.pdf; Broadberry, Stephen et al. 2010. *English medieval population: reconciling time series and cross sectional evidence*. https://warwick.ac.uk/fac/soc/economics/staff/sbroadberry/wp/medievalpopulation7.pdf; Vision of Britain: http://www.visionofbritain.org.uk/; 'Table of population, 1801-1901', in *A History of the county of Oxford*: Volume 2, ed. William

Page (London: Victoria County History, 1907), 213–224. British History Online. http://www.british-history.ac.uk/vch/oxon/vol2/pp213-224; Wrigley, Edward Anthony, Roger Schofield, Ronald Demos Lee, and Jim Oeppen. 2010. *The population history of England, 1541–1871: a reconstruction.* Cambridge: Harvard University Press.

3.   Tiller, Kate and Giles Darkes, eds. 2010. *An historical atlas of Oxfordshire.* Oxfordshire Record Society. Vol. 67.

4.   Selected towns and parishes of Oxford for illustration. The numbers for the total population of Oxfordshire (pre- and post-1974 boundaries) have been divided by 15 to show them on a similar scale.

5.   Other parishes both large and small were evaluated but this group shows both typical examples (mainly steady graph lines along bottom) and the extremes – massive leap in Oxford city parishes compared to everywhere else.

6.   OFHS Search Services statistics, May 2020.

7.   Nash, James in Tiller, Kate and Giles Darkes, eds. 2010. *An historical atlas of Oxfordshire.* Oxfordshire Record Society. Vol. 67.

8.   Dyer, Christopher. 2018. Local societies on the move in the middle ages: migration and social mobility in England 1100–1500. *BALH The Local Historian.* 48(1).

Four

Migration in and around Oxfordshire

Sue Honoré

Introduction

People have lived in Oxfordshire since prehistoric times, but it is only since the development of surnames that we have been able to trace individual families successfully. The county is bounded by the Cotswold hills to the west and the Chiltern hills to the south-east, yet neither are steep and impenetrable to travel. Ancient trackways grew into Roman roads, with good passage from west to east, along what is now the A40 from Wales and Gloucestershire, and from north to south through Banbury to Oxford and Southampton. The salt ways from Droitwich through the north Cotswolds also formed important trackways. Several waterways were navigable, but most especially the Thames river provided an easy way to travel and transport goods through Oxfordshire. The location of Oxford means that it was often used as a stopping-off point on journeys from the northern counties and Midlands, as well as from Wales to London. Oxfordshire market towns such as Banbury, Henley and Thame became key trading points. Therefore, although small, Oxfordshire has for a long time been a place of movement.

How, why and when did people move to Oxfordshire? Where did they come from? When they were in the county, where did families move to and what drove them to change homes? Who stayed put and who moved frequently?

Immigration to Oxfordshire

As shown in Chapter 3, people came to Oxfordshire mainly from the west, south and north, following the core travel routes, and then settled in these border regions of Oxfordshire.

Movements from the west tended to be based on farming, especially sheep farming, as well as trade to and from Wales and ports such as Bristol. Until the eighteenth century several wealthy families, from the north of England in particular, invested in manors or farmland in the Cotswolds and into Oxfordshire as a way of securing a foothold in a convenient location closer to bigger trading areas and with access to London politics and society. In some cases Oxfordshire properties may have been the core family estates, but more often it was a manor or estate purchased as a supplemental location for business purposes, for cadet (lower) branches of the family or merely for show of wealth. Turnover was particularly high in the sixteenth to seventeenth centuries, however, with families remaining for only a short time. The prominent landowners became active in Parliament especially in the eighteenth century – such as George Lee, Viscount Quarrendon of Ditchley, the Spencer family of Blenheim Palace, Sir James Dashwood of Kirtlington, Henry Perrot of North Leigh and Thomas Viscount Parker of Shirburn Castle.[1] These estates will have required large numbers of workers who may have been sourced locally but also migrated from further away in Oxfordshire and other more distant family estates.

Specific trades, such as textile manufacture in Witney, brickmaking in Nettlebed, stone extraction in Stonesfield and major building projects in Oxford will have drawn workers from across the country. The university also attracted support services and tradespeople to the city, and may have encouraged graduates to stay in the county. Successful market towns attracted workers from the surrounding areas. Breweries in places such as Hook Norton, Oxford and Henley provided beer for travellers and inns supplied accommodation, food and a change of horses for those on the move.

There was some religious immigration, mainly in the nineteenth century, with groups settling near to those who held the same beliefs or whom they had known beforehand. In fact, migration was often driven by family and business connections, and this was certainly true in Oxfordshire, with evidence of waves of people moving to locations with known contacts. As shown by the case study of Witney described in Chapter 3, young people tended to move for their first jobs or when they were newly married, leaving the family home. Those in service or farm workers may have moved with their employers to other estates owned by the same employer, or to other local employers, frequently during their lives.

As a sample, some names that came to Oxfordshire from elsewhere can be seen in Table 6.

Spratley/Pratley	Yorkshire
Lankshear, Osbaldeston	Lancashire
Davis, Evans, Jones, Williams, Thomas	Wales
Blackwell, Dumbleton, Hiatt, Iles, Pearce, Preddy/Preedy/Priday, Snowshill, Trotman	Gloucestershire
Alderman, Batchelor, Buckingham, Gomm, Joyner, Quainton	Buckinghamshire
Blagrave, Illsley, Lambourne, Tidmarsh	Berkshire

Table 6. Surnames from other historical counties.

Home parish surnames

Professor David Hey, a well-known family and local history researcher, talked about 'country' – a local area that people knew well based on their personal experience. He believed that in every area there were 'core families' (and hence surnames) that belonged to these countries and remained there for many generations. He claimed that: 'Most people probably travelled, if they travelled at all, only short distances. Core families were to be found in virtually every community'.[2]

Much of Hey's research was based around his native Yorkshire; Oxfordshire, being much more dynamic and easily traversed, may not have had such strong evidence of static families, but the case studies below explain some of the surname distribution and movement in Oxfordshire.

Here the term 'home' is roughly equivalent to David Hey's 'country'. It is a single parish or cluster of nearby parishes up to about five miles distant where a surname remains over a long time, ideally with baptisms from at least the sixteenth century onwards. The surname is not found in any significant numbers elsewhere in Oxfordshire.

Although this is a judgement call, overall 54% of the 408 Oxfordshire surnames investigated seemed to have a home location, mainly in the west, north and south of the county. Some examples are included below.

Cherrill

Cherrill is a classic example of a name which had a very strong individual home parish and remained there or in neighbouring parishes over the period from 1537 to 1899. This name may have come originally from the place name Cherhill near Calne, Wiltshire, but once in Oxfordshire it is found almost exclusively in the parish of Dorchester. Cherrills appear in the lay subsidies back to the 1550s in Dorchester, as well as Court Rolls and wills but the parish registers only survive back to 1638. The name is found elsewhere in a few burials (e.g. 1593, Abingdon) and marriages (1543, Warborough) before that. If the neighbouring parishes which border Dorchester are included (Marsh Baldon, Chiselhampton, Drayton, Warborough, Brightwell, Little/Long Wittenham, Clifton Hampden, Nuneham Courtenay) then the name stayed within about two miles of Dorchester for over 250 years. Until the late nineteenth century over 93% of Oxfordshire baptisms for Cherrill were within eight miles of the village. In fact, the furthest Oxfordshire parish where Cherrill was found was Stokenchurch at 14.6 miles away, with only one baptism.

Drinkwater

The name Drinkwater is strongly focused in the parish of Enstone, where it is present from the 1560s, and also in nearby parishes of Tackley, Chadlington and Wootton, which together make up 38% of all Drinkwater baptisms.

Brice

For Brice, 62% of the baptisms from 1537 to 1899 come from Charlbury, Combe and Witney – just three parishes, with early numbers strong in Witney from the 1550s, although there are burials from the 1530s in Abingdon. There is potential that this is a locative name representing Brize (Norton).

Dunsdon

This name is found in the two Hanney parishes in the Old Berkshire area of the county from the 1570s, which make up 58% of total Dunsdon baptisms.

Regional surnames

Some surnames had a slightly broader spread across a region of Oxfordshire, as the following examples show:

Clack

Figure 25. The Clack family outside their home in Clanfield.

The Clack family was firmly rooted in the south of the county and was thriving, particularly in the period 1750–1850, with 52% of the Clack baptisms in an area extending to about five miles from Clanfield (the parish with the greatest number of overall baptisms), stretching south into western 'Old Berkshire' and north up into the parishes immediately above Clanfield (Figure 26). A quarter of the baptisms occurred in the southern half of the west of Oxfordshire – west and slightly north of Witney. The other large grouping of Clack baptisms was in the remainder of the Old Berkshire area of Oxfordshire and the south-east tip of Oxfordshire – so extending to the whole of modern southern Oxfordshire. There were a small number of baptisms in Oxford, including modern suburbs such as Summertown and in the east, mainly around Thame.

Early baptisms for this surname occurred in places such as Waterperry, Tetsworth and Waterstock in the east of the county but died out in the seventeenth century. By the 1620s there were a couple of men producing children in Crowmarsh Gifford and several in South Stoke in the 1670s–1680s, but baptisms in these parishes diminished as numbers increased in west Oxfordshire – in places such as Shilton from the 1660s and Ducklington, then spreading to Black Bourton, Bampton, Broadwell, and most especially in Clanfield (from the 1680s), all being neighbouring parishes, but also in Stanton Harcourt and further afield such as Harwell in the nineteenth century. The family were gentlemen and successful farmers, tradesmen and yeomen initially, but by the mid nineteenth century were mainly agricultural labourers.

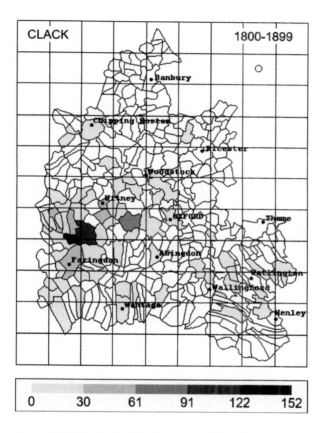

Figure 26. Clack, Oxfordshire baptisms and burials 1800–1899.

Munday

There is a similar story for the surname Munday. About 54% of all Munday baptisms occur in seven parishes (Aston Rowant, Chinnor (mainly residents of Henton), Ewelme, Henley, Nettlebed, Sydenham and Thame) – all in the same area of the south-east of the county (Figure 27). Although early records show the name in areas of the Vale of White Horse and west Oxfordshire (such as Great Coxwell, Sutton Courtenay, Woodstock, Bampton) and Oxford, it is the group in the Henley and Thame areas that thrive. The surname was in Woodstock in the fifteenth century, but it not known if the different branches are connected. Again, this family had several well-off members in the sixteenth to eighteenth centuries, including substantial yeomen in the south-east of the county, as well as several Oxford graduates and tradesmen such as vintners, brewers, butchers and fishmongers.

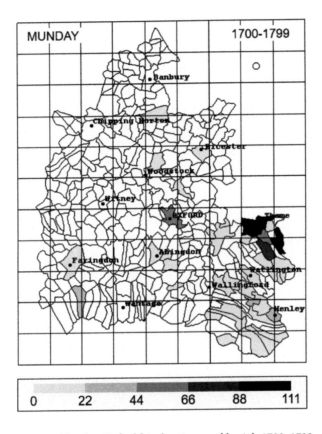

Figure 27. Munday, Oxfordshire baptisms and burials 1700–1799.

Calcutt

Calcutt was a name present in North Leigh in west Oxfordshire from early on and lasted for a considerable period, where the families managed farms until the late nineteenth century. Only then did baptisms in nearby Cogges surpass those of North Leigh; neighbouring Witney was also strong in this period (Figure 28). The name was also common in the Banbury/Wardington/Hook Norton/Deddington area, where the families had resided for a long period, becoming Methodists in the nineteenth century. The Calcutts have been in Oxfordshire since medieval times and the family of Richard Calcutt (d. *c*.1550) includes Sir Walter of Williamscote and Thomas of North Leigh, linking the families of the Hook Norton/Banbury/North Leigh areas.

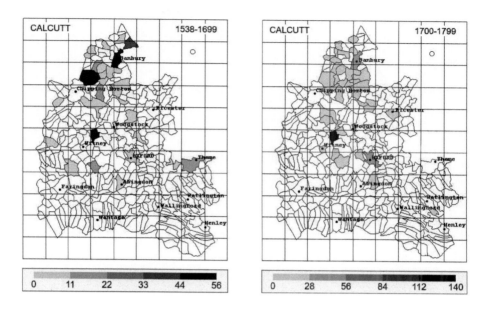

Figure 28a and b. Calcutt, Oxfordshire baptisms and burials 1538–1799.

Hirons

Hirons was based strongly in northern parishes right from the start of parish records, with particularly high numbers in Banbury, Wardington, Horton, Great Tew, Deddington and Barford St Michael, although some families existed in more central parts of the county at various times, most especially in 1650–1749. There were very few Hirons families in the south – which made up only 6% of the baptisms for this surname. The Hirons family in Wardington survived with lands from the sixteenth to nineteenth centuries.

Summary of home and regional names

From our research, the west of Oxfordshire has the largest number of examples that have a home territory, especially in the parishes of Shipton-under-Wychwood, Bampton, Witney and Charlbury. The north also demonstrates a long-term settling of families, especially in Banbury, Deddington, Adderbury, Cropredy and Tadmarton. Those in the south are focused around Henley, Wallingford, Great Milton and the Benson and Ewelme parishes. Eastern parish clusters are far rarer, with Bicester and Thame featuring. Of course, the records for many of these parishes have managed to survive for a long period, which helps. The named examples above show that some families came to Oxfordshire in the late medieval period into the sixteenth century, invested in land, survived the Civil War, profited from enclosure and managed to continue to own property in the county for several centuries afterwards, without moving far from their initial holdings.

Examples of other Oxfordshire surnames with a strong home base include those shown in Table 7.

Surname	Home parish(es)	Other strong parishes
Absolom	Wallingford	Cholsey/Hinton Waldrist
Baston	Bampton	Cumnor/Ducklington
Beesley	Warborough	
Churchill	Banbury/Deddington/North Aston	
Costard	Benson & Chinnor	
Dunsdon	Hanney	
Elderfield	Harwell	
Florey	Standlake	
Frewin	Henley/South Stoke/Ipsden/Caversham/Blewbury	Toot Baldon/Great Milton
Gulliver	Banbury	
Havell	Cholsey/South Stoke	
Heritage	Bicester	
Hiatt/Hyatt	Shipton-under-Wychwood	
Hosier	Standlake	
Lardner	Charlbury & Stonesfield	Witney & Shipton-under-Wychwood
Luckett	Hook Norton	
Mullington	Churchill	
Norcutt	Swyncombe	

Puffett	Broadwell	
Pulcher	Iffley	
Pusey	Denchworth/Uffington/Wantage/Abingdon	
Quarterman	Chalgrove/Garsington	
Rolls/Rowles	Witney	
Shayler	Shipton-under-Wychwood	
Townsend	Witney	Standlake, Shipton-under-Wychwood
Tustin	Adderbury/Banbury/Milcombe	
Warner	Benson & Ewelme	
Whicheloe	Appleford	
Wilsdon	Woodstock	

Table 7. Home/regional Oxfordshire names.

Population peaks in two places

Another pattern shown by several names is the 'two peak', and here a name may flourish in one parish and much later in another. The challenge is working out if the change is caused by a migration of one family or a new family appearing from elsewhere.

Lock

Lock is an interesting surname in that it is found throughout the county from the far north, with early records, for example, in Horley, near Banbury, down to Warborough and Henley in the south (Figure 29). Yet over 20% of the baptisms occur in only two places – Bicester and Minster Lovell. Given that the early Minster Lovell parish records are missing, the number may be even higher (no Lock baptisms extant in Minster Lovell for 1537–1649).

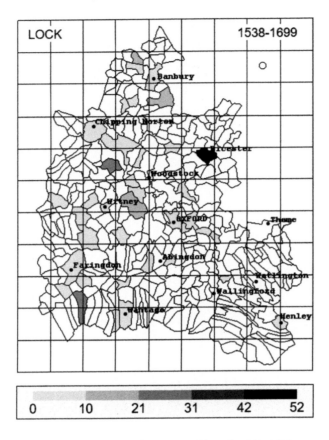

Figure 29. Early Lock baptisms and burials 1538–1699.

As Oxfordshire is relatively small, the population of a given surname in a given parish may actually be one single family. Looking at the Bicester population, that appears to be true, based on Nicholas Lock who lived in the seventeenth century and produced five generations of direct descendants in that town (although there is an earlier William buried in 1547). There are very few baptisms in surrounding parishes. The early Locks were successful butchers. Nicholas's most prolific children were William and Edward and they, along with their brother Benjamin, founded the main dynasty of this family, reaching into the early nineteenth century. But many of the children died early, as did the wives of the Lock men and some lines daughtered out with no sons. Others will have moved on from Bicester. Some went to Oxford and elsewhere, although not all have been traced. The Bicester Locks lasted roughly 200 years from 1600–1800.

Most Locks seem to be called John or William. Tracing Nicholas Lock, which is a fairly unusual first name for this family, throws up several early records in London as well as Kent (including the Feet of Fines in Ruxley, North Cray in 1467), Yorkshire, Norfolk and Somerset, so origins are difficult to confirm. Closer to home there are Nicholases in an area near Cirencester in Gloucestershire as well as Henley, Caversham and Charlbury in the sixteenth century, and Oxford and Black Bourton in the seventeenth century. The family were also Quakers, especially those around the Faringdon/Uffington area. So finding origins even for the 'Nicholas' branch(es) is a challenge, but it is possible that some Locks came from London directly to Bicester or through the Henley area and may also have come to Oxfordshire via Gloucestershire. There may well have been a migration from Warwickshire and Northamptonshire into the Banbury area.

Figure 30. Pether's builders working on restoring Minster Lovell Mill in the 1920s. Included are three members of the village Lock family: Back row on left, John Lock; front row second from left, Lovell Lock and third from left, Ernest Lock.

In contrast to Bicester, west Oxfordshire housed the majority of the Oxfordshire Locks, with 40% of baptisms in several interlinked parishes with frequent small migrations between them. The Minster Lovell Locks also fall into one single family, but in other respects it differs from Bicester. There were seven generations from the mid seventeenth century up to the late nineteenth century, but each generation had three to six males producing families in the village – and they were prolific. Several of these families had between eight and eleven children. The wives did not tend to die early and therefore stayed with the family unit throughout, providing stability and childcare. Where ages at death were documented, or could be calculated, they show that Lock men also lived long lives – many into their eighties and with an average age of sixty-five years from 1816–84. Those that left the village tended to move locally within a short distance. Key occupations were in stonemasonry or carpentry but also textile work. Like other Oxfordshire villages, however, the families deserted in the later nineteenth century and moved further afield for work, including overseas. Therefore most of the people in Minster Lovell died of old age, as there were few younger people remaining and few baptisms.

The Lock story is not all that unusual and any given Oxfordshire parish may have only one foundation family with a given surname. The challenge for family historians is tracing back from that foundation person to confirm that they were the first immigrant to that village and also to discover if that person was the first in Oxfordshire.

Sparrowhawk

The name Sparrowhawk is an ancient one, existing before the Norman Conquest,[3] but in Oxfordshire it occurs in two distinct clusters, one centred around the Bampton area (eight parishes) in west Oxfordshire and the other around Whitchurch/Sonning area (seven parishes) in the south-east of the county. The two clusters show the same population highs and lows over time and share some common first names such as Richard, Thomas and John, but it is not known if they are one common family. There are other early records in surrounding counties such as Gloucestershire, Berkshire, Wiltshire and Warwickshire, however.

Urban names

Over time there was movement into towns from the countryside following changes in land management practices. Some Oxfordshire surnames have a long association with towns, such as Gardener/Gardner, Needle, Wootton and Warland; others became urban names over time as people took up new employment, such as those with the Gillett and Viner surnames. Some names may have stayed in a given locality, but others, with contacts and relatives in other towns, may have migrated longer distances between the more urban areas of Oxfordshire (and those of local counties).

Names such as Gardener, Harris, Howse, Shepherd, Hirons, Lovejoy, Phipps, Radband, Tredwell and Yates occurred in the towns of Banbury, Henley and Thame in the 1537–1899 period, but with different population levels in different towns. Figures 31 and 32 show the varying fortunes of four of the names in Banbury and Thame. The Thame example, with negligible numbers of all names until the eighteenth century, highlights how local history helps to understand surname populations. Although Thame had been a market town since medieval times, it had a big expansion in the eighteenth and nineteenth centuries, attracting people to live and work in its market and trading areas, mainly from nearby villages.[5]

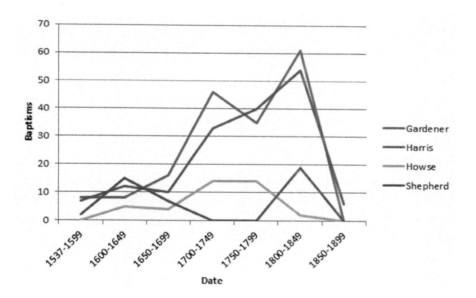

Figure 31. Gardener, Harris, Howse and Shepherd baptisms in Banbury.

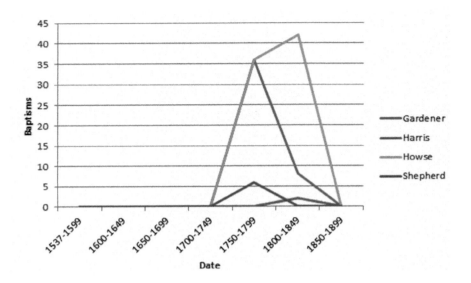

Figure 32. Gardner, Harris, Howse and Shepherd baptisms in Thame.

Some surnames existed in reasonable numbers in three different-sized locations in Oxfordshire – village, town and city, but numbers grew enormously in the Oxford city parishes from the mid eighteenth century. An example, Crapper, is shown in Figure 33, appearing in records from the sixteenth century in the village of Adderbury, and from the eighteenth century in the town parish of Abingdon St Helen's as well as Oxford and its current suburbs. Other names with a similar story in these three parishes include Blay, Cox and Salmon.

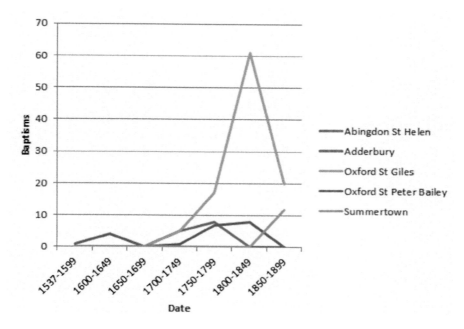

Figure 33. Crapper distribution in Adderbury, Abingdon and Oxford areas.

The above examples show population numbers, but not precise family migration patterns, which are now explored through a few case studies.

Family migration examples

Ferriman

One way to look at the movement of a family is to search for all records of that family within original sources and then to map the name by location and by time.

The surname Ferriman is usually defined as originating from a person who keeps a ferry. The name is thought by some to come from Yorkshire, but given Oxfordshire's many rivers and with mentions of named ferrymen at Toot Baldon in 1257, Sandford-on-Thames in 1295, Bablock Hythe in the twelfth and thirteenth centuries, Osney in 1467 and several other riverside locations, it may well be that the surname arose locally in Oxfordshire/Berkshire.[6] The Thames in particular acted as a key method of transport and river crossings were (and are) essential in the county.

From 1500, early occurrences of the name were in Sonning, Berkshire (although no connection with the Oxfordshire group has been found), but also in a relatively small cluster of parishes from the Abingdon area along the Ridgeway in the Vale of White Horse (marked as '1' in Figure 34). There is a marriage in Denchworth in 1541 and a baptism in Abingdon in the 1560s. It is possible that these early families may well be related, with residency circulating around nearby villages. In the early seventeenth century there were three strong groups – in Northmoor, Oxford and Burford as well as a spread to Marcham and Garford (marked '2'). From the 1660s the name was recorded in several parishes near to Burford as well as spreading southwards in the Vale of White Horse (marked '3'). Finally, looking at the early eighteenth century (marked '4'), it could be found moving north and east. The name then became very firmly rooted in Leafield, providing the greatest number of records into the late eighteenth and nineteenth centuries. The family were well known there for running the George Inn, and later generations even included a sea captain or two, harking back to old times.

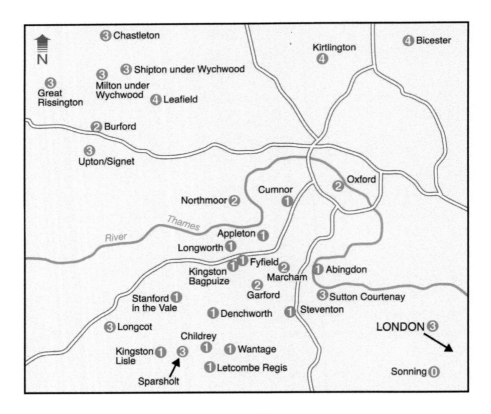

Figure 34. Location of the surname Ferriman from 1510–1750.
Key: 0 = early Berkshire; 1 = 1530–1610; 2 = 1600–1650; 3 = 1660–1700; 4 = 1700–1750.

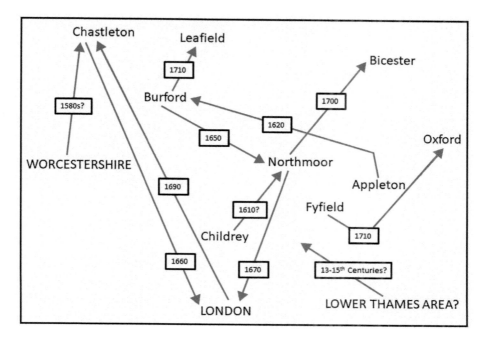

Figure 35. Approximate decades of Ferriman migration with key locations.

One item to note in terms of parish records is that the wealthier Northmoor Ferriman family travelled to Oxford to record many of their life events. A given baptism, marriage or burial place may not signify residence.

The Ferriman family may have come from an old ferry-managing family somewhere on the Thames and did not move far from medieval times to the nineteenth century, gradually fanning out in south-west Oxfordshire. There are other connections with London and potentially Worcestershire.

Other examples of migrating families include:

Pratley

Like Ferriman, Pratley became a very common name in Leafield. Its origins were possibly from near Beverley in Yorkshire, or even from a Norman name. It has been variously spelled Sprotley, Spratley and eventually Pratley from the mid seventeenth century. The Oxfordshire family came via Maids Moreton in Buckinghamshire to South Newington near Banbury in about 1540 with a descendant, William, moving to Leafield and founding a large dynasty there. In the period from 1537–1899 over 70% of the baptisms for

Pratley were in five nearby parishes in west Oxfordshire – Leafield, Shipton and Ascott-under-Wychwood, Hailey and Finstock. Once settled, this family had a strong sense of 'home', limited to a very small area of the county.

Blencowe/Blinco

This name seems to have originated from Blencow in Cumbria[4] but came into Oxfordshire possibly in several waves of related families from Northamptonshire (around Middleton Cheney) and Buckinghamshire. They were in Charlton-on-Otmoor and Horley in the late sixteenth century, as well as the general Banbury/Adderbury area and Thame in the early seventeenth century. The family later became more prominent in Oxford city. There was a known illegitimacy in 1803 which means that some Blencowe families today may not have come from a male genetic Blencowe surname line. This example demonstrates that political lines such as county boundaries had no real meaning to people, who moved freely within a small geographic area.

Lindars

Lindars as a surname is found in the Sandford St Martin/Chipping Norton area in the north-west of the county in the late sixteenth and seventeenth centuries, but died out there and flourished in south-east Oxfordshire in Tetsworth from the 1730s through to the end of the nineteenth century. The family produced five generations in the Chipping Norton area, but John Lindars (b. 1705) then married Elizabeth Allen in Thame and migrated to Tetsworth, where their children were born, and founded a dynasty of at least another five generations in this area. Although other Lindars families were found in southern Oxfordshire and in the London area as well as further afield, such as Norfolk, this family story is a classic one of one family member moving location but, through subsequent stability in the new region, causing a hotspot for a surname in a small geographic area.

Dumbleton: a case study

Tracing surname movements can be a challenge, especially when the name is common and may have several starting points. It is also tricky during the time between the scant medieval records and the sixteenth century, but a

Figure 36. The village of Dumbleton in Gloucestershire, probable origin of the Dumbleton surname, and burial place of Patrick Leigh Fermor.

mini one-name study involving parish records, wills, (verified) family trees and other documents combined with DNA may help. As an example, the surname Dumbleton is shown here (Figure 37) with a focus on the families from 1500–1800, although more than eleven generations have been traced on some lines. Dumbleton is said by most surname dictionaries to have arisen from the village of Dumbleton in Gloucestershire, only about twenty miles north-west of Chipping Norton. It is a particularly common surname for the relative population size of Oxfordshire, Warwickshire and Gloucestershire. The families in this period were generally farmers, ranging from yeomen to agricultural labourers, but also commonly involved in trades such as blacksmithing and shoemaking.

The majority of the traceable Oxfordshire Dumbletons seem to have come from Tadmarton and the nearby village of Swalcliffe, mainly as the offspring of Thomas Dumbleton (*c*.1508–1569) of Tadmarton who had multiple marriages and many children (who in turn were fairly prolific). Although many of the Dumbleton family remained over the generations in these two villages and the general area near Banbury, it is surprising how quickly the surname spread out. In 150 years the family had covered a large portion of

Oxfordshire. Some migrations were gradual, with a son moving one or two villages away from his father. Others were more dramatic. The family was not restricted by political county boundaries and there were two-way movements between Oxfordshire and Gloucestershire, Worcestershire, Warwickshire and Northamptonshire in particular. Migration was not random: some sons seemed to follow earlier family migrants, especially to the Milton/Adderbury area; to Shipston-on-Stour; to the Chastleton area near Moreton-in-Marsh; and to the area of Buckinghamshire on the border with Oxfordshire near Piddington, Ludgershall and Boarstall.

There were also several populations just outside Oxfordshire, which may in time prove to be connected to this line, including a well-to-do family in the Batsford/Bourton-on-the-Hill area (located between Dumbleton and Oxfordshire) in the early sixteenth century with Dumbleton first names in common with the Oxfordshire branch. There was another group in south Warwickshire, and one in Northamptonshire in the Middleton Cheney/Chacombe/Marston St Lawrence region. There were also a few Dumbletons in early times in southern Oxfordshire near Cuddesdon, Berrick Salome and Chalgrove who have yet to be connected, along with one family in Caversham and another in the Bicester area. However, all these families lived in a fairly concentrated area of England.

The map shows only a few of the earlier movements of the Dumbletons out of Tadmarton and Swalcliffe, otherwise it would become too difficult to read, but it does highlight how one branch of a family can spread out from a central point and create subsequent hubs of migration.

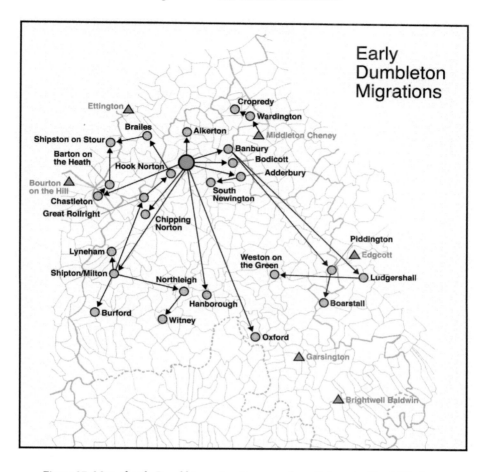

Figure 37. Map of early Dumbleton migration away from Tadmarton/Swalcliffe (large blue circle) to other parts of (mainly) Oxfordshire, shown by orange circles. Populations with connections unconfirmed are marked by green triangles. For clarity the map does not show all Dumbleton populations.

A summary of some of the early migrations is shown in Tables 8 and 9.

Migration to	Migration date (approx.)	Migrant	Onward migrations
Swalcliffe	1550s–70s	Brothers John (d. 1602), Richard (d. 1610/11) & Edward (1549–)	(see next table)
Banbury	By 1611	William married in Banbury 1611	
Milcombe	By 1629	Jonathan (1629–) Records of Dumbletons in Milcombe 1558/1589 but connection unknown.	South Newington (from 1653)
Shipton/ Milton-under-Wychwood	By 1656	Daniel (1635–1679)	Great Rollright (1675–1700) then Hook Norton (1760s) and Brailes, Warks (c.1800); Burford (by 1702) then London; North Leigh (1690–1700) then Witney (1720s); Lyneham (1680s)
Alkerton/ Shenington	1680s–1700	John (1662–1717)	Shutford (1730s)
Oxford	By 1690s	Benjamin (1668–)	
Grimsbury (Banbury)	By 1723	Joseph (1669–)	Ludgershall, Bucks (by 1750) then possibly to Weston-on-the-Green but also may have come from Shutford; Piddington (by 1755) then Boarstall, Bucks (by 1787)

Table 8. Dumbleton migration locations from Tadmarton.

Migration to	Migration Date (approx.)	Migrant	Onward migrations
Milton/ Adderbury	1550s–1580s	John (there by 1629) or Richard (d. 1586), Luke there by early 1600s.	Bodicote; South Newington
Easington (Banbury)	1570–1602	Edward (*c.*1540s–1603)	
Shipston-on-Stour (Warks)	Before 1602	William son of Richard – d. 1602 Shipston-on-Stour	
Hanborough	*c.*1610–1630	Edward (*c.*1570s–1643)	
Chastleton	1630s–1640s	Richard (1611–) (but in females Margaret daughter of George was a servant at Chastleton to George Osbaston. She died in the 1590s there.)	Barton-on-the-Heath, Warks (by 1680) then Todenham to Shipston-on-Stour, Warks (1700s)
Chipping Norton	By 1681	Ferdinando (b. *c.*1650s)	William to London (1690) then returned to Witney

Table 9. Dumbleton migration locations from Swalcliffe.

Although some emigrants left Oxfordshire early on, once into the mid eighteenth century movement became much more frequent and extended to more distant places, with Oxfordshire Dumbletons being more common in London, Birmingham, the West Country, Yorkshire and overseas. Each of the Dumbleton lines that had moved some steps away from Tadmarton/Swalcliffe created new jumping-off platforms for migration to even more distant new homes around the world.

Migration driven by jobs: shepherds in Minster Lovell[7]

John Gillett was born in Brize Norton in 1804 and moved to Manor Farm in Minster Lovell in 1833 as the farm bailiff, remaining until ousted in 1874 by his employer. He had a strong reputation as a renowned breeder of Cotswold sheep, winning numerous prizes at the Royal Show and other competitions.

Gillett must have encouraged business to the village. He held annual sheep sales advertised in *Jackson's Oxford Journal* and other local and national papers: 'fine sheep from the celebrated stock of Mr John Gillett'.[8] Several shepherds worked in the village. They may have discovered Minster Lovell through these sheep sales. To work for John Gillett would have been a prestigious post and even working for one of the other village farms would have been a stepping-stone to being associated with a famous breeder.

Figure 38. Sheep shearing in the village of Minster Lovell.

Apart from John Gillett, the earliest records of shepherds in Minster Lovell in this period were Thomas Hickman, who married in 1821, and James Cripps, who was in the 1841 census, having moved from Lew. In the same period Joseph Gosling and Thomas Sadler were in nearby Asthall and in Swinbrook along with Isaac Mills. Both Thomas Hickman and Thomas Sadler had been born in Curbridge, only nine years apart in the 1780s, so would have known each other well. This core group was joined in Minster Lovell in the 1850s by Robert Coppin from Alvescot, Noah Hayden from East Hanney near Wantage, and George Holborough from Great Barrington via Coln Rogers in Gloucestershire. The clearance of Wychwood Forest for pasture during this decade will have increased the need for shepherds. The 1860s saw the greatest number of shepherds, with the Sadlers (father and son), Gosling, Hickman, Ayris, Coppin, Holtom, Dipper and Stevens families.

Name	Before Minster Lovell	In Minster Lovell (est.)	After Minster Lovell
John Gillett	Brize Norton; Asthall Leigh	1833–1874	Bruern; Fairford
James Cripps	Lew	1835–1847	Witney; Crawley
Noah Hayden	East Hanney; Fawley, Berks; East Hanney	1852–1858	?
Thomas Hickman	Curbridge; Little Rissington, Glos; Bourton-on-the-Water, Glos; Ablington, Glos	1855–1864 (death) (possibly in ML c.1818–1821)	
Joseph Gosling	Broadwell; Asthall; Swinbrook; Brize Norton	1855–1866 1875–1888	Ditchley; returned Minster Lovell; after 1888?
Isaac Mills	Black Bourton; Swinbrook; Bledington, Glos	1857–1860	Asthall; Bampton; Eastington, Glos; Black Bourton
George Holborough	Great Barrington, Glos; Coln Rogers, Glos	1858–1863	Curbridge; Enstone; Winchcombe, Glos

Robert Coppin	Alvescot; Little Rissington; Sherborne, Glos	1862–1863 (death)	
Thomas (& Thomas) Ayris	Ducklington	1861–1865	Ducklington; Hardwick; Stanton Harcourt
Edward Holtom		1866–1873	Westbury-on-Severn, Glos; Brize Norton
Thomas (& James) Sadler	Curbridge; Combe; Asthall; Swinbrook; Asthall; Swinbrook; Langley	1868–1870 (Thomas, death) 1868–1915 (James, death)	
James Stevens	Brize Norton	1868–1874	Bampton; Witney
George (& Thomas) Dipper	Ducklington; Curbridge; Ducklington	1870–1872	Taynton; Swinbrook; Widford; Witney; Thomas then to Handsworth, Staffs to work in ironworks

Table 10. Shepherds who worked in Minster Lovell and other locations.

These shepherds moved four to eight times at the peak of their careers, mostly in local circles and often to the same few farms. They probably knew each other and key ('good') employers through their occupational networks. The map (Figure 39) shows a circle of about thirty miles diameter, but with most movements occurring within eight miles of Minster Lovell.

Figure 39. Map showing places sixteen shepherds worked in their careers. Minster Lovell indicated by a star.

By the 1870s farming was in decline. The Minster Lovell branch of the Agricultural Labourers' Union went on strike for more money in 1872 and, although they achieved their aim, it may have been a watershed moment. John Gillett's employers, the Taunton family, sold Manor Farm in 1874 and dismissed him. He moved to Tangley Farm near Bruern, north of Burford, taking over from his son, but went bankrupt in 1881 and ended his days living with his daughters in Fairford in Gloucestershire. He and his family are buried in Minster Lovell. James Cripps and Thomas Sadler died in this decade and the others moved on. Joseph Gosling had moved to Ditchley, another large estate in the 1860s, but he returned to Minster Lovell along with James Sadler as the sole surviving shepherds from this group through the 1880s.

Larger families

There were several names in Oxfordshire that occurred in many places and it is very difficult to untangle them and produce accurate family trees. Without a definitive written record going way back in time and DNA tests we may never know how many lines of a given family are actually connected, even if they remained in a small area of Oxfordshire. Examples of such names include Townsend (mainly in the Abingdon, Banbury and Witney areas); Timms (occurring in 120 parishes but most commonly Ascott-under-Wychwood, Barford St Michael, Bicester, Brize Norton and Cropredy); Green (widespread but high in Faringdon and Great Coxwell); and Wheeler (across the southern half of Oxfordshire). Cross is an example of a name which may have had multiple origins or may have been a simple story of movement to increasingly larger conurbations for work with successive generations. The Cross surname in Oxfordshire may have started with rural workers in areas such as Chadlington, Shipton-under-Wychwood, and Charlbury, where on average there were more families but fewer children, but ended up in Cowley and Abingdon where, of the families there, four produced seven or eight children apiece (two of the fathers being successful maltsters).

Emigration from Oxfordshire

Although emigration is not covered in detail in this book, the graphs in Chapter 3 show how many names dropped dramatically in Oxfordshire in the nineteenth century. Over 2.7 million people left southern England between 1841 and 1891,[9] including large numbers from agricultural regions of Oxfordshire. Emigration from Oxfordshire to places within the British Isles followed the same trails in a reverse direction as those used for immigration into Oxfordshire – south mainly to London, north to the West Midlands, especially Birmingham, to Lancashire/Yorkshire for factory work and west to the coal areas of south Wales. There was mass migration overseas to the USA, Australia, Canada and New Zealand. In terms of free migrants, whole family groups often moved together, including young in-laws and grandparents as well as neighbours from the same village or town. Families were often encouraged by earlier migrants from home, not just for economic reasons, so researching a wider community may help to find the fate of individuals who have gone missing from Oxfordshire records.

Destination countries often have excellent records on immigrants, and the families themselves took souvenirs and documentation of home, more likely preserved due to their sentimental value, all of which can prove invaluable to family history researchers. DNA is also beginning to link overseas families with locations back in England.

Summary

Many families in Oxfordshire may have stayed in a home location for several generations, but others moved, often driven by the need for work. Migration paths may be driven by geography (road or water networks), by family members thriving in a new area, by increasing industrialisation and services in the nearest towns and cities or by training or work opportunities offered by a family social or business network. In order to research family movements, here are some hints and tips:

- Go back in time: find the earliest records for a given surname – in Oxfordshire, in the UK and Ireland and across the world.
- Make use of all types of documentation which may help trace migrations. There is no one single source with all the answers. Apart from the usual documents on genealogical websites, make use of early wills which may describe a relative in another place; look for medieval references and manorial documents; check village and local histories.
- Trace families by location rather than just family trees. A location study combined with dates may help to reveal migration patterns. Try to develop a timeline of locations, and plot families on maps.
- Use occupations to surmise where a family may have moved.
- Networks cause migrations – research associated family lines, friends and neighbours and work colleagues to find what might have drawn someone to migrate. Look for wealthy local families who may have taken servants, gardeners and farm workers with them to new locations.
- Larger families with many sons will tend to increase the spread of a family from one location to another as several males look for work.
- Although surname research focuses on the male members of a family, trace females as well, as their married names and locations may give clues to later family migrations.

- Use DNA to help confirm how many lines with a given family were the same in Oxfordshire and elsewhere. DNA also helps connect with relatives who may have information that you do not possess.
- Search major cities such as London and Birmingham and overseas if families vanish, especially in the nineteenth century.

Notes

1. Collins, Ted and Michael Havinden. 2005. Long term trends in land ownership 1500 to 1914: Berkshire and Oxfordshire. *Oxoniensia*. LXX. https://oxoniensia.org/oxo_volume.php?vol=70.

2. Becket, John. 2016. Professor David Hey: an appreciation. *BALH The Local Historian*. 46(2).

3. Reaney, Percy H. and R. M. Wilson. 2005. *A dictionary of English surnames*. Oxford: Oxford University Press.

4. Reaney and Wilson, op. cit.

5. 'Thame: Trade, industry and agriculture', in Lobel, Mary, ed. 1962. *A history of the county of Oxford: Volume 7, Dorchester and Thame Hundreds*. London: Victoria County History. British History Online. http://www.british–history.ac.uk/vch/oxon/vol7.

6. Chance, Eleanor *et al.* 1979. *A history of the county of Oxford: Volume 4, the City of Oxford*, ed. Alan Crossley and C. R. Elrington. London: Victoria County History. *British History Online*. http://www.british–history.ac.uk/vch/oxon/vol4; Lobel, Mary D., ed. 1957. *A history of the county of Oxford: Volume 5, Bullingdon Hundred*. London: Victoria County History. *British History Online*. http://www.british–history.ac.uk/vch/oxon/vol5; Lobel, Mary, ed. 1962. *A history of the county of Oxford: Volume 7, Dorchester and Thame Hundreds*. London: Victoria County History. British History Online. http://www.british–history.ac.uk/vch/oxon/vol7; Baggs, A. P. *et al.* 2004. *A history of the county of Oxford: Volume 14, Bampton Hundred (Part Two)*, ed. Simon Townley. London: Victoria County History. *British History Online*. http://www.british–history.ac.uk/vch/oxon/vol14; Townley, Simon, ed. 2016. *A history of the county of Oxford: Volume 18*. Woodbridge, Suffolk: Boydell & Brewer for the Institute of Historical Research. *British History Online*. http://www.british–history.ac.uk/vch/oxon/vol18.

7. Honoré, Sue. 2012. *Family ties: migration in the village of Minster Lovell 1830–1880*. Thesis for Advanced Diploma in Local History. University of Oxford.

8. *Jackson's Oxford Journal*. 1843. 29 December.

9. Boyer, George R. 1997. *Labour migration in southern and eastern England, 1861–1901*. Cornell University. https://ecommons.cornell.edu/bitstream/handle/1813/75799/Boyer15_Labour_Migration.pdf?sequence=1.

Five

Oxfordshire Surnames Derived from Place Names

Richard Merry

Introduction

Many families acquire their surnames from place names. These are termed toponymic surnames and are a form of locative (location-related) surname, such as Oxford or London, that are usually distinct from topographical surnames that derive from general landscape features such as 'hill' or 'ford', though some surnames could be from either. Similarly, place names (toponyms) such as Buckland, Brooklands, Stonehill, Stockwell or Woodford can be topographical as well. A toponymic origin for surnames such as these may present an impossible problem. Names such as Buckingham, Clanfield, Enstone, Fifield, Henley and many others are familiar place names in Oxfordshire and surnames are likely to be associated with these places. Other surnames, such as Busby, Chillingworth, Frogley, Huckwell, Ludlow and Mobberley, are from further afield, Huckwell (Heuqueville) being one of many with French origins. For Oxfordshire, locative names have been discussed in detail by McKinley.[1] Studies such as those of Cheshire, Mateos and Longley,[2] and Cheshire, Longley and Singleton,[3] have investigated the regional clustering of British surnames and found strong regionalisation using statistical approaches, but the distribution of toponymic surnames may represent unique circumstances and also contribute to geographic clustering.

Figure 40a and b. Two of the Oxfordshire place names that appear as surnames in the county.

It is tempting for family historians to use a toponymic surname as evidence that the location was the place of origin of the family bearing this surname and was acquired when surnames became general. While this may often be true, some people may have gained their surnames for other reasons. They might have been a servant in a manor or of a landholder bearing the surname, the place just being one of several places where the person had been previously resident. The surname might have been assumed as required by the terms of an inheritance, or a surname could have been given to a foundling.

It is possible that several individuals departing from the same place settled in other, different places and all acquired the same toponymic surname, but they may or may not have the same paternal line. Well-researched family histories and Y-DNA evidence may be the only way of distinguishing the descendant families. Wherever the origin, these surnames tie the holder to a place for whatever reason and mostly imply that the holder may have moved from somewhere else. In 1881 there were only three people with the surname Oxford resident in Oxfordshire[4] and four in Berkshire, but eight other counties had more than fifty holders of the surname. It is not always true that the source of a surname is a matching place name that is nearby. The Kislingbury surname, derived from a place in Northamptonshire, was mainly found in Surrey and Oxfordshire in 1881 and not at all north of Oxfordshire.

This chapter considers the many 'place-name' surnames found in the parish registers and other early sources for post-1974 Oxfordshire. If the surnames were associated with Nonconformist families they are less likely to appear in the parish register records which were used in the discussion that follows.

The geographic origins of place-name surnames present in Oxfordshire

Clues to finding the places of origin of toponymic surnames may usually be found in the main dictionaries of surnames such as Reaney and Wilson,[5] and Hanks, Coates and McClure,[6] or in gazetteers and atlases.[7] Considerable scholarship in these sources has found the likely locations. Ordnance survey maps may help, either historic or modern online versions,[8] but it is not uncommon for small historic places to be missing from modern maps so that some detective work is needed to find a likely place. The surname dictionaries may give indications such as 'location unknown' and add 'possibly in west Oxfordshire'. Other sources that might give clues to locations are among the place indexes of published indexes of the earlier Hundred Rolls, probate records (The Index Library), Feet of Fines or other listings. Surnames that are clearly from other countries are not uncommon, some being present in Oxfordshire from very early times (for example, de Oili to Doyley and de Anuers to Danvers). Detailed discussion of English place names can be found among the publications of the English Place Name Society including those by Gelling for Oxfordshire[9] and Berkshire,[10] and also Whynne-Hammond.[11]

For many surnames, such as Ashby, Aston, Ashton, Barton, Grafton, Milton, and Whitton, a number of possible locations may be found. It may be likely that the appropriate location of origin is within or near Oxfordshire, especially in early times when most people may not have moved far from their origins, but this may not always be so and several locations of origin should not be discounted.

Figure 41. Some familiar Oxfordshire place names that are found as surnames, taken from signs around the county.

Perhaps the best place to find surnames that are also place names is from the parish registers. Surname listings prior to the introduction of parish registers in 1538, and later in some listings such as Hearth Taxes, were often somewhat selective of the people recorded. Landholders, officials, clergy, tradesmen or those appearing in law courts were more likely to be recorded, and they may not have recorded the 'ordinary' folk who appear in parish registers. It is also more likely that a surname present in the parish registers before about 1600 may survive to the present day, unless it was initially very uncommon.

Figure 42. Buckingham Street in Grandpont, Oxford.

To gain some idea of the frequency of place names as surnames, about 2000 surnames were assessed from among the Oxfordshire parish registers and some earlier sources covering post-1974 Oxfordshire which includes the northern part of the former Berkshire. These known and probable toponyms were located and their Ordnance Survey grid locations found. Where there were several possible locations, the most likely location closest to Oxfordshire was usually chosen. The search made was not completely exhaustive, but covers a fair representation. A small number of these were not considered because a location could not be found, they were felt to be too ambiguous, it was difficult to be certain, or they had a high likelihood of having an alternative meaning. Of the total of 2000 surnames investigated, about 400 (20%) were thought likely to be place names. Several surnames were of a general geographical nature: Cornish, England, Fleming, Gascoine, Holland, Ireland (Erlelond), Scot and Welch. Twenty-eight surnames were most likely derived from place names in France, including Cantwell, Chaundy, Florey, Glanville, Havell, Louch, Maisey and Sessions. Janaway is thought to indicate Genoese origins and Danvers derives from Antwerp (Anvers). A few surnames were also county names: Galloway, Kent, Pembroke and Wiltshire.

As might be expected, the majority of the remaining surnames (346) could be located among English counties. The thirty-eight counties are listed in Table 11. As also might be expected, most place names used as surnames in Oxfordshire (73) are likely to have come from that county. With the exception of Lancashire, the next most likely sources may be from those counties closest to Oxfordshire.

County	Number	County	Number	County	Number
Oxfordshire	73	Somerset	7	Shropshire	4
Gloucestershire	29	Cambridgeshire	6	Bedfordshire	3
Berkshire	21	Yorkshire, West Riding	6	Cornwall	3
Buckinghamshire	18	Cheshire	5	Cumberland/Cumbria	3
Wiltshire	16	Devon	5	Hertfordshire	3
Lancashire	15	Dorset	5	Middlesex	3
Warwickshire	15	Kent	5	Norfolk	3
Northamptonshire	14	Leicestershire	5	Durham	2
Staffordshire	13	Nottinghamshire	5	Essex	2
Hampshire	11	Suffolk	5	Surrey	2
Derbyshire	8	Sussex	5	Northumberland	1
Worcestershire	8	Yorkshire, North Riding	5	Yorkshire, East Riding	1
Lincolnshire	7	Herefordshire	4	**Total**	**38**

Table 11. Listing of the counties of origin and number of possible place names that have been recorded as surnames found in Oxfordshire. Place names are counted once.

These place names were extracted from Oxfordshire parish registers, the 1539 and 1542 muster rolls and the Feet of Fines 1485–1509. A few of these surnames were recorded earlier at the named location, even as early as the Hundred Rolls of 1279. These early recordings may not necessarily be the same family as recorded by around 1500. As mentioned above, it is probable that many of the surnames may also have derived from one of the places having the same or similar names in other counties.

Locations of the place names

Most (376) of the locations of the place names that could be associated with surnames recorded in the parish registers and muster rolls are shown in the map in Figure 43, and detail of the Oxfordshire area is shown in Figure 44. Again, locations closest to Oxfordshire were chosen when multiple locations were possible. The dates of first record for the surnames ranged from before 1540 to 1724.

Figure 43. The location of places in Britain where the place names were present as surnames in Oxfordshire from about 1500 to 1725. Genmap UK version 2.31 (Archer Software) was used with Ordnance Survey grid references to produce this map.

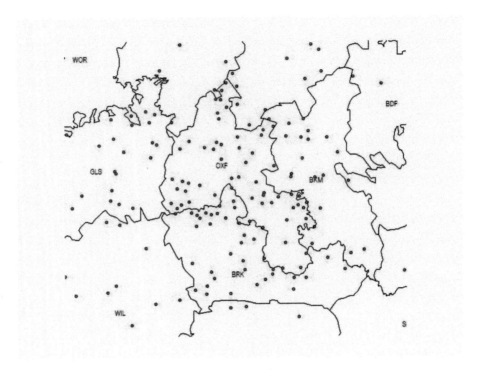

Figure 44. Detail from Figure 43 showing the locations of places also recorded as surnames in pre-1974 Oxfordshire.

The distribution of places contributing surnames to Oxfordshire becomes increasingly concentrated with closeness to the county, as outlined in Table 11 and as might be expected. Figure 43 may give the impression that there may be a concentration of locations near the borders of the pre-1974 county. There are many reasons why a family with a place-name surname settled in Oxfordshire. Some people from other parts are known to have settled in the county because of association with forestry, the wool industry, leather processing and as employees of landholders, among other reasons. Only detailed family history research and a certain amount of luck that records still exist may give clues to origins. It may be that the surname was only acquired after arrival at the Oxfordshire parish of residence.

The locations of the mapped place names are quite dispersed and it leads one to wonder which pathway to Oxfordshire the original holder of the place-name surname may have used. Did the parish of first record indicate that surnames from the north were first recorded in the north of Oxfordshire, and so on? This is unlikely to be known with certainty as parish records only show life events – baptisms, marriages and burials – not necessarily where the new arrivals first lived. However, an analysis of more than 300 place-name surnames suggests that there was often a relationship of the location of the parish of first record in Oxfordshire with direction of the place name to the north, south, east, west or Thames Valley, especially if the place was in a neighbouring county or where there was a longstanding migration route, such as from Wales. In other instances the direction of origin was not obvious.

Parishes of first record

These toponymic surnames appeared in the parish registers at a modern Oxfordshire location from 1538 to 1724. Not all parish records began in 1538, and some records have been lost, but most were recording by about 1600. A total of 377 surnames that derived from place names were recorded in a parish from these (usually baptismal) registers over this period of time. Of these, fifty-seven parishes first recorded one place-name surname, twenty-six recorded two, and twelve each recorded three or four. The parishes recording the greatest number of toponymic surnames are presented in Table 12. The most (thirty) were recorded at Abingdon. Cropredy and Banbury between them recorded thirty-three and, as mentioned above, these names may show no consistency of location of origin with proximity to the north of Oxfordshire. Oxford parishes first recorded only thirteen of these surnames despite the presence of students and academics from further afield. A selection of surnames derived from place names recorded from the parish registers with their year of first record and county of origin is presented in Table 13.

Parish	Number	Parish	Number	Parish	Number
Abingdon	30	Cuddesdon	12	Great Milton	5
Cropredy	17	Witney	12	Langford	5
Banbury	16	Henley	8	Shipton-under-Wychwood	5
Bicester	16	Steventon	7	Taynton	5
Bampton	15	Spelsbury	6	Warborough	5
Oxford	13	Stanford in the Vale	6	**Total (all parishes: 377)**	167

Table 12. Oxfordshire parishes of first record of toponymic surnames.

Parish	Surname	Year first in parish registers	Likely origin of place name*
Abingdon	Assendon	1539	OXF
	Beckinsale	1553	LAN
	Cherrill	1593	WLT
	Filbee	1548	NOR
	Lapworth	1560	WAR
Cropredy	Elkington	1541	NTH
	Hanwell	1547	OXF
	Maule	1550	France
	Newbury	1563	BRK
	Tarver	1620	LAN
Bampton	Cheney	1542	France
	Maisey	1539	France
	Orpwood	1542	OXF
	Preedy	1553	SOM
	Warwick	1540	WRK
Banbury	Dudley	1574	WOR
	Gascoine	1602	France
	Moreby	1584	YKS

	Wallington	1619	HRT
	Wheatley	1564	OXF
Bicester	Beamsley	1692	YKS
	Burson	1561	STF
	Grantham	1594	LIN
	Hillsdon	1563	BKM
	Horwood	1551	BKM
Oxford	Barlow	1600	DER
	Cambray	1601	France
	Lambourne	1535	BRK
	Pembroke	1664	Wales
	Wetherall	1587	CUM

* County names (pre-1974) are indicated by their Chapman code.

Table 13. Selected place-name surnames from the top six parishes in Table 12 with year of first record in the parish registers and likely or closest place of origin.

The records of first appearance of these toponymic surnames in the parish registers were counted from before 1540, then in five-year intervals to 1725. Their distribution over time is shown in Figure 45. Of the 377 surnames, about 75% were present in Oxfordshire before 1600. There may be a general tendency for some more distant English toponyms to have been first recorded later, but not universally so. For example, Busby (Yorkshire or Leicestershire) was recorded at Horley in 1541 (and much earlier in other records) and Osbaldeston from Lancashire was recorded at Spelsbury in 1558.

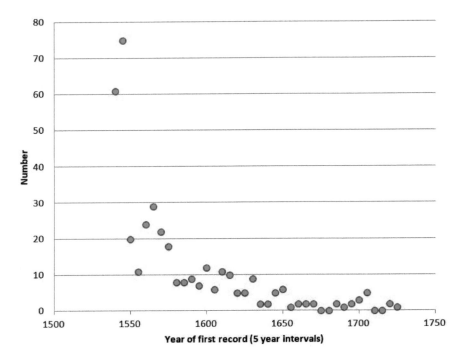

Figure 45. The number of toponymic surnames recorded in the Oxfordshire parish registers over time (before 1540 to 1725).

Conclusion

- Place names have contributed many family names to the people of Oxfordshire and the points presented below show their importance and aspects that should be considered.

- It is likely that about 20% of the surnames present in Oxfordshire derive from place names (toponyms).

- About 80% of these were already present in the county by 1600.

- Many of these surnames could have their origins from several locations with the same or similar names and it is not possible to be definite about the likely location without good family history or other evidence.

- Keeping this in mind, mapping the likely locations of places shows that these place names used as surnames are mostly to be found in the present-day county or in neighbouring counties.

Notes

1. McKinley, Richard Alexander. 1977. *The surnames of Oxfordshire*. London: Leopard's Head Press.

2. Cheshire, J., P. Mateos, and P. A. Longley. 2009. Family names as indicators of Britain's regional geography. CASA Working Paper Series, 149. http://www.casa.ucl.ac.uk/ working papers/paper149.pdf.

3. Cheshire, J. A., Paul A. Longley, and Alex D. Singleton. 2010. The surname regions of Great Britain. *Journal of Maps*. 6(1). pp. 401–409. DOI: 10.4113/jom.2010.1103.

4. Archer, S. 2017. *The British 19th century surname atlas*. Archer Software CD-ROM.

5. Reaney, Percy H. and R. M. Wilson. 1997. *A dictionary of English surnames*. Oxford: Oxford University Press.

6. Hanks, Patrick, Richard A. Coates, and Peter McClure. 2016. *The Oxford dictionary of family names in Britain and Ireland*. http://public.ebookcentral.proquest.com/choice/ publicfullrecord.aspx?p=4745339.

7. Smith, F. 1968. *A genealogical gazetteer of England*. Baltimore: Genealogical Publishing Company.

8. https://osmaps.ordnancesurvey.co.uk.

9. Gelling, Margaret and D. M. Stenton. 1953. *The place-names of Oxfordshire* (Vol. 1). Cambridge: Cambridge University Press.

10. Gelling, Margaret. 1976. *The place-names of Berkshire*. Cambridge: English Place-Name Society.

11. Whynne-Hammond, Charles. 2007. *English place-names explained*. Newbury, Berkshire: Countryside Books.

Six

Medieval Bynames and Surnames in Langtree Hundred and the Wychwoods

Simon Draper and Simon Townley

This chapter looks at thirteenth- and fourteenth-century bynames and emergent hereditary surnames in two separate areas of Oxfordshire – Langtree Hundred in the south-east Oxfordshire Chilterns, and an area around Wychwood Forest in the west of the county on the edge of the Cotswolds, both of them areas recently studied by the Victoria County History.[1] The chief source material is the Hundred Roll survey of 1279[2] and the lay subsidies of 1306, 1316 and 1327,[3] which together provide a systematic body of material for the period in which descriptive bynames were beginning to solidify into hereditary surnames.

Names are discussed using the widely accepted categories of locative, relationship, occupational, status-related and nicknames,[4] which can sometimes be hard to distinguish. Locative bynames include toponymics derived from a place of origin (e.g. de Norton), and topographical names derived from features in the landscape or within a particular settlement (e.g. atte cross or atte wood). Relationship names include patronymics (X son of Y) and other names derived from an ancestor's forename (e.g. Godwin, Simmons), along with explicit descriptions of relationship (e.g. Cosun).[5] Occupational names are ostensibly self-explanatory, although some could actually be nicknames, as could also certain status-related names such as (le) bishop, knight or abbot. Other nicknames derived most commonly from character traits or physical appearance. How far such bynames were already hereditary in the thirteenth and early fourteenth centuries is often unclear, certainly amongst the lower social levels with which this chapter is primarily concerned. The weight of evidence suggests, however, that they would certainly not have been hereditary for long, meaning that a locative or occupational name is likely to have applied to an individual's forebears a generation or two earlier, if not necessarily to that individual him- or herself.[6]

Reference has been made throughout to the *Oxford Dictionary of Family Names in Britain and Ireland* (2016), and to the wider Oxfordshire context provided by Richard McKinley's *Surnames of Oxfordshire* (1977),[7] building on P. H. Reaney's seminal *The Origin of English Surnames* (1967). The chapter concludes with a brief comparison of bynames in the two areas, and some comments on their post-medieval survival.

Figure 46. The parishes in the Wychwood Forest area (green) and Langtree Hundred (yellow) discussed in this chapter. Although boundaries have changed, the Wychwood area includes Milton-under-Wychwood, Shipton-under-Wychwood, Ascott-under-Wychwood, Lyneham, Cornbury Park, Wychwood, Langley, Leafield and Ramsden. The Langtree parishes are Crowmarsh Gifford, Newnham Murren, Mongewell, North Stoke, Ipsden, Checkendon, Goring, Whitchurch and Mapledurham.

Langtree Hundred[8]

Langtree was one of the smaller hundreds of medieval Oxfordshire, although by 1279 it encompassed all or part of nine ancient parishes running up from the Thames into the Chiltern hills: from north to south, Crowmarsh Gifford, Newnham Murren, Mongewell, North Stoke, Ipsden, Checkendon (part), Goring, Whitchurch and Mapledurham (part). Characteristically for south Oxfordshire, all nine were 'strip parishes', taking in cross-sections of the varied landscape and its natural resources including the river itself, meadows, open fields, woods and heaths. Owing to the chalk geology water was often scarce, most people in the hills depending on ponds for their supply, but springs broke out on the lower slopes where chalk met clay. Medieval settlement was similarly varied, from clustered or linear villages and hamlets often containing the parish church down by the river, to scattered hamlets and isolated farms on the slopes and in the hills.[9]

Such stark contrasts in the hundred's landscape and pattern of settlement are clearly reflected in the bynames and surnames of its inhabitants in 1279,[10] 1306,[11] and 1327.[12] Topographic names (referring to local geographical features) account for over a quarter of the approximately 400 listed names (not necessarily unique names or individuals) studied. In the more tight-knit riverside villages and hamlets, some occupants bore names indicating the locations of their houses in relation to others within the same settlement. Boveton ('above town'), Streetend and Townsend all suggest a degree of physical separation (and by implication higher actual or perceived social status) from closely packed neighbours,[13] whilst names meaning 'on the corner', 'in the bend' or 'in the lane' may also serve to denote visual prominence.[14] Two names ('at the mill' and 'at the hospital') make reference to notable buildings,[15] one to a bridge[16] and another (Stonehouse) apparently to a dwelling constructed from a rare and distinctive material in a region where virtually all buildings apart from churches were timber-framed.[17]

Figure 47. Mapledurham watermill built in the fifteenth century.

Moving into the Chilterns, and reflecting the more dispersed settlement pattern found there, several people bore names referring to water sources. Some were unnamed springs or streams,[18] but others were named ponds, including Homer ('pond in a hollow') in Ipsden,[19] and lost examples such as 'Brademere' ('broad pond') and 'Wythemere' (perhaps 'withy pond') both in Checkendon[20] and 'Stamereswell' ('stone pond well') in Mapledurham.[21] Some names referred to prominent landscape markers, such as lone trees (beech[22] and pear[23]), a white stone,[24] a cross (perhaps a crucifix mentioned in a charter of 966)[25] and a burial mound,[26] whilst others derived from enclosures (Garston, Haw and Haycroft)[27] and buildings (e.g. Wick[28] and Smerecot[29]). However, most referenced natural landscape features, among which valleys,[30] hills,[31] fields,[32] slopes,[33] heaths[34] and woods[35] all feature prominently.

Toponymic names (derived from named places) were less common, but still account for around an eighth of all names. Some reflect obvious lordly connections with Normandy (e.g. Coudray, Chausey, Mohun),[36] but more difficult to explain are the Norman toponymic names borne by two Ipsden cottagers in 1279,[37] unless illegitimacy was involved, or they were merely given lordly names either as nicknames or to reflect servitude.[38] Other lords and freeholders were named from their estates (e.g. Hardwick, Huntercombe),[39] whilst places within the hundred also feature in a few names borne by tenants who may have migrated locally, from one manor to the next (e.g. Mongewell).[40] Immigration into the hundred from surrounding regions is suggested by names derived from toponyms in Oxfordshire (Asthall, Piddington, Shirburn),[41] Berkshire (Abingdon, Blewbury, Brightwalton, Burghfield, Clapcot, Cookham, Harwell, Lambourn)[42] and Buckinghamshire (Buckingham, Hogshaw, Ilmer),[43] and individuals from further afield are indicated by the names Budiford,[44] Colchester,[45] and Lavington.[46]

Figure 48. The Old Smithy owned by the Baker family of Cowley. From left: Fred Baker, unknown man, Mr Giles Baker (snr) and George Baker. The cart belonged to Silas Turner, Cowley's carrier.

Occupational and status names (a quarter of the total) generally reflect those more widely found in medieval rural England (e.g. Baker, Carpenter, Carter, Clerk, Hayward, Miller, Marshall 'farrier', Reeve, Shepherd, Smith, Vacher 'cowherd'),[47] but interaction with the Berkshire cloth industry is suggested by a few names denoting tailors and weavers.[48] The presence of a Spicer (spice-dealer) in 1306 is probably explained by the proximity of Crowmarsh Gifford to the market town of Wallingford.[49] More distinctively local crafts and trades appear in names connected to the river (e.g. Fisher and perhaps Rammer),[50] woodland crafts (e.g. Turner and perhaps Besemere),[51] and the pottery and tilemaking industries (e.g. Crock, Tiler).[52] Status names only sometimes accurately reflected a person's social status. John and Ralph le Frankleyn ('freeman') were indeed freeholders in 1279.[53] However, William le Cotier ('cottager') was a free tenant,[54] and John le Justice probably bore an hereditary surname that originated as a status name with his father Robert *dictus justiciarius* ('called the judge').[55]

The remainder of the names studied comprise an almost equal mix of relationship names and nicknames, of which the former derive from both native English personal names (e.g. Baldwin, Coleman, Loveday, Sweetman, Wineman)[56] and introduced Norman ones (e.g. Bernard, Bertram, Gerard, Gilbert, Reynold),[57] with two Welsh personal names (Owain and Hywel) also represented, perhaps suggesting immigration from Wales.[58] However, the individual who bore the hereditary surname Welsh (Waleys) in Goring in 1279 apparently could trace his ancestry back through three or four generations similarly named to Ralph Walensis, son of William Druval (d. by 1174), the Norman lord of that manor,[59] and any Welsh connections are obscure, unless Ralph had once served with the English army in Wales. Why the English family of Newnham Murren freeholders was so named remains similarly mysterious,[60] and the name Scot borne by an Ipsden cottager in 1279 could just as easily derive from the medieval personal name Scot as the ethnic descriptor.[61] John le Breton and Robert le Franceys, however, presumably did have Breton and French ancestry, although the latter's father was Robert le Mouner 'miller' of Benson.[62] The nickname Newman, recorded in three parishes, was probably given to men newly arrived and settled into a manor.[63] Most other nicknames made reference either to personal appearance or character traits, of which the former are exemplified by Belebouche 'beautiful mouth',[64] Cras 'fat',[65] Gaunt 'slim',[66] and Gernon 'moustache',[67] and the latter by Duce 'sweet',[68] Giler 'deceiver',[69] Marmion 'monkey, brat',[70] and Wernegold 'hoard gold' (presumably for a mean person).[71] More enigmatic is Tophorn, which could mean 'ram's horn',[72] perhaps with bawdy connotations,[73] and it would be tempting to associate Tredewater ('tread water') found in Whitchurch with a Thames boatman operating from the wharf there,[74] although of course no relevant evidence can be adduced.

The Wychwood Area[75]

The study area for Wychwood comprises seven places formerly included in the large ancient parish of Shipton-under-Wychwood: Leafield, Ramsden, Langley, Lyneham, Ascott- and Milton-under-Wychwood, and Shipton itself. Most lie in the Evenlode valley, with Leafield and Ramsden occupying higher ground a little further south, separated from the other places (until its clearance in the 1850s) by the 4400-acre Wychwood Forest and Cornbury park. Though the forest remained royal property, woodland around its fringes belonged to adjoining manors and parishes, providing (with the forest itself) carefully controlled woodland grazing, woodland resources, and opportunities for poaching. Even so the area relied primarily on traditional Cotswold sheep-corn farming, pursued within a mixed framework of small private closes and large open fields.[76] The Hundred Rolls and lay subsidies for these places provide a database of nearly 300 names borne by some 520 individuals, amplified by names from the 1381 poll tax and from forest and other records.[77]

Figure 49. Members of the Barrett family in Wychwood Forest on Whit Monday 1898.

Wood-related names

Despite the woodlands' local importance, the proportion of bynames with woodland associations is small (no more than 4.5% of the total). The purpose of bynames, after all, was to distinguish individuals bearing a very limited range of (mostly Norman-French) forenames, and in an area with large amounts of woodland topographical names derived from woodland features would be of limited use.

Exceptions included the bynames 'underwood' (found in Leafield and Ramsden on the forest edge), 'at the ash' (in Lyneham and Ascott), and 'walde' (also in Leafield, and meaning 'wooded region, forested land, upland').[78] The name 'woderoue' (noted in Milton in 1306–27) may relate to a row of houses at or near a wood, but could equally derive from Middle English 'woderove', referring to sweet woodruff (a sweet-scented plant).[79] The name Roke (preserved in Oxfordshire in a Chiltern place name near Benson) referred usually to someone living by a prominent oak tree, resulting from a misdivision of Middle English 'atter oke'. The name 'le Rok', found in Langley in 1279, was perhaps more likely derived from Middle English 'rok(ke)' (rock or distaff), however, despite Langley's position on the forest edge.[80] The name Lye (recorded in 1381) is more certainly wood-related, derived from Middle English *legh*, and denoting wood pasture or a cleared area within woodland.[81] By then, however, the name was almost certainly hereditary, and could in any case have originated as a locative byname derived from the nearby villages of North or South Leigh. Some other names are less obviously wood-related without local knowledge. Richard de Boynhale, for instance, was named from Ascott's Boynal Wood on the forest's northern edge, and was himself a woodward, living presumably in an outlying cottage some distance from Ascott village by the river Evenlode.[82]

Figure 50. A girl on a donkey in Chinnor in 1905. The racks on the donkey are for carrying bundles of wood used by chair turners.

Perhaps more surprising is the relative absence of occupational names reflecting wood-related employment, although as much of that was probably seasonal and combined with farming or other activities, it may not have always stood out as a defining characteristic. Partial exceptions are the names 'le potter' and 'le crocker' (both denoting a potter), found in Ascott (1272) and Leafield (1272 and 1327). Both places may have produced the distinctive Wychwood pottery found across the area, and though pottery manufacture is not in itself a woodland trade, it did rely on brushwood for fuel as well as on local clay.[83] The name 'le co(l)lier' (for a charcoal burner) is found at nearby Ditchley,[84] and the trade itself is recorded in Ascott, Ramsden, and neighbouring Finstock. Its practitioners, however, bore unrelated bynames –

a reminder that while occupational names can shed light on local activities, their absence is not necessarily significant.[85] The names 'turner' and 'brush' (respectively describing someone who fashioned small wooden objects on a lathe or made besoms from brushwood) occur in Shipton, but only in the 1380s, and so were probably both hereditary and imported.[86] Given the Wychwood context, it is tempting to associate the local names 'wodhorn' and 'horn' with hunting horns, although both names are capable of other interpretations.[87]

At a higher social level, the name 'forester' was borne by the thirteenth-century lords of part of Lyneham manor. By then the name was certainly hereditary, and disappeared from the township after Jordan le forester's daughter married into the Fiennes family of Herstmonceux (Sussex), whose own name became attached to the manor.[88] The hereditary royal foresters of Wychwood (discussed below) bore unrelated bynames and surnames,[89] and so too did the various woodwards recorded in several parishes across the area from the thirteenth century.[90] The surname Woodward nevertheless survived locally in the 1640s.[91]

Other bynames

The area's remaining bynames were typical of the region, the largest proportion being relationship names, followed by nicknames and occupational names, topographical names, toponymics drawn from particular places, and a handful denoting either status or broad geographical origin. Several are ambiguous, the byname Heynes, for instance (listed in Milton in 1316) being possibly relational (from the Middle English personal name Hain), topographical (denoting a dweller by an enclosure), occupational (denoting a servant), or a nickname (denoting a 'mean wretch' or 'niggard').[92]

Relationship names mostly derived from male forenames, sometimes in a pet form as with the Lovekins of Shipton, Ramsden, and Milton.[93] A significant number incorporated Old English or Anglo-Scandinavian rather than Norman-French forenames, suggesting that such personal names had remained in local use.[94] Others (Enote, Letice, Mariot) derived from female personal names,[95] perhaps reflecting settlement of holdings on a widow or daughter a generation or two earlier, and so making identification with the female line important. Nicknames (as elsewhere) chiefly referred to character traits or physical appearance, more positive examples (probably sometimes used ironically) including Makeblithe, Welikempt (well turned-out), and

Smart (brisk or vigorous),[96] while William le riche was Ramsden's wealthiest taxpayer in 1316.[97] Some status-related names such as 'le knyht' or 'le freeman' may have also been nicknames, especially when borne by villeins,[98] although others (including 'bond' and possibly 'le bor' for unfree tenants) were no doubt literal.[99]

Figure 51. Long-standing rural family occupations, such as thatching.

Occupational names reflect the area's agrarian economy and common rural trades, as in the names 'carter', 'shepherd', 'hayward', 'reeve', and 'day' (dairymaid),[100] or the numerous examples of 'smith' and 'miller', of whom John faber (i.e. smith) at Lyneham was required to make ironwork for the lord's ploughs, showing that his name was still literally descriptive.[101] The names 'le quareour' (quarrier), 'le spicer', 'le taylor', and 'le couper' reflected Milton and Shipton's slightly wider range of trades, Milton's quarries continuing into modern times.[102] Topographical names identified those living by the cross or by the 'oven' (perhaps a forge or common bakehouse), by a road bend or gate, by a brook, stream or well, by a (probably stone or clay) pit, by the heath or meadow plot, or above the 'town' or village.[103] Some such names suggest outlying cottages or farmsteads, although the theme is much less marked than in the Chilterns with its scattered upland settlement.[104] Less usual topographical bynames included 'del hulwerk' (i.e. hillwork), referring apparently to a large rectilinear earthwork near modern Lowbarrow House in Leafield.[105]

Toponymics referring to other towns or villages provide evidence of migration, although places can be hard to identify, and of course not all migrants bore such names. McKinley's analysis of toponymics in Chadlington Hundred as a whole concluded that long-distance migration amongst lower-status tenants in the twelfth to fourteenth centuries was relatively rare,[106] a conclusion broadly supported by the Wychwood evidence. Identifiable bynames nonetheless suggest some limited movement between places in west Oxfordshire and from Gloucestershire, Warwickshire, Berkshire, and the Welsh Marches,[107] and migration is further suggested by names such as Devenish, le Newman, and (possibly) le Breton or Scot.[108] Holders of assart land in Ramsden in 1279 included several people named from neighbouring places, presumably either outsiders taking up newly available land or incomers doing the same,[109] while McKinley also noted an unusual preponderance of bond tenants in Lyneham who were named from other places.[110]

Figure 52. Langley farmhouse at Shipton-under-Wychwood on the edge of the forest.

Names derived from people's own place of residence were rare below lordly level, and were largely confined to freeholders. The most striking example is that of the de Langley family, hereditary foresters of Wychwood Forest, who from *c.*1208 took their name from their manor of Langley on the forest's northern edge, probably in imitation of more socially prestigious landholding families. Before then successive generations of the family had been known by the name of Rasur, originally denoting a barber or razor-maker, although by then they were already foresters, and the name (like de Langley later on) was clearly treated as hereditary.[111]

Conclusion

Overall, the broad pattern of bynames in Langtree Hundred and the Wychwood area was typical of the south Midlands generally. A significant proportion of topographical bynames in Langtree were drawn from ponds and landscape features reflecting the Chilterns' scattered upland settlement and general lack of surface water, while a significant number around Wychwood (albeit a low percentage overall) had woodland connotations, although woods featured also, unsurprisingly, in the Chilterns. Toponymics in both zones reflect only small-scale movement within the immediate area and from adjacent counties, save for lordly connections with Normandy. Relationship names and nicknames were of a common type, and occupational names, too, largely reflected the areas' agrarian economies, with occasional references to woodland crafts or to more specialist trades. The clustering of several people with the same byname (e.g. the Smarts in Lyneham or the Salemans in Leafield and Ascott)[112] suggest that some such names were becoming hereditary, as many of those borne by higher-status lords and freeholders already were. Others, however, may have remained fluid considerably later.

In both areas both the 1381 poll tax lists and early sixteenth-century subsidy rolls show a significant turnover of names, and by the 1520s very few of the thirteenth-century names recorded in these villages were still in use – the result, presumably, of increased mobility in the centuries following the Black Death, combined with the possible adoption of new hereditary names, and family extinctions in the male line.[113] Some names did continue, however, amongst them not only such widespread names as Taylor, Carter or Newman, but also Underwood (in Wychwood) and English and Justice (in Langtree).[114] Perhaps the most striking survival was the Ascott name of Chaundy, whose history has been traced in the village from the twelfth century (in its original Norman French form of Chenduit) through to the death of its last Ascott holder in 1965.[115]

Figure 53. Gravestone of Emma Elizabeth and John Chaundy at Ascott-under-Wychwood.

Notes

1. *Victoria County History of Oxfordshire* [*VCH Oxon.*] 2019. XIX: Wychwood Forest and Environs; XX: The South Oxfordshire Chilterns (forthcoming).

2. *Rotuli Hundredorum temp. Hen. III & Edw. I* (Record Commission, 1812–18) [*Rot. Hund.*], II, 726–46 (Chadlington hundred, incl. Wychwood parishes), 774–82 (Langtree hundred).

3. The National Archives [TNA], E 179/161/8–10.

4. Hanks, Patrick, Richard A. Coates, and Peter McClure. 2016. *The Oxford dictionary of family names in Britain and Ireland.* [*ODFNBI*] Intro. section 3.3.

5. TNA, E 179/161/9 (Rog. Cosun in Leafield, John Symond in Milton-u-Wychwood).

6. For general discussions, *ODFNBI*, intro. section 3.4; R. McKinley. 1977. *The surnames of Oxfordshire* (English Surnames Series III), 7–40.

7. See notes 4 and 6 above.

8. This section written by Simon Draper.

9. See *VCH Oxon.* XX. Forthcoming. Medieval bynames in neighbouring Ewelme hundred (*VCH Oxon.* XVIII, 2016) are discussed in S. Mileson and S. Brookes. Forthcoming. *Peasant perceptions of landscape: Ewelme Hundred, South Oxfordshire, 500–1650,* chapter 5.

10. *Rot. Hund.* II, 774–82.

11. TNA, E 179/161/10.

12. Ibid. E 179/161/9.

13. e.g. Thos Buvetun (Littlestoke in Checkendon, 1279), Wm Bovetoun (North Stoke/ Ipsden, 1327); Walter ate Stretende (Crowmarsh, 1279); Wm ate Tunesende (Gatehampton in Goring, 1279); cf. McKinley, *Surnames of Oxon.* 42; *ODFNBI*, s.v. Bowton, Streeting, Townsend.

14. e.g. Wm in Angulo (Whitchurch, 1279); Hen. in la Hurn (North Stoke, 1279); Edith in la Lane (Mongewell, 1306); cf. *ODFNBI*, s.v. Hearn, Lane.

15. Adam ad Molendinum (Whitchurch, 1279); Hen. atte Spitele (Newnham, 1327). The former presumably refers to Whitchurch Mill and the latter to the leper hospital at Crowmarsh: *VCH Oxon.* XX (Crowmarsh Gifford).

16. Reginald de Stokbrugg (Crowmarsh, 1279); Ric. de Stokbregge (Newnham, 1306); Ric. Stoke[b]rugge (Newnham, 1327). For Stockbridge, *VCH Oxon.* XX (Crowmarsh Gifford).

17. Alan Stonhous (Mapledurham, 1327). An alternative toponymic origin in Stonehouse (Glos.) is theoretically possible but perhaps unlikely: cf. *ODFNBI*, s.v. Stonehouse.

18. e.g. John de Fonte (North Stoke, 1279); Hugh de Brok (Crowmarsh, 1279); Walter de la Lake (Mapledurham, 1279); cf. *ODFNBI*, s.v. Well, Attwell, Brook, Lake.

19. e.g. Rob. de Holemere (North Stoke, 1279); M. Gelling. 1953. *The place names of Oxfordshire* [*PN Oxon.*], I, 57.

20. Rob. de Brademere, Gilbert de Wythemere (Checkendon, 1279); *PN Oxon.* I, 47.

21. Ric. de Stamereswell (Mapledurham, 1279); Geof. de Stanmereswelle (Mapledurham, 1327).

22. e.g. James de la Beche (Whitchurch, 1279); Geof. ate Bech (Whitchurch, 1327); *ODFNBI*, s.v. Beech. However, it is possible the Whitchurch family of freeholders was descended from the de la Beches of Aldworth (Berks.): T. R. Gambier-Parry, ed. 1932. *The Goring charters 1181–1546*, II, lxxxvi–xciii; *VCH Oxon.* XX (Whitchurch).

23. Ric. Puryman (North Stoke/Ipsden, 1327); *ODFNBI*, s.v. Perryman. Pearman was later a common local surname.

24. Wm de la Wyteston (Newnham, 1279); Jn atte Whitestone (Newnham, 1327). For Whetstones End near Stoke Row, *VCH Oxon.* XX (Newnham Murren).

25. Walter de Cruce (Newnham, 1279); Rob. ad Crucem (Newnham, 1306); *VCH Oxon.* XX (Newnham Murren).

26. Juliana de Dusteburwe (Crowmarsh, Newnham, 1279). Either a barrow or a rounded hill: cf. M. Gelling and A. Cole. 2000. *The landscape of place names*, 145–51.

27. Jn atte Garstone 'at the grass enclosure' (North Stoke/Ipsden, 1327); Rob. de Hawe 'of the enclosure' (Goring, 1279); Wm a la Heycrofte 'at the hay croft' (Ipsden, 1279); cf. *ODFNBI*, s.v. Garston, Haw, Haycroft.

28. e.g. Rob. de Wik (Ipsden, 1279); Thos de la Wyk (Mongewell, 1279); cf. *ODFNBI*, s.v. Wick. For Wicks Wood, *VCH Oxon.* XX (Mongewell).

29. Alice de Smerecot (Ipsden, 1279). The name probably means 'smiths' cottage': cf. E. Ekwall. 1960. *The concise Oxford English dictionary of place names* (4th edn), s.v. Smethcote. *PN Oxon.* I, 59 notes the Ipsden field-name Smithcutt shaw.

30. e.g. Matilda Cumbe (Goring, 1279); Rob. de la Dene (Mapledurham, 1279); cf. *ODFNBI*, s.v. Coombe, Dean. Laurence atte Combende (Goring, 1279) presumably lived at Coombe End: *VCH Oxon.* XX (Goring).

31. e.g. Jn ate Helle (Whitchurch, 1306); Arnold ate Hulle (North Stoke/Ipsden, 1306); Gilbert de la Suthhulle 'of the south hill' (Whitchurch, 1279); cf. *ODFNBI*, s.v. Hill. Path Hill in Whitchurch was sometimes still known as South Hill in the 1740s: *VCH Oxon.* XX (Whitchurch).

32. e.g. Wm a la Felde (Checkendon, 1279); Hen. ate Velde (North Stoke/Ipsden, 1306): cf. *ODFNBI*, s.v. Field.

33. e.g. Hugh de Buthelesor 'of the house (Old English *bothl*) slope' (Mongewell, 1279); Emma de Chalcore 'of the chalk slope' (Goring, 1306). For Chalcore, *PN Oxon.* I, 51; *VCH Oxon.* XX (Goring). Both names have as their second element Old English *ōra* 'slope': Gelling and Cole, *Landscape of place names*, 203–10.

34. e.g. Rob. de la Bruer (Newnham, 1279); Simon ate Hethe (Goring, 1306); cf. *ODFNBI*, s.v. Heath.

35. e.g. Jn le Frith (Whitchurch, 1279); Walter de la Grave (Checkendon, 1279); Ric. de la Legh (Mapledurham, 1279); Hugh ate Wode (North Stoke/Ipsden, 1306); cf. *ODFNBI*, s.v. Firth, Grove, Leigh, Wood, Attwood.

36. e.g. Thos de Coudrai (Goring, 1327); Jn de Chausy (Mapledurham, 1279); Jn de Mohun (Goring, 1327), from Coudrai (Seine-Inférieure or Eure), Chaussy (Seine-et-Oise), Moyon (La Manche): cf. *ODFNBI*, s.v. Cowdrey, Chasey, Moon.

37. Rob. Gizors, Rob. Pikeneye (Ipsden, 1279), from Gisors (Eure), Picquigny (Somme): cf.

ODFNBI, s.v. Pinkney.

38. McKinley, *Surnames of Oxon.* 204–6.

39. e.g. Wm de Herdewik (Whitchurch, 1279); Walter de Huntercumbe (Newnham, 1279); cf. *VCH Oxon.* XVIII, 348; XX (Whitchurch).

40. Walter de Mongewelle (Newnham, 1327).

41. e.g. Walter de Esthall (Mongewell, 1279); Ric. de Pidington (Mongewell, 1279); Roger de Schereborne (Goring, 1279).

42. e.g. Nic. de Abindon (Newnham, 1306); Rob. de Blebur' (Goring, 1279); Rob. de Brihtwalton (Newnham, 1279); Jn de Burwefeld (Mongewell, 1279); Thos de Clopcote (Crowmarsh, 1327); Wm de Cokham (North Stoke, 1279); Simon de Harewell (Goring, 1279); Wm de Lambourn (Whitchurch, 1306).

43. Jn de Bukingham (Crowmarsh, 1279); Rob. de Hoggessae (Ipsden, 1279); Hen. de Yllemere (Ipsden, 1279).

44. Nic. de Budiford (Checkendon, 1279), probably from Bidford (Warws.): J. E. B. Gover *et al.* 1936. *Place names of Warwickshire*, 201. A less likely provenance is Bideford (Devon).

45. Ric. de Colecestr' (Crowmarsh, Newnham, 1279), presumably from Colchester (Essex).

46. Geof. de Lavynton (Goring, 1327), probably from Market or West Lavington (Wilts.) rather than other places so named: *ODFNBI*, s.v. Lavington. The family name is found in Gambier-Parry (ed.), *Goring charters*, where it is hypercorrected to Launton. However, Launton (Oxon.) cannot be the source of the name, since its medieval forms are 'Langeton' or similar: *PN Oxon.* I, 228.

47. e.g. Ric. le Bakare (North Stoke/Ipsden, 1327); Ralph Carpenter (Crowmarsh, 1279); Hugh Carectar' [i.e. carter] (Checkendon, 1279); Hugh Clerico [i.e. clerk] (Newnham, 1306); Roger Haywardes (Whitchurch, 1306); Jn Molend' [i.e. miller] (Whitchurch, 1279); Walter le Mareschal (Goring, 1327); Geof. Preposito [i.e. reeve] (Mongewell, 1306); Ric. Bercar' [i.e. shepherd] (Ipsden, 1279); Jn Faber [i.e. smith] (Whitchurch, 1279); Alex. le Vacher (Crowmarsh, 1327); cf. *ODFNBI*, s.v. Baker, Carpenter, Carter, Clerk, Hayward, Miller, Marshall, Reeve, Shepherd, Smith, Vacher.

48. e.g. Andrew le Taylur (Newnham, 1279); Wm le Taillour (Whitchurch, 1327); Rob. Tixtor [i.e. weaver] (Goring, 1306); Jn le Webbe (Goring, 1327); cf. *ODFNBI*, s.v. Taylor, Webb; McKinley, *Surnames of Oxon.* 148–9; *VCH Oxon.* XX (overview).

49. Hen. Spicer (Crowmarsh, 1306); cf. *ODFNBI*, s.v. Spicer; *VCH Oxon.* XX (Crowmarsh Gifford).

50. e.g. Phil. Piscatrix [i.e. fisher] (Goring, 1279); Thos le Rammer (Crowmarsh, 1327), perhaps derived from Anglo-Norman French *rameur* 'oarsman, rower'.

51. e.g. Hen. le Turner (Goring, 1279); Wm Besemere (Whitchurch, 1279), perhaps 'besom-maker': *ODFNBI*, s.v. Bessemer.

52. e.g. Roger Crok (North Stoke, 1279); Ric. Tegulator [i.e. tiler] (Crowmarsh, 1279); cf. *ODFNBI*, s.v. Crock, Tyler; *VCH Oxon.* XX (overview).

53. Jn & Ralph le Frankleyn (Gatehampton in Goring, 1279); cf. *ODFNBI*, s.v. Franklin; McKinley, *Surnames of Oxon.* 126–8.

54. Wm le Cotier (Goring, 1279); cf. *ODFNBI*, s.v. Cother.

55. Jn le Justice (Ipsden, 1279); McKinley, *Surnames of Oxon.* 21.

56. e.g. Adam Baldewyne (North Stoke/Ipsden, 1327); Phil. Coleman (North Stoke, 1279); Wm Luvedey (Mongewell, 1279); Wm Sweteman (Goring, 1279); Hen. Wynnemane (Whitchurch, 1327); cf. *ODFNBI*, s.v. Baldwin, Coleman, Loveday, Sweetman, Winman.

57. e.g. Thos Bernard (Ipsden, 1279); Roger Bertram (Whitchurch, 1279); Wm Gerard (Crowmarsh, 1279); Thos Gileberd (Mapledurham, 1279); Nic. Reynald (Goring, 1327); cf. *ODFNBI*, s.v. Barnard, Bartram, Gerard, Gilbert, Reynold.

58. Wm Ywun (Goring, 1279); Walter Howeles (Whitchurch, 1327); cf. *ODFNBI*, s.v. Ewen, Howells.

59. Walter le Waleys (Goring, 1279); Gambier-Parry (ed.), *Goring charters*, I, xliv, lxvii; *VCH Oxon.* XX (Goring); cf. *ODFNBI*, s.v. Wallis.

60. e.g. Geof. Anglicus [i.e. English] (Newnham, 1279); Geof. le Engleys (Mongewell, 1279); Benedict Lenglissch (Crowmarsh, 1327); *VCH Oxon.* XX (Newnham Murren); cf. *ODFNBI*, s.v. English.

61. Hen. Scot (Ipsden, 1279); *ODFNBI*, s.v. Scott. Scots Farm and Scots Common in Ipsden are presumably named from this family: *VCH Oxon.* XX (Ipsden).

62. Jn le Breton (Crowmarsh, Newnham, 1279); Rob. le Franceys (Littlestoke in Checkendon, 1279); McKinley, *Surnames of Oxon.* 21; cf. *ODFNBI*, s.v. Breton, Brittain, Francis.

63. e.g. Wm le Neweman (Ipsden, 1279); Thos le Nyweman (Mongewell, 1279); Thos le Neweman (Whitchurch, 1279); cf. *ODFNBI*, s.v. Newman; McKinley, *Surnames of Oxon.* 75, 203.

64. Wm Belebuck (Goring, 1279). The family features in Gambier-Parry (ed.), *Goring charters*, I, xxxv and passim, with variant forms including Belebouche, Belebuche, Belebuck.

65. e.g. Ric. le Cras (Whitchurch, 1279); cf. *ODFNBI*, s.v. Grace. Cray's Pond in Goring is perhaps named from this family: *VCH Oxon.* XX (Goring).

66. e.g. Hugh le Gant (Checkendon, 1279); cf. *ODFNBI*, s.v. Gaunt.

67. e.g. Phil. Gernon (Mongewell, 1306); cf. *ODFNBI*, Gernon.

68. Wm Duce (Whitchurch, 1279); cf. *ODFNBI*, s.v. Dowse.

69. Wm le Giler (North Stoke, 1279); *Middle English Dictionary* [MED], s.v. gilour.

70. e.g. Thos Marmion (Checkendon, 1327); cf. *ODFNBI*, s.v. Marmion.

71. Thos Wernegold (North Stoke/Ipsden, 1327); *MED*, s.v. wernen, gold.

72. Rob. Tophorn (Crowmarsh, 1279); Thos Tophorn (Crowmarsh, 1327); *MED*, s.v. tup(pe), horn; cf. *ODFNBI*, s.v. Topham, citing the early bearer Wm Toppeheved, for which the meaning 'ram-head' is suggested.

73. Reaney, P. H. 1967. *The origin of English surnames*. Routledge & Kegan Paul, 292–3.

74. Wm Tredewater (Whitchurch, 1279); *MED*, s.v. treden, water; *VCH Oxon.* XX (Whitchurch). For similar nicknames, cf. *ODFNBI*, s.v. Treadaway, Treadwell.

75. This section written by Simon Townley.

76. *VCH Oxon.* XIX, 1–4, 14–15, 29–30, and passim. The forest itself was uninhabited save for isolated hermitage-cum-chapels, park buildings at Cornbury, and (by the later

Middle Ages) a few scattered forest lodges: ibid. 256–8.

77. *Rot. Hund.* II, 726–46; TNA, E 179/161/8–10; C. C. Fenwick, ed. 2001. *Poll Taxes of 1377, 1379 and 1381*, part 2 (British Academy Records of Social and Economic Hist. n.s. 29), 332–4 (Shipton and Langley only); B. Schumer, ed. 2002. *Oxfordshire forests 1246–1609* (Oxfordshire Record Society 64).

78. *Rot. Hund.* II, 735–6 (Underwood), 743 (*de fraxino)*; TNA, E 179/161/8–9 (atte nassche; walde); cf. *ODFNBI*, s.v. Nash, Underwood, Would.

79. TNA, E 179/161/9–10; *ODFNBI*, s.v. Woodrow, Woodruff.

80. *Rot. Hund.* II, 739; *ODFNBI*, s.v. Rock, Nock (atten oke); cf. *Rot. Hund.* II, 744 (Rob. le Ston'). For the place name Roke, *VCH Oxon.* XVIII, 34.

81. Fenwick, ed. *Poll Taxes*, 334; *ODFNBI*, s.v. Leigh.

82. *VCH Oxon.* XIX, 89, 103.

83. Ibid. 16, 104, 143–4.

84. Schumer, ed. *Oxfordshire forests*, 56.

85. Ibid. 57. 64; *VCH Oxon.* XIX, 15, 89, 104, 229. The Ascott charcoal burner (noted 1398) was William atte Nashe (i.e. at the ash), although by that date his name was probably hereditary.

86. Fenwick, ed. *Poll Taxes*, 332–3; *ODFNBI*, s.v. Brush, Turner (including other possible origins). Cf. the Whitchurch name Besemere (above, Langtree, occupational names).

87. TNA, E 179/161/9, s.v. Ascott D'Oyley and Leafield; ibid. DL 43/8/14; Fenwick, ed. *Poll Taxes*, 332 (Horn); cf. *ODFNBI*, s.v. Horn. Derivation from Woodhorn (Northumb.) seems unlikely.

88. *VCH Oxon.* XIX, 170–1. Cf. also William Forster: Fenwick, ed. *Poll Taxes*, 332; *ODFNBI*, s.v. Forester, Forster.

89. de Langley (formerly Rasur): below (other bynames).

90. e.g. Schumer, ed. *Oxfordshire forests*, pp. 45–9, 66, 68; *VCH Oxon.* XIX, 103.

91. e.g. J. Gibson, ed. 1994. *Oxfordshire and North Berkshire Protestation Returns and tax assessments 1641–42* (Oxfordshire Record Soc. 59), 97; cf. Gloucestershire Archives, D9125/3/26, fol. 34.

92. TNA, E 179/161/8; *ODFNBI*, s.v. Hayne, Haynes. Possibly also from Haynes (Beds.).

93. TNA, E 179/161/8–9; *ODFNBI*, s.v. Lovekin, Luckin. Recorded as a Ramsden forename in 1279: *Rot. Hund.* II, 736. Cf. Edekin (*Rot. Hund.* II, 735).

94. e.g. Alfred, Baldwin, Colling, Osmund: *Rot. Hund.* II, 730, 735–6; *ODFNBI*; cf. McKinley, *Surnames of Oxon.* 211–15.

95. *Rot. Hund.* II, 730–1, 743; *ODFNBI*, s.v. Ennett, Lettice, Marriott.

96. *Rot. Hund.* II, 730, 743; TNA, E 179/161/9, s.v. Ascott D'Oyley, Lyneham; McKinley, *Surnames of Oxon.* 23, 264–5 (Welikempt, Welekempd); *ODFNBI*, s.v. Smart; cf. ibid. s.v. Makepeace.

97. TNA, E 179/161/8. The name seems to have been occasionally confused with Richards, but survived locally into the 17th century: ibid. E 179/161/9; Schumer, ed. *Oxfordshire forests*, 127, 132; Gibson, ed. *Protestation Returns*, 97.

98. *Rot. Hund.* II, 730 (le freeman, both villeins); TNA, E 179/161/8, s.v. Lyneham (le

knyht); cf. McKinley, *Surnames of Oxon.* 3–4, 202; *ODFNBI*, intro. 3.3.4.

99. *Rot. Hund.* II, 735; TNA, E 179/161/9, s.v. Shipton; *ODFNBI*, s.v. Bond, Bore (suggesting the nickname 'boar', though association with Old and Middle English *(ge)būr* also seems possible).

100. Noted at various dates (sometimes Latinised) in Ascott, Langley, Leafield, Lyneham, Ramsden, Shipton: *Rot. Hund.* II, 726–46; TNA, E 179/161/9; Fenwick, ed. *Poll Taxes*, 332–4.

101. For John, *Rot. Hund.* II, 743. Smith and miller (or *faber* and *molendinarius*) occur repeatedly in e.g. *Rot. Hund.* and TNA, E 179/161/9.

102. *Rot. Hund.* II, 738; TNA, E 179/161/8–10; *VCH Oxon.* XIX, 60–3, 184–6, 199–202. Cf. Fenwick, ed. *Poll Taxes*, 332–3 (Slattere).

103. atte cross or *de cruce*; atte novene or offene; *in angulo* (at the corner); atte barre (gate); atte broke, atte watere, *de fonte*; atte putte; atte hethe; atte medpleck (meadow + plekke, a patch of land); bovetun: *Rot. Hund.* II, 726–46; TNA, E 179/161/8–10. Cf. *ODFNBI*, s.v. Oven, Barr, Pitt, Medcroft; McKinley, *Surnames of Oxon.* 42–5.

104. Cf. above, Langtree hundred.

105. *Rot. Hund.* II, 735; *VCH Oxon.* XIX, 129–30. The term 'hulwerk' also referred to the South Oxfordshire Grim's Ditch through Ramsden.

106. McKinley, *Surnames of Oxon.* 69–80.

107. e.g. de Bedeford (Bidford, Warws., or Bideford, Devon?); de Chivele (Chieveley, Berks.?); de Coleshulle (Coleshill, Glos.?); de Lodebur' (Ledbury, Herefs., or Lydbury, Salop?); de Risendon (Rissington, Glos.?): *Rot. Hund.* II, 735, 743; TNA, E 179/161/8–9. West Oxon. places referenced in toponymics included Bloxham, Chadlington, Fifield, Fulbrook, Hailey, Hanborough, Minster Lovell, Salford, and Taynton.

108. *Rot. Hund.* II, 731, 735, 738; TNA, E 179/161/8–10, s.v. Ascott, Lyneham, Milton. Scot could equally be a relationship name from the Middle English personal name Scot: *ODFNBI*.

109. *Rot. Hund.* II, 736, including men named from Hanborough, Hailey, Delly End in Hailey, and Wilcote; cf. VCH Oxon. XIX, 229.

110. McKinley, *Surnames of Oxon.* 72.

111. Ibid. 17–18; *VCH Oxon.* XIX, 48.

112. *Rot. Hund.* II, 735, 743; TNA, E 179/161/8–9.

113. Fenwick, ed. *Poll Taxes*, 332–4; TNA, E 179/161/170; E 179/161/177. Leafield saw a further largescale turnover in local surnames between the 17th and 19th centuries: *VCH Oxon.* XIX, 146; B. Schumer. 1991. 'Woodlanders: the village of Leafield and the Pratley family, 1851–71' (London Univ. Diploma in the History of the Family), 9, 33.

114. TNA, E 179/161/170; E 179/161/177; E 179/162/233.

115. Draper, S. 2017. Chaundy: the history and origins of an Oxfordshire surname. *Oxoniensia.* 82. pp. 359–61.

Seven

Advertising Family Businesses
in Oxfordshire

Sue Honoré

Unlike today, when companies have names such as ABC Taxis and Heavenly Bread, earlier businesses in Oxfordshire and elsewhere were named after the owners, instilling great pride in their trade and providing an easy way to know who managed the business. This chapter is designed to highlight some of the ways family historians can find out about such businesses in Oxfordshire, especially in the nineteenth and twentieth centuries.

Figure 54. A motorcycle delivery vehicle belonging to J. Pratley, baker and confectioner.

Trade directories

Finding records, particularly images of family-run businesses, is becoming much easier. Increasingly, trade directories can be found online (see, for example, the University of Leicester's collection for Oxfordshire: (http://specialcollections. le.ac.uk/digital/collection/p16445coll4/search/searchterm/Oxfordshire/field/ place/mode/exact/conn/and/order/nosort). There is also a useful guide to trade directories which can be found at https://www.oxfordshirehistory.org. uk/public/directories_free.htm. Although directories did not include everyone (entries needed payment), and were often a year out by the time they were published, they can be an invaluable source of information for the changing population of a village over time, a useful source for tracing ancestors who may have moved and to discover when businesses were handed on to a family member on the death of the proprietor. They might also provide clues as to the name of an employer of a young man if his trade and location is known. Advertisements can also be found in other directories such as the Post Office Directory or locally printed village directories.

Shopfronts

Shops themselves usually had the name of the proprietor over the door, or in some cases painted on the building itself. Window displays could be elaborate, showing the variety of goods for sale, again providing extra background on an ancestor. Photographs and illustrations of Oxfordshire shops and business premises can be found on Oxfordshire History Centre's site www.pictureoxon. org.uk. Picture Oxon collections include a notable survey of 1940s and 1950s Oxford shopfronts. Records and publications, including some images of local businesses, can be found in Oxfordshire History Centre (OHC)'s archive and local studies collections by searching Heritage Search, OHC's online catalogue. Collections relating to Oxfordshire businesses may also be found in several local museums. They can be seen in local history books written about specific Oxfordshire localities, such as the *Changing Faces* series. When there was a special event such as a royal jubilee, the end of a war, a market or a special national/local holiday then shops were often decorated and images will have found their way into local newspapers. Shops in a town centre or

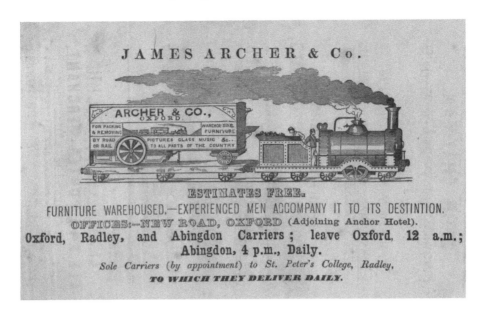

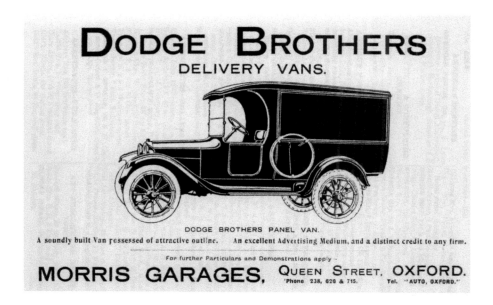

Figure 55. (a) An advert for Archer & Co., from the 1871–2 Post Office Directory of Oxford; (b) advertisement for Royal Oxford sausages from John Wiblin, butcher, in Kelly's Oxford Directory of 1907; (c) advertisement for Dodge Brothers' delivery vans at Morris Garages on Queen Street, Oxford, from Kelly's Oxford Directory of 1921.

near a village square may well be recorded in these pictures. Newspapers can be accessed at the OHC and some libraries, as well as from sources such as the British Newspaper Archive (www.britishnewspaperarchive.co.uk) and newspapers.com (www.newspapers.com). The British Newspaper Archive has an increasing number of titles, including key publications for Oxfordshire such as *Jackson's Oxford Journal, The Oxford Times* and *Banbury Advertiser*. Oxfordshire History Centre holds collections of titles not yet available online.

Delivery vehicles

Goods needed to be delivered, and carts (and more recently, vans) may have shown a company logo. Again, local history books, the OHC and museum collections and even private family records may contain useful information. Where picture dating is possible, based on the clothing of the individuals or given landmarks, then an image may help family historians to identify individuals in the photo.

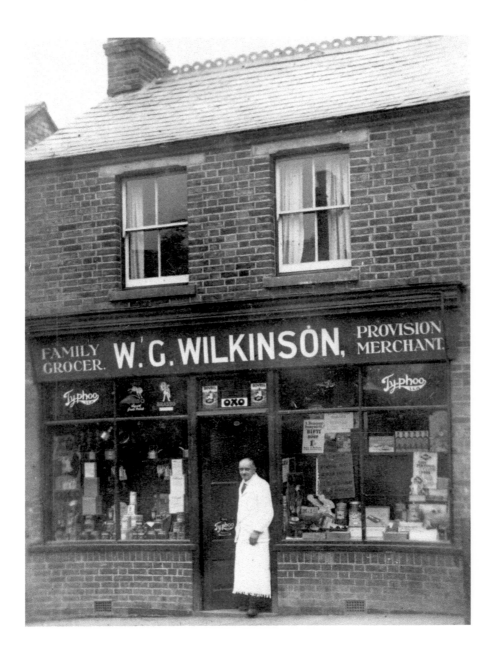

Figure 56. (a) 39 Crescent Road, Cowley, a general grocery store run by William Wilkinson. Image taken in the late 1930s/early 1940s; (b) Nos. 118–120 Magdalen Road, Oxford, Smart Faulkner & Co Quality House grocer's shop, with an advertisement hoarding for Boffin's bread on the side; (c) 71 and 71a Sheep Street, Bicester: Coxeter's furnishing shop and A. E. Electrical shop; (d) Castle's fruiterers and seedsmen of Wantage, with Mr W. Castle standing at the door; (e) E. Butler & Son grocer's shop in Windmill Road, Headington; (f) Shop front of A. Baker & Company (1898) Ltd, tobacconists at 135 High Street, Oxford; (g) Scrivener's, a family shop which started as a tailor's and ended as a toy and wool shop in Bicester, with Miss Carrie Scrivener standing at the door; (h) the striking walls of Lamprey & Sons in the Market Place, Banbury.

Figure 57. (a) W. M. Harris, butcher and fishmonger, making deliveries; (b) Fred Skuse, baker and grocer and Bob Blake with the Skuse delivery van; (c) the lorry and builders at Bartlett Brothers Builders in Witney; (d) the Upstone paint van outside the shop in Porlock, Somerset, run by Albert Louis Upstone (1899–1977), who came from an Oxfordshire family; (e) W. Hobbs, hardware seller, delivery van; (f) another grocer's van, Adams & Son of Bladon.

Posters/Flyers

Special occasions such as sales, or the delivery of a particular consignment of goods, could prompt a shop owner to create a poster which was hung in prominent places locally. Being fragile and often printed on cheaper paper, many will not have survived, but there are examples of such flyers in collections found in museums and archives. Businesses may also have printed catalogues, business cards or postcards advertising their businesses, which have a greater chance of surviving. Those who could afford it would post larger advertisements in trade directory pages, signifying a more profitable business or an owner attuned to the value of advertising. If a business was big enough or run by a prominent family, then examples of the documents may be found in family collections accessible via the National Archives Discovery site (https://discovery.nationalarchives.gov.uk) or local archives and museums. The John Johnson online collection (http://johnjohnson.chadwyck.co.uk/) is another valuable resource which includes trade cards and other ephemera and can be accessed using a library card.

The Best Breakfast in the World

'Not eating your breakfast, this morning, dear?'

'No, this Bacon isn't as good as usual. This isn't COTTRELL'S, is it?'

'I'm sorry dear, but my grocer had sold out of COTTRELL'S BACON, so I had to have some other kind, which he said was "quite as good"'

'Well darling, it is not anywhere near as good, so please get COTTRELL'S, as I do like to start the day well, with a good breakfast'

COTTRELL'S PRIZE MEDAL BACON

FOUR PRIZE MEDALS AWARDED FOR
WILTSHIRE CURED BACON AGAINST ALL ENGLAND

FINEST QUALITY OBTAINABLE

Be sure and ask your Grocer for Cottrell's Bacon and see that you get it

COTTRELL'S SAUSAGES are THE BEST
TRY THEM

Sole Manufacturer: J. E. COTTRELL, Abingdon, Berks.

Keep The Home Firms Earning

Figure 58. (a) Early printed advertisement for the White Lion family and commercial hotel and William Page, wine and spirit merchant, of Banbury; (b) advertisement for Hitchman & Co. Pale Ale and Stout Brewers, Chipping Norton; (c) full-page Cottrell's bacon advertisement from Oxford Monthly, vol. 12, 1935.

Other methods

Advertising could be put on the actual goods sold, if there was space. Glass or earthenware bottles from breweries, drink manufacturers or chemists' medicine bottles are common. Sometimes small plaques were added to mechanical goods and farm equipment. Wrappers or shopping bags may survive in a few cases. These artefacts can often be found in museum exhibits. Gravestones may be marked with the carver and photographs may have the photographer printed on the back. Some people have researched businesses within a given trade or local area and can provide history of when an owner operated (e.g. www.cartedevisite.co.uk for photographers; Stephanie Jenkins' Headington site: www.headington.org.uk).

Figure 59. (a) A cake wrapper from Oliver & Gurden of Oxford; (b) bottles used by Hitchman & Co. Brewery of Chipping Norton.

Surveys

Knowing an exact address or position on a map for a given business can be useful for family history researchers. Many ideas have already been mentioned above, but there may be other useful sources. From time to time surveys were undertaken by government bodies or individuals in a given area. These surveys may provide a wealth of information on shop names, owners and exact locations. There may also be images or very detailed descriptions of the buildings. Historical maps may also be labelled with business names. For Oxfordshire, some examples of surveys and other location-based sources include:

- The Historic Environment Records/Sites and Monuments Records from Historic England (https://historicengland.org.uk, with some records available on Picture Oxon).
- Oxford City Council Heritage Register (again, many images on Picture Oxon).
- The Vale & Downland Museum, Wantage.
- Generic photographers, such as Taunt and Packer who travelled around photographing locations, which may be found on some postcards for sale in antique shops or at fairs as well as online.
- Maps drawn up for government or legal purposes such as tithe maps, district valuation maps (both available from www.oxfordshirehistory.org.uk) or maps produced for land sales.
- The *Victoria County History* of Oxfordshire volumes may also contain business owner names and dates (www.british-history.ac.uk/search/series/vch--oxon).
- Last, but not least, local history societies for individual towns and villages. Information may be found in printed or photographic form but also in the knowledge of the society members.

Figure 60. One of the avenues in the Covered Market built by John Gwynn in the late eighteenth century, showing several butchers' stalls advertising their goods in the foreground and even a bicycle advertising Gibbard's butchers.

Summary
Finding advertisements for a family business can lead to datable photographs of family members, maps and address listings detailing exact locations, a history of a business in a given town or village, dates when a business existed, goods sold, newspaper articles on the business, and relatives' names – all of which can enhance the information of the history of an Oxfordshire family.

Eight

Oxfordshire Village Life: Changes in the Nineteenth Century

Charles Eldridge

Introduction

The nineteenth century would bring great changes to rural life in England; families would flock to the growing cities or new countries with the promise of higher wages and better living conditions. Others left as their cottage industries became part of the Industrial Revolution. Two factors in many Oxfordshire villages were enclosure and the industrialisation of farming practices; the former would deny ordinary agricultural labourers and smallholders land to support themselves (and thereby they would have to rely on parish relief) whilst the latter would reduce the need for casual farm labourers, replacing people with machines. Enclosure had its benefits; it allowed better crop rotation and planting techniques, and encouraged land conversion and reclamation that led to increases in crop yields and acreage of farmlands that fed the country as the population in England grew from less than 10 million (in 1801) to around 30 million (in 1901).

This chapter tells the story of four medium-sized parishes that between them spread across the historical county of Oxfordshire (Figure 61).

Figure 61. Location of the four Oxfordshire parishes described in this chapter.

1. Central Oxfordshire: Bletchingdon

Figure 62. Driving cattle through Bletchingdon, past the Black's Head Inn, early twentieth century.

Bletchingdon parish includes the hamlet of Enslow on the River Cherwell (and from 1790, the Oxford Canal) to the west of the main village. Bletchingdon village was originally built around a green, but the north-side houses were demolished when Bletchingdon Park was modified and later rebuilt by the Annesley family in 1783–5, who continued to live there through the nineteenth century. In Enslow, there was a stone quarry and flour mill. Bletchingdon's common lands were enclosed by agreement between the Lord of the Manor, the rector and the tenants in 1622 which predates the first use of an enclosure act in Oxfordshire by 100 years. Until the nineteenth century, most of the eastern part of the parish was uncultivated heathland used for sheep. High-quality meadowland along the banks of the Cherwell encouraged some arable farming, but most of the land remained grassland until around 1840.

2. South Oxfordshire: Chalgrove

Figure 63. The timber-framed manor house at Chalgrove dating from about 1450.

Chalgrove parish includes the hamlet of Rofford to the north-west. Enclosure occurred late in Chalgrove (1843) though, like Bletchingdon, Rofford was enclosed during the seventeenth century. Chalgrove originated as a linear village surrounded by open fields, occupying a site on the banks of Chalgrove stream.

The major landowners were Oxford colleges (Magdalen and Lincoln). During the nineteenth century, the parish remained predominantly agricultural, with sheep, cattle and some corn production. Rofford contained a few larger farms, whilst Chalgrove supported small-scale farmers and cottagers who benefitted from common grazing rights. Chalgrove brook flows south of the village, passing near the church, and formerly powered several mills.

3. North Oxfordshire: Tadmarton

Figure 64. A group of villagers in Tadmarton in the 1920s.

Tadmarton parish, south-west of Banbury, splits into two communities – Upper Tadmarton includes the church, manor house, the Lampet Arms and a group of farmhouses. The hamlet of Lower Tadmarton was probably the original settlement, with scattered buildings and a farm near the mill. It lies at the junction of a prehistoric track used by Welsh drovers, still in use into the nineteenth century. Both communities retain much of their original character today, with many of the houses which were listed in the Hearth Tax of 1665 surviving. By 1797 much of the parish seems to have been pasture or meadow. During the nineteenth century, three generations of MacDermots held the manor, with Manor Farm being occupied by tenants. Another landowner was Captain Lampet, who built The Highlands near Lower Tadmarton and owned an agricultural machinery factory in Banbury. The Highlands was also let out to tenants as the captain did not want to live surrounded by 'all those sheep'.

4. West Oxfordshire: Brize Norton

Figure 65. Barnes Stores, Brize Norton, on the main road through the village.

Brize Norton lies on the northern edge of the Thames valley beside the old Bampton to Burford and Witney to Gloucestershire roads. The East Gloucestershire Railway was built through the parish and a railway station opened in 1873 south of the village. The village occupies the parish's central area and includes two farms: Manor and Grange. There were six outlying farmsteads. After enclosure in 1776, several farms were improved and a new farmstead (Kilkenny Farm) was created. The large farms created continued with only minor changes for almost a century. From the late eighteenth to the mid twentieth century, farmers continued to practise arable-based mixed farming. Sheep remained the principal livestock.

These parishes were chosen for this study as they were of similar acreage and population throughout the nineteenth century (see Table 14), though the present-day populations are quite different. All four parishes show gradual growth in population until 1841 or later (16–59% increases) with, in some cases, more rapid declines until the end of the century (21–45% decreases) and into the twentieth century.[1]

| | Acreage | Population by date | | | | | | | | | | | |
		1801	1811	1821	1831	1841	1851	1861	1871	1881	1891	1901	2011
Bletchingdon	2654	503	521	570	641	638	673	659	693	602	649	549	910
Chalgrove	2385	518	506	569	549	691	616	549	527	512	429	379	2830
Tadmarton	2070	387	377	401	355	404	450	411	434	357	320	301	541
Brize Norton	3277	453	475	528	627	687	720	716	695	639	610	537	938

Table 14. Parish size and population.

Census and population

Fields recorded in the census

Using the 1841 to 1911 census information for each parish, the following sections look at how changes in Britain affected the lives and roles of the common folk within these parishes. As there were significant changes in the villages in the early 1900s, the inclusion of the 1911 census data helps to emphasise late nineteenth-century trends.

Each census gathered slightly different information. The 1841 census did not identify specific birthplaces or exact ages whilst, in general, only the occupation of the head of each household was recorded. The 1851 census documented birthplaces and an increased diversity of occupations.

For most of the farms in 1851, the census included the acreage and number of labourers employed. It also highlighted those regarded as paupers or receiving relief; this was probably to assess the impact of Poor Law unions and workhouses created in the late 1830s. Later censuses do not indicate those receiving relief. From the 1891 census onwards, less information is given about farms. In the 1911 census new information is given on length of any marriage and, if appropriate, the number of children from that marriage.

Population change

When comparing age, birthplace and gender data for each parish population, similar trends were seen for all four parishes:

- average ages for both males and females increased from mid 20s to early 30s between 1841 and 1911. The most dramatic changes occurred after 1891;
- the percentage of inhabitants born within the parish declined from 56–71% (1851) to 49–56% (1911) – the effect in Bletchingdon was less than the other parishes; and
- there were marginally more males in Chalgrove, Tadmarton and Brize Norton though the imbalance seems to disappear by 1901.

When looking at age distribution (Figures 66–69) there is consistency in that the most common group were children aged one to nine, followed by young people of ten to nineteen with a gradual decrease by (age) decade from there on. The total Chalgrove population was highest early on (691 in 1841) with Tadmarton and Brize Norton peaking in 1851 and Bletchingdon in 1871. The biggest population drop for 1841–1911 occurred in young people under twenty, who as a cohort fell between 11% (Brize Norton) and 20% (Bletchingdon) more than the percentage drop for the total population of each village; the middle-aged were relatively stable and the older population increased.

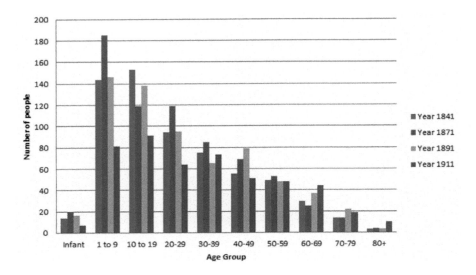

Figure 66. Bletchingdon population by age for 1841, 1871, 1891 and 1911.

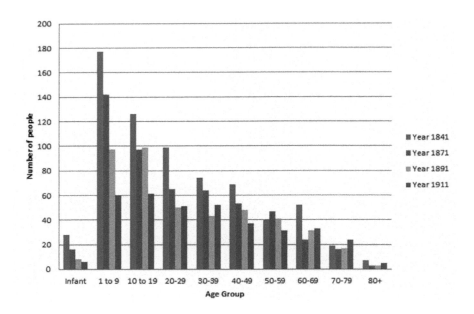

Figure 67. Chalgrove population by age for 1841, 1871, 1891 and 1911.

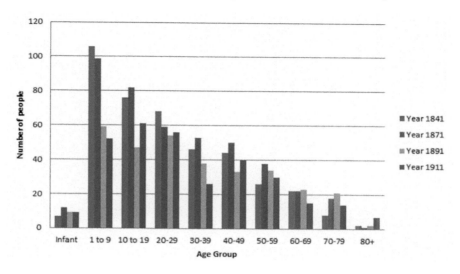

Figure 68. Tadmarton population by age for 1841, 1871, 1891 and 1911.

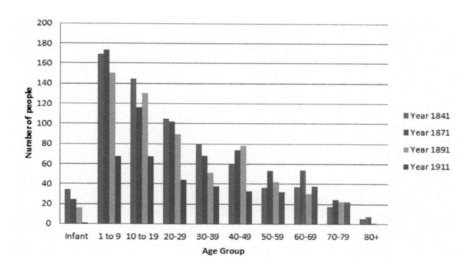

Figure 69. Brize Norton population by age for 1841, 1871, 1891 and 1911.

Some aspects of population change are explained by a drop in births (baptisms) after 1891; this was confirmed by examining the Bletchingdon parish register where the number of baptisms dropped from circa nineteen per year from 1810–1890 to fifteen per year in 1891–1900 and to nine per year from 1901–1910.

Factors impacting the population of the villages

Agricultural decline

The nineteenth century in England was a difficult time for farming. There had been an earlier depression between 1815 and 1835 which impacted these four villages as well as the rest of the county, with landlords and tenants suffering financial ruin, such that large areas of farmland were entirely abandoned, though most of the poor could still rely on parish relief. From 1836 until 1846, agriculture flourished until the Corn Laws (which were designed to keep grain prices high to favour domestic producers) were repealed. Between 1873 and 1879, British agriculture suffered from wet summers that damaged grain crops. Cattle farmers were hit by foot-and-mouth disease, and sheep farmers by sheep liver rot. Imports from overseas, particularly grain from the USA and sheep/meat from Australia and New Zealand competed with local Oxfordshire produce in the second half of this century.

Mechanisation

New agricultural machinery was developed in blacksmiths' workshops, starting with ploughs aligned in series that improved corn production. From the 1820s, a wide variety of animal-powered machinery was developed, especially for improving the efficiency of cutting and threshing grain, although primitive methods of cutting corn with hand tools were still used into the twentieth century. A new seed drill was developed in Oxfordshire to sow more efficiently. In 1870, George Dew, diarist and Poor Law official, wrote that a farmer (W. P. King of Rectory Farm), near Bletchingdon '… has a new reaping machine which cost near upon £30 … He says he can save 4 shillings an acre in the expense of cutting his corn and it is calculated to do the work of 16 men with only one man and two horses'.[2] As the century progressed, steam-powered engines drove both farm machinery and new railways across Oxfordshire.

In Tadmarton, the arrival of landowner Captain Lampet mid-century probably changed the lives of many families; his engine-driven threshers reduced the number of labourers required, and ensured enough work that the engine driver lived in the village from 1861 onwards.

Machinery also destroyed the hand-lacemaking which once flourished in the south Midlands. Hand-stitched boots were superseded by machine-made products from Northampton or Leicester. Tailors declined as mass-produced clothing became available. The decline in parish populations also affected those involved in the building trades. Those that serviced the horse economy, i.e. blacksmiths and carpenters/wheelwrights, survived somewhat longer until the motor vehicle undermined their trades in the twentieth century.

Enclosure and tenant farms

The Enclosure Acts (1604–1914)[3] combined smaller scattered strips of land into larger estates for the wealthier landowners, often allocating poorer land to small farmers. Most importantly, they removed common grazing rights, depriving many villagers of part of their livelihood and ability to support their families by using shared grazing fields. Each of these four villages had a different story on the impact of enclosure.

The early seventeenth-century enclosure of Bletchingdon had allowed the establishment of a dozen or so tenant farms that covered most of the parish, with some of the heathland being reclaimed as farmland. Farm acreage was larger than in other parts of the county, as shown in Table 15. Whilst some tenant farmers were born and bred in Bletchingdon (such as the Bartletts and several generations of the Rogers family), most were from neighbouring parishes.

One example of incomers was the West family, who came from Rousham and farmed the Greenhill Farm. They specialised in breeding and showing of their long-wool sheep and won medals and cups as far away as Birmingham, London and Paris.

Acreage	Men	Boys	Farm	1851	1861	1871	1881
400–500	11–18	4–5	Home Farm	H. Bartlett	H. S. Bartlett	A. H. Bartlett	H. J. Bartlett
300–480	7–10	4–5	Stonehouse	J. Holliday	J. Holliday	T. Shrimpton	
345–380	14–17	5	Greenhill	W. West	T. West	T. West	
150–160	2–4	1–2	Manor Farm	S. Rogers	S. Rogers	T. Rogers	T. Rogers
140–260	2–7	2	Heathfields	G. R. Walker	J. Hatwell	W. Boddington	W. Arnold
130–150	1–3	1–3	Frognest		E. Tuffrey	E. Tuffrey	E. Coleman
120–200	2–4	1	Heath	W. Butler	E. Emberlin	E. Emberlin	
120–130	1–3	2	Diamond	S. Gregory	R. Gregory	J. Rogers	J. Rogers
95–120	3	1–2	Staplehurst	J. Peake	J. Peake	T. Enser	J. F. Haines
75	2+	1	Grove		J. Warland	S. Walton	S. Walton
60–130	2–4	1–2	Underdown	.	C. N. Bartlett	W. T. North	
235	8		Not listed	J. Walton			
200	7		Not listed	C. Harper			
50	2	1	Cottage				W. Enser

Table 15. Tenant farms in Bletchingdon.

The Rogers family, who came from neighbouring Kirtlington via Tackley, farmed the Manor Farm for four generations until the whole estate was sold in 1967. Details of farming life were recorded in farm records[4] and the census and included the names of the workers in 1851: Stephen Tomlins (aged 40), William Bullock (37), John Savin (17), Alfred Marlow (14), Charles Woodford (11), William Boffin (17) and Elizabeth Tomlins (46). In later censuses, fewer labourers were used and often there was one boy who may have only worked during the ploughing season, such as Charles Woodford in 1851.

Prior to the 1851 census, most of the tenant farmers had been locals and included the following families listed in both 1795[5] and the 1841 census: Painter, Baker, Butler, Cox, Eustace, Bayley, Budd, Peverell and Haines. From 1851 there was higher turnover in farm tenants.

Chalgrove had nine fields that covered 1764 acres at the time of enclosure in 1845.[6] The average field size was smaller than Bletchingdon, but still large, with arable (mostly wheat) covering two-thirds of the parish. The proportion of arable rose to three-quarters by 1870, with meadows supporting 70 horses, 67 dairy cattle, 1960 sheep and 186 pigs. Following the agricultural depression in the 1870s, arable land fell to less than half, with pasture supporting a large number of cattle (277).

In contrast, Tadmarton had 37 small closes (less than 4 acres) when the village was enclosed in 1776, with fifteen proprietors including the rector and the churchwardens. Enclosure did not substantially affect the pattern of land ownership. Fifty-five years later, thirteen proprietors were assessed for land tax, of whom only four were owner occupiers with a much larger number (12) of tenant farmers. By 1851 farms were generally small or alternatively in the region of 100–270 acres farmed by families with the surnames such as Austin, Bloxham, Colegrave, Garrett, Salmon and Wilks, along with the Rector Thomas Leg who had 166 acres. Like Chalgrove, animal husbandry increased later in the century; by 1892 Lower Tadmarton Farm was described as a first-rate sheep farm and two-thirds of another farm was pasture.

From the early nineteenth century a considerable proportion of Brize Norton had become owner-occupied. In the 1851 census, nine substantial farmers occupied 2824 acres with individual holdings ranging from 215 to 469 acres. From 1817, William Worley, his son and grandson were successive part-owners of Manor Farm, the last becoming sole owner and the owner of other farms. After 1877, Christ Church amalgamated the John Worley farms to form the larger 845-acre Manor Farm. As such, Brize Norton followed the model of the larger farms of Bletchingdon and Chalgrove.

Figure 70. Charles Gillett of Brize Norton.

Brize Norton's principal farmers survived the late agricultural depression, tenants presumably being assisted by rent reductions: the rent of Manor Farm was reduced during the 1880s by 38%. Again, the farms changed from largely arable to mixed farming. In 1863 two large central farms were described as turnip, barley and stock farms. From 1817 Charles Gillett and his descendants owned and worked Kilkenny Farm. John Gillett created a flock of Oxford Down half-breed sheep which was regarded as outstanding in Oxfordshire.

In the 1870s there was a branch of the National Agricultural Labourers' Union in the village with the chairman of the district's executive committee being Joseph Eggleton, a Brize Norton inhabitant and Primitive Methodist preacher.

Poverty

Poverty impacted upon the residents of these villages, as they struggled to survive, affecting the demographic structure, mortality and crime rates.

The Chalgrove Friendly Society was established in 1840 for workers aged 14–45 unable to work due to sickness or injury. Poverty and poor housing may have encouraged some to leave, while others looked to agricultural trade unionism. The loss of common grazing land may explain an increase in the number of recorded paupers in this parish from thirteen in 1841 to forty-three only ten years later. In a study of 1892,[7] Chalgrove parishioners were described as being poor and discontented and their conditions in terms of housing, pay, amenities and relations with their employers were considered to be worse than in most of the surrounding villages.

Robert Laurence, Vicar of Chalgrove from 1832 to 1885, campaigned for better accommodation for the poorer farm workers but this brought him into conflict with the landowners (the Oxford colleges); he was also secretary of the local agricultural labourers' trade union, demonstrating church support for the poor, as in Brize Norton.

In 1803, seventeen persons were regularly given parish relief in Tadmarton, but two years later, the number had more than doubled and remained around thirty adults for the next two decades. By 1830 there were forty on the overseers' books, including nine widows and at least six orphans, with £740 spent on poor relief. Before the passing of the Poor Law Amendment Act in 1834, expenditure had declined.

In 1802–3, forty-two adults and eighty-nine children (28% of the population) were regularly relieved in Brize Norton. By 1814–5, the numbers had increased to ninety-three adults. Weekly payments to individuals for illness and unemployment were recorded from 1825 to 1833. The overseers arranged the bringing of coal from Eynsham for the poor (which continued for the rest of the century) and made occasional payments for shoes and treatment at the Oxford Infirmary.

Migration

Given the challenges of nineteenth-century village life, population changes in these villages can be explained largely by migration. The movement of young single adults and families to nearby towns, industrial cities and abroad occurred throughout the century but especially after 1870. Some migration was premeditated by Poor Law unions trying to drive out the poor, whilst for others it was a family decision, forced by bad harvests or a lack of agricultural work. Some residents were relocated to the local workhouses in nearby towns that opened in 1835–6 and could house up to 1500 inmates in total across the four locations.

Individual examples of emigration from Oxfordshire included:

- In 1845, forty-two of the poorest villagers left Tackley for a new life in Australia, funded by the parish. They left Liverpool on the *Cataraqui* but all lost their lives in a shipwreck off the coast of Tasmania. Their story is told by the Tackley Local History Group[8] and elsewhere.
- George Dew, the relieving officer for Bicester Union, wrote the following in his diaries:

'In 1871, a young family from Lower Heyford emigrated to Canada after raising the fares by subscription of local people (Dew donated a half crown) whilst late in the year another young man from Lower Heyford sailed for the USA.'

'In 1872, more agricultural labourers refused to work at 10 shillings a week and left for work in Birmingham.'

'In 1874, various ships of emigrants left for New Zealand – most were farm labourers including two more families from Upper Heyford and Caulcott and two families from Islip.'[9]

Occupations
Outdoor occupations

Figure 71. Hornsby traction engine owned by the Smith family, who lived in Lesters Cottage (behind engine) until 1911. Left to right: Arthur Smith jnr, Arthur Smith snr, Frank Edmonds (driver), unknown, Jim Preston, Jim Preston snr, unknown.

As job descriptions became more specifically defined over the century, the generic 'agricultural labourers/farm labourers' dropped (Figure 72). At the same time there was an increase in the number of gardeners, gamekeepers, grooms/coachmen and farm bailiffs ('estate management' category, Figure 73). The use of more vehicles to assist farming led to the increased role of the carter, and roles such as engine driver or engine man appeared with mechanisation. The numbers involved in animal husbandry (shepherds, dairymen, etc.) did not decline and in some cases increased marginally with time as these were tasks that were not yet mechanised.

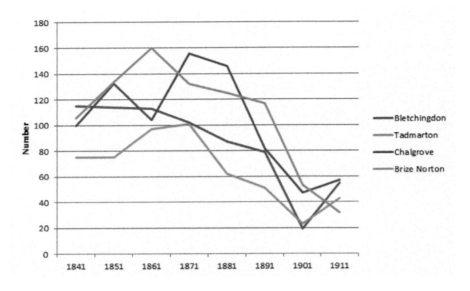

Figure 72. Agricultural labourer/farm labourer jobs in all four villages 1841–1911.

Bletchingdon

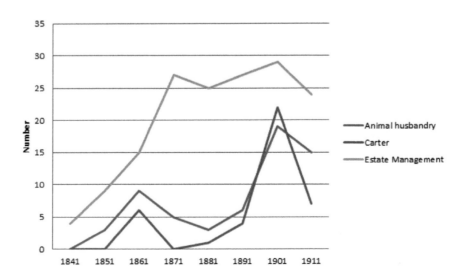

Chalgrove

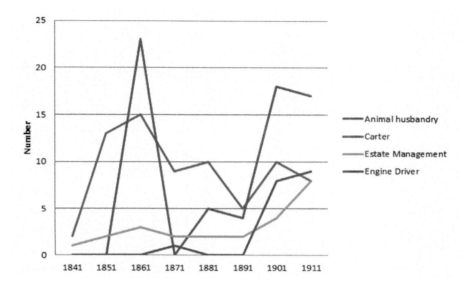

Tadmarton

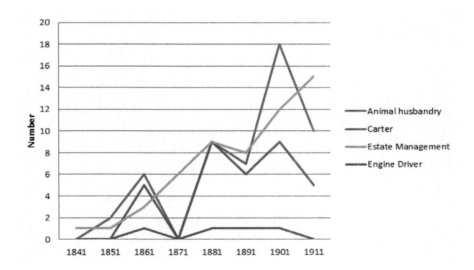

Brize Norton

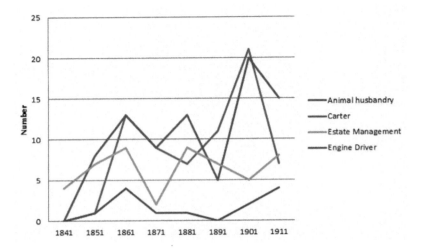

Figure 73. Other agricultural jobs by village 1841–1911.

The overall number of farmers did not change much in all four locations, indicating that the number of farms may have been relatively stable or, as some farms merged, the owners of smaller landholdings described themselves as being in the farming business (Figure 74).

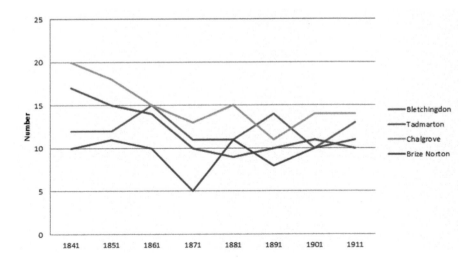

Figure 74. Farmers in all four villages 1841–1911.

In Brize Norton, some families engaged in secondary activities. One of the Akers families became market gardeners from at least 1853 to 1881 and Thomas Gillett (of Kilkenny Farm) was a corn dealer and seedsman. From the 1850s to 1880s four carpenters and wheelwrights were sometimes recorded as makers of agricultural machines and implements. From 1864 to 1877 there was also a manufacturer of artificial manure.

Over half of each parish's population is not listed with an occupation in most of the censuses (usually married women and children). Nevertheless, around 50% of the working population was declared as engaged in outdoor farm employment across the parishes. The overall decline in the parish population in the late 1800s aligns with a decline in the numbers involved in farming and outdoor occupations.

Indoor servants

In terms of indoor servant roles, there was some fluctuation, as seen in Table 16.

In Bletchingdon, the main variations were dictated by the number of servants at Bletchingdon Park at the time of the census return and the purchase of Heathfield House by Viscount Valentia in 1869 as a dower house. The later censuses also included some retired senior servants (housekeeper, cook) listed who had previously worked at Bletchingdon Park.

Apart from the more specific domestic servants at the manor houses, many of the larger farms and households had general (farm) servants who were normally girls from the village employed between leaving school and marriage whilst some of the tenant farmers remained unmarried and employed a housekeeper. There was one oddity in the use of the term 'housekeeper'; many of the married women in Chalgrove were documented as 'housekeepers' in the 1881 census, which was not the conventional use of the word, so that the numbers for this census are inaccurate.

The picture was similar in the other three parishes. There was a decline in the general servant role towards the end of the nineteenth century, possibly as young females had already left the village with their family or found work in local market towns or London.

Occupation	1841	1851	1861	1871	1881	1891	1901	1911
Bletchingdon								
Housekeeper / Cook		7	7	4	7	5	8	6
Nurse / Nursemaid		3	2	7	6	3	4	4
Housemaid / Other Maids		2	7	5	7	9	13	8
Butler / Footman		3	3	2	3	4	4	3
Valet / Lady's Maid		1	5	6	1	5	3	1
Governess / Tutor			1	1		2	2	
Charwoman / Laundry Maid		4	7	8	12	10	5	5
General Servant	43	24	14	23	23	25	7	8
Total	**43**	**44**	**46**	**56**	**59**	**63**	**46**	**35**
Chalgrove								
Housekeeper / Cook		4	9	2	31		6	8
Nurse / Nursemaid		1	2	4			2	2
Housemaid / Other Maids			1		1		4	5
Governess / Tutor				2	1			
Charwoman / Laundry Maid		4	1	3	1		3	2
General Servant	34	8	19	13	11	7	10	16
Total	**34**	**17**	**32**	**24**	**45**	**7**	**25**	**33**
Tadmarton								
Housekeeper / Cook		4	7	10	10	3	8	8
Nurse / Nursemaid		1	2	3	3	2	1	2
Housemaid / Other Maids		1	2	3	4	3	5	5
Footman / Lady's Maid			2	2				

	1841	1851	1861	1871	1881	1891	1901	1911
Governess / Tutor							1	
Charwoman / Laundry Maid			1	2	2	2		1
General Servant	27	21	13	14	7	9	8	8
Total	**27**	**27**	**27**	**34**	**26**	**19**	**23**	**24**
Brize Norton								
Housekeeper / Cook		3	7	9	5	3	2	5
Nurse / Nursemaid		1		1	2	1		
Housemaid / Other Maids			1	1	1	2	2	1
Governess / Companion			1				2	1
Butler / Valet							1	
Charwoman / Laundry Maid		3		4	2		1	
General Servant	33	21	12	15	18	16	3	10
Total	**33**	**28**	**21**	**30**	**28**	**22**	**11**	**17**

Table 16. Indoor servant occupations as shown in census from 1841 to 1911.

Other occupations

Table 17 lists the remaining occupations within Bletchingdon and around Enslow. The village contained the normal trades of a village or small town. It is not surprising that there were a number of carpenters, wheelwrights and blacksmiths to support the local farms though the number of butchers, bakers and grocers seems high for a rural village; it is probable that these were to support fresh food for the Bletchingdon Park and Heathfield House households.

Occupation	1841	1851	1861	1871	1881	1891	1901	1911
Butcher / Baker / Grocer	6	9	7	7	11	13	6	6
Blacksmith	3	4	4	3	2	2	2	1

Carpenter / Joiner / Wheelwright	9	7	10	10	6	4	3	6
Sawyer		5	1	1	1	1	1	
Slater and Plasterer / Thatcher	1	1	1	1				1
Shoemaker	10	9	8	7	4	1	1	1
Tailor / Dressmaker / Draper	2	10	1	3	5	8	7	2
Lace Maker / Milliner / Gloveress		1	2	5	1	3		
Publican / Innkeeper / Ostler	1	5	4	2	3	2	4	2
Dealer / Carrier	3	5	2	2	1	4	2	3
Sub Postmaster / Mistress / Parish Clerk				2		1	1	1
Miscellaneous Occupations		2	2	2	2	4	5	8
Subtotal (Bletchingdon Village)	**35**	**58**	**42**	**45**	**36**	**43**	**32**	**31**
General Labourer	16	1	1			8		6
Wharfinger	1	1	2	1	1	1		
Coal Dealer / Labourer			2		5	3	6	6
Brickmaker / Bricklayer / Tile Maker	2		2	1	1	1	2	6
Miller / Miller Labourer / Corn Merchant	2	1	2	3	2	4	5	4
Boatman / Boatbuilder / Canal Labourer	4	1	2	2	1		3	

Stonemason / Labourer / Store Dealer	3	3	1	3	5	9	8	2
Stone Quarry Labourer		6	10	12	5	9	6	6
Road Labourer		2		1		5	2	3
Railway Labourer / Platelayer		9	2	11	3			
Railway Porter / Clerk / Signalman		2	1	1	2	3	4	
Railway Policeman		1	1					
Station Master (GWR)				1	1		1	1
Subtotal (Enslow)	**28**	**27**	**26**	**36**	**26**	**43**	**37**	**34**
Total	**63**	**85**	**68**	**81**	**62**	**86**	**69**	**65**

Table 17. Trades and other professions (Bletchingdon).

The second group of trades based in Enslow relates to the import of cheap coal from the canal, the stone quarry which serviced local building projects, and the development of the railways to the west and south of the parish. Enslow railway station was opened in 1850 as part of the Great Western Railway from Oxford to Banbury.

Figure 75. Narrowboat families on the Oxford Canal.

Whilst some boatmen and their families are shown in Bletchingdon during the early censuses, none remain later on. Initially one or two boatmen worked and lived on their canal boats whilst their families remained in the parish. Later, the whole family lived on the boat. As the canal became less commercially attractive, some returned to work in other roles in the village, including the Bazeley family.

Table 17 also shows the demise of the village shoemaker to be replaced by factory-made shoes, the increase in railway workers and the introduction of local post offices and the telegraph. The village also gained new skills such as a local midwife (nurse) and a hairdresser.

Two carriers were mentioned in the 1841 census for Chalgrove (Joseph Gray and Richard Bellson); one of them running to Thame, Wallingford and Oxford. The business continued in the 1860s, but was gradually reduced to twice-weekly visits to Wallingford. Post was delivered through Wallingford or Tetsworth. A sub-post office on Chalgrove High Street was run in 1851 by the carrier's daughter, and in 1899 (when run by the farmer Frederick Mander), it was a money-order office and savings bank.

Table 18 lists the other occupations in Chalgrove and shows a similar range of trades to Bletchingdon with a few additions (cooper, watchmaker and lime maker) though these trades would disappear after the 1861 census as people moved to more urban locations or the trade died out locally.

Occupation	1841	1851	1861	1871	1881	1891	1901	1911
Butcher / Baker / Grocer	6	8	7	6	6	11	1	4
Blacksmith / Farrier / Harness Maker	5	4	4	5	6	6	1	3
Cooper	2	1	2					
Carpenter / Joiner / Wheelwright	4	4	4	6	5	4	3	4
Clockmaker & Watchmaker	1	1						
Sawyer / Woodman	1	2						
Thatcher		2	1	1	2	1		
Shoemaker	3	4	5	4	1		2	2
Tailor / Dressmaker / Needlewoman	3	7	8	12	4	1	1	2
Lace Maker / Straw Bonnet Maker		2		1				
Publican / Innkeeper / Maltster	4	3	2	3	4	5	1	5
Hawker / Dealer / Carrier	4	1	4	2	1	1		2
Postmistress / Post Worker / Parish Clerk		2	1					3
General Labourer				1		4	2	3
Lime Maker			1					
Miller / Millwright	1	2	1	2	4		2	5
Stonemason / Labourer	1	1	1	1	1			
Road Labourer		1				1	1	1
Policeman			1					2

Miscellaneous Occupations		1	2				2	2
Total	**35**	**46**	**44**	**44**	**34**	**34**	**16**	**38**
Pauper / Parish Relief	12	42	14	1		8	3	1

Table 18. Trades and other professions (Chalgrove).

Table 19 shows the data for Tadmarton, which contains similar trades to Bletchingdon and Chalgrove. With around ten farms in the parish, several carpenters, wheelwrights and blacksmiths were needed to support farm maintenance, though the sharper decline in blacksmiths compared to the other villages suggests that the use of horses became limited over time. The number of butchers, bakers and grocers fluctuated throughout the century. These numbers did not increase in the last census with the full occupancy of Highlands Mansion and Highlands Villa, so it is possible food was sourced from Bloxham or Banbury by this time. The parish was poorer, reducing demand for local goods and services. Without a nearby railway or canal there was less need for general labourers.

Occupation	1841	1851	1861	1871	1881	1891	1901	1911
Butcher / Baker / Fruiterer / Grocer	3	4	1	4	5	3		3
Blacksmith / Farrier	2	5	3	3	1			1
Carpenter / Joiner / Wheelwright	5	6	4	5	6	1	6	4
Weaver / Hurdle Maker	3				1	1		
Sawyer		3	1					1
Plasterer / Thatcher			1				1	
Shoemaker	4	5	1	3	5	2	2	
Tailor / Dressmaker / Draper	2	1	1	2	5	4	1	2
Lace Maker / Milliner		3		1				1

Publican / Innkeeper / Maltster	2	3	1	5	5	2	2	2
Hawker / Dealer / Carrier / Higgler	2	2	1	4	2	3	1	1
Postmistress / Parish Clerk		1	1	2		1	1	1
General Labourer		12			3	3		
Lime Burner		2		2				2
Miller / Millwright		2	2	2	2	1		
Stonemason / Labourer			1	1	1	2	1	
Road Labourer						1	2	1
Policeman			1	1	1			
Miscellaneous Occupations	1	3	3	3	2	4		6
Total	**24**	**52**	**22**	**38**	**39**	**28**	**17**	**25**
Pauper / Parish Relief		12	3		11	1	7	

Table 19. Trades and other professions (Tadmarton).

Table 20 lists occupations within Brize Norton, providing similar results to Bletchingdon apart from the focus on stonework and malting.

In the late seventeenth century, commercial malting expanded in Brize Norton. Until the early nineteenth century, there were usually two to four active maltsters. From 1880 onwards, there was a single maltster presumably renting the main malthouse.

Quarries adjoining land in the open fields were mentioned in the seventeenth and eighteenth centuries and Brize Norton supplied building stone to Bampton's expanding population. Stoneworking was dominated by the Timms family, who had lived in the parish from 1773. Seven of eight stonemasons listed in 1841 were family members, as were all six masons in the 1881 census. Numbers thereafter declined, but one business survived into the twenty-first century with Patrick Timms undertaking Cotswold stonewalling and other building work.

Occupation	1841	1851	1861	1871	1881	1891	1901	1911
Butcher / Baker / Confectioner / Grocer	4	12	14	15	13	18	10	6
Market Gardener							2	
Blacksmith	1	2	4	2	3	2	1	
Carpenter / Drill Maker / Wheelwright	7	6	7	4	4	5	7	2
Weaver	1							
Sawyer			2		1			
Slater / Plasterer / Builder	2	1	1		2	2	1	
Shoemaker	6	8	9	8	4	3	2	
Tailor / Dressmaker / Draper	3	6	7	11	5	11	7	4
Gloveress / Milliner			2	3		2	1	
Publican / Innkeeper / Maltster	2	2	8	5	3	2	3	1
Hawker / Dealer / Carrier / Higgler	2	4	2	3	2	1	1	2
Postmistress / Parish Clerk		1	1	1		3	1	
General Labourer				12	1	4	8	7
Stonemason / Labourer	8	12	20	17	8	7	13	5
Road Labourer / Surveyor					1	1	4	8
Railway Labourer / Platelayer					3	3	5	1
Railway Porter / Station Master					2	1	3	2
Coal Dealer / Coal Merchant's Labourer					1	1	2	1

Quarrier / Quarryman	1	1	1				2	1
Police Officer			1					
Miscellaneous Occupations		3	7	2	4	3	3	4
Total	**37**	**58**	**88**	**83**	**58**	**69**	**76**	**44**
Pauper / Parish Relief		15	2	18	1	1		

Table 20. Trades and other professions (Brize Norton).

Family surnames

Bletchingdon

Many of the common surnames present in nineteenth-century censuses for Bletchingdon arrived in the village in the period 1740–1780. Between 1750 and 1901, the parish population increased from 353 to 503[10] with immigration from neighbouring parishes as the village prospered under the management of the Annesley family. However, many of the incoming families were poor. The following list shows how these families filled many of the labouring roles:

- Taylor – mainly agricultural labourers or stone quarry labourers;
- Ward – agricultural labourers or general labourers;
- Tomlins – agricultural labourers;
- Bazeley – agricultural labourers though some became boatmen, with subsequent families living along the canal system around Coventry and Nuneaton;
- Hickman – some worked as gardeners as well as agricultural and railway labourers;
- Cripps – agricultural labourers;
- Baker – butchers and small-scale farmers;
- Kirtland – worked in a variety of roles from farmer, blacksmith, cordwainer or grocer to more menial roles as stone quarryman, carrier or boatman;
- King – one of the village's blacksmiths;

- Bullock – initially worked as agricultural labourers but successive generations moved up in society with roles as gamekeeper, coal merchant, miller, groom, and finally Charles Bullock became the parish clerk and steward to the Valentia family in the late nineteenth century;
- Collett – arrived in the late 1800s as stonemasons;
- Peverell – the men were agricultural labourers whilst the women appeared to be village laundresses; and
- Harper and Bartlett families – tenant farmers in the first half of the nineteenth century.

The story was similar for the other villages.

Chalgrove

Some of the long-term residents of Chalgrove, who were mostly agricultural labourers, had the surnames Atkins, Belson, Brown, Burton, Cherrill, Coles, Fletcher, Goode, Gray, Gunston(e), Guntrip, Herbert, Hicks, King, Munt, Paine, Peedell, Smith, Spicer, Stone, Weed(o/e)n, Wheeler, Williams, Wood(w)ards and Young. Some of the principal farmers over the century were Billing, Cannon, Franklin, Hatt, King, Nic(k/h)olls, Stevenson and Young. The Belcher family specialised as stonemasons; White as harnessmakers; Peedell as coopers; Hatt as butchers; Smith and Faulkner as shoemakers; Phelps (along with Auger and Goode) as carpenter/wheelwrights; and Rym(e/a)ll as blacksmiths, along with Brown, Barnett and others. Jobs later in the century involved bricklaying (Brown, Goode, Phelps) and acting as agricultural engineers for traction engines (e.g. Belson, Gray, Hurst, Smith, Williams, Woodwards). Several families managed public houses or sold beer and ran grocery or bakery shops over the nineteenth century.

Tadmarton

In Tadmarton most of the early nineteenth-century residents were local or from nearby Warwickshire parishes. Surnames held by long-term residents this century, such as Austin, Barlow, Bodfish, Bourton, Box, Cartwright, Elmore, Freeman, French, Gardener, Howkins, Morby, Preedy, Turner and Young, were in agricultural labourers' jobs, although some moved into other roles towards the end of the century. The core farmers were Austin, Garrett, Salmon and Wilks. The Hitchcox, Howkins and Wells families practised shoemaking and the Meadows and Shirley families were carpenters. The role of miller was often shared with farming as in the Cherry, Tatum and Sims families and the role of publican was also a part-time job supplementing farming, held by various people such as the Austin, Green, Blakeman and Pargeter families. The Green and Newport families had a wide range of roles in the village over a long period, from agricultural labourer to schoolteacher.

Brize Norton

Brize Norton also had long-standing agricultural labouring families such as the Akers, Butler, Clack, Drinkwater, Faulkner, Hunt, Joynes, May, Miles, Parker, Pearce, Sollis, Stevens/Stephens, Upston(e), Wade, Wiggins, Wilkins and Winfield families. The farmers were Gillett, Lay, Lord, Gardner and Morley, along with another wave such as the Sturch family towards the end of the century. However, the village was dominated by the Timms family businesses in stonemasonry and later the building trade, pulling in other local workers such as Bye, Dipper, and Radburn in stonework, Hart and Sil(l)man in quarrying and Nunney in the slate trade as well as several building labourers. The Akers family provided long-term confectionery and baking for the village but also worked the land. The Holtom family were the longest serving shoemakers along with others such as Greenaway, Hambridge and Tuckwell. The Cooper, Hall, Powell, Pratt and Drinkwater families were in the beer trade. The Hollis family were mechanics and later in the century men with surnames such as Gunn, Cambray, Phipps, Tuckwell and Wade became involved in machinery and the railways. Other long-standing families with multiple occupations included Cox, Gardner and Smith.

Summary

The nineteenth century was one of change brought about by enclosure and land ownership, improved transport links, mechanisation and trade. In rural Oxfordshire these changes impacted farming practice and produce, as well as requirements for agricultural jobs, and inevitably led to increased levels of poverty and migration. These four villages, of comparable size in different parts of the county, with some variation in residents and occupations, were nevertheless very similar and were likely to be typical of most other Oxfordshire villages in that century.

Notes

1. Further information on these four parishes can be found in the VCH Oxfordshire series. For Bletchingdon: Lobel, Mary D., ed. 1959. *A history of the county of Oxford: Volume 6, Ploughley Hundred.* London: Victoria County History. *British History Online;* for Chalgrove: Townley, Simon, ed. 2016. *A history of the county of Oxford: Volume 18.* Woodbridge, Suffolk: Boydell & Brewer for the Institute of Historical Research; for Tadmarton: Lobel, Mary D. and Alan Crossley, eds. 1969. *A history of the county of Oxford: Volume 9, Bloxham Hundred.* London: Victoria County History; for Brize Norton: Colvin, Christina *et al.* 2006. *A history of the county of Oxford: Volume 15, Bampton Hundred (Part Three),* ed. Simon Townley. London: Victoria County History.

2. Dew, George James, and Pamela Horn. 1983. *Oxfordshire village life: the diaries of George James Dew (1846–1928), relieving officer.* Abingdon: Beacon Publications.

3. UK Parliament. 2021. *Enclosing the land.* https://www.parliament.uk/about/living-heritage/transformingsociety/towncountry/landscape/overview/enclosingland/.

4. Humphries, Vanadia. 2003. *Memoirs of Bletchington: an Oxfordshire village.* Ox in the Circle Publications for the Parish Council of Bletchington, Oxfordshire.

5. EurekA Partnership. 2002. *The people of Bletchingdon.* Stoke Mandeville: EurekA Partnership on behalf of Eileen Bartlett and Angela Hillier.

6. Oxfordshire History Centre Enclosure Handlist. https://www.oxfordshire.gov.uk/sites/default/files/file/history-collections/Enclosurehandlist.pdf.

7. Sources: Research by Kevin Poile and the Chalgrove Local History Group (https://chalgrovelocalhistorygroup.org.uk) and Townley, Simon, ed. 2016. *A history of the county of Oxford: Volume 18.* Woodbridge, Suffolk: Boydell & Brewer for the Institute of Historical Research.

8. Tackley Local History Group. *Tackley Local History Group.* https://www.tackleyhistory.org.uk/.

9. Dew, George James, and Pamela Horn. 1983. *Oxfordshire village life: the diaries of George James Dew (1846–1928), relieving officer.* Abingdon: Beacon Publications.

10. Lobel, Mary D., ed. 1959. *A history of the county of Oxford: Volume 6, Ploughley Hundred.* London: Victoria County History.

Nine

Tracing Coopers in Oxfordshire

Sue Honoré

Introduction

This chapter looks at a specific trade in Oxfordshire – coopers or barrel makers – in order to investigate the location and stability of surnames in the county and the interaction between surnames inside and outside Oxfordshire. The search was based on apprenticeship records, freedom of city records, poll tax, trade directories, census, wills, baptism/marriage/burial information, family trees and other miscellaneous records from 1547 to 1895. It will not have captured every cooper in the county, but should provide a reasonable record.

Although this study focuses on coopers, there is much that could be applied to other tradespeople in and from Oxfordshire.

Figure 76. A series of sketches from W. Pyne of coopers at work.

The coopering population

In total the study produced 514 names of coopers which included both apprentices and masters. Out of this total, 207 were on apprentice lists. There were 347 masters' names. Forty-one individuals were able to be traced as both apprentices and masters. The number of 514 does not equal the total number of individual people because some were on both lists and others shared names with their relatives and could not always be separated out. Another group did not have apprenticeship records available online, but appeared to train with their father, uncle or another relative in a less formal arrangement and stayed in the local area; they were traced through records such as censuses and trade directories. A third group trained in London and appeared to remain there. In total 32% of the people had an accurate or good history of their lives from apprentice to adult cooper.

The apprentices were drawn mainly from the middle 'tradesman' classes, although there were a surprising number whose fathers were wealthy yeomen who appeared to be pushing their second and subsequent sons to have a reputable trade to fall back on. There were some from the labouring classes, but these were much less common.

The masters were located across Oxfordshire but not every village needed a cooper and they were concentrated in the bigger towns or close to brewery sites. Often multiple generations or relatives of the same family worked in the same town. Some of the key names involved from larger towns are shown in Table 21.

Place	Surnames
Banbury	Austin, Charles, Clarson, Cook, Fox, Franklin, Green, Kilby, Lamber, Lidiard, Luckman, Taylor
Bicester	Baker, Bull, Capel, Carter, Dagley, Edenbrough, Hancock, Hazel, Lait, Timberlake
Henley	Bennett, Brookman, Browne, Cope, Cox, Deavon, Hartred, Hayward, Johnson, Lovegrove, Pratt, Reeves
Oxford	Alder, Allen, Archer, Ayres, Betts, Bland, Bolton, Boswell, Boyce, Burton, Carr, Carter, Clarke, Clift, Colton, Combs, Cook, Cowdry/Coldry, Cox, Day, Goodman, Grey, Hall, Hayes, Hedges, Hudson, Hughes, Hutt, Jackson, Jagger, Jones, Kyrke, Lowe, Parker, Pain/Payne, Pink, Plowman, Prickett, Robertson, Robinson, Rogerson, Rone, Savory, Sawyer/Sayer, Smith, Soanes, Stevens, Taylor, Toms, Tubb, Walker, Whitton, Wickson, Wise/Wife, Wospe, Wright
Thame	Goodson, Hall, Hunt, Long, Peedell, Staples
Watlington & Wallingford	Banister, Cope, Hall, Hunt, Keeley, May, Maxey, Ryder, Wells
Witney	Ayres, Clark, Fisher, Flower, French, Harris, Holloway, Keene, Matthews

Table 21. Surnames of coopers in larger towns of Oxfordshire.

There were also instances of coopers in several smaller locations, including Bampton (Williams family), Burford (Francis/Baylis), Caversham (Harding), Charlbury (Collett/Hanks), Culham (Wase/Wade), Deddington (Powers/French/Franklin), Faringdon (Noad/Ockwell), Hook Norton (Luckett/Wyton), Mollington/Alkerton (Boot/Goldby), Standlake (Eaton) and Woodstock (Garrett/Godfrey), plus a few other towns and villages. There were usually only one or maybe two cooperage businesses in these smaller places.

Locations

Figure 77. Morland coopers at Abingdon in the 1890s.

For those who were apprentices in Oxfordshire and for whom their origin could be traced through apprenticeship documents, 90% came from within Oxfordshire, followed by 6% from the bordering counties (Gloucestershire, Berkshire, Buckinghamshire, Northamptonshire, Warwickshire and Wiltshire). However, apprentice coopers did come from far away to train in the county – including from Dorset, Hampshire, Huntingdonshire (Cambridgeshire), Lancashire, Yorkshire, Shropshire and Wales.

All those who came from distant counties, apart from one, trained in Oxford, so the city was a draw to longer distance travel, perhaps to a master with a good reputation, providing future work prospects or to train with someone with a family connection. The peak of distant apprentices in Oxfordshire occurred in the sixteenth century (63%) with the majority of the rest in the eighteenth century, which was a period of population expansion. In the seventeenth and nineteenth centuries, apprentices from elsewhere were not so common, at least for coopers.

There is an imbalance between those who came to Oxfordshire to train or were local apprentices and those who left the county for education. It is astounding to see that 24% of the Oxfordshire-born apprentices left for London to train. London was obviously a strong draw and, given that nearly 60% of all traceable apprentices in this study stayed in the place they trained to continue to live and work, there was a definite skills drain of coopers from Oxfordshire to London, particularly to the Shoreditch dockland area. Those going to London tended to come from the south of Oxfordshire (56% of the total), with 24% from the west and the rest from Oxford and the north. These results probably reflect the geographic proximity between the locations as well as the more common trade routes and social networks connecting Oxfordshire to other places.

Even if they trained in Oxfordshire, several coopers left the county once qualified. Locations include seagoing areas such as Portsea in Hampshire, Kingston upon Hull and Bristol as well as industrial centres such as the Midlands including Birmingham (Henry Hancock), and Reading (James Adnett). Others left for the counties bordering Oxfordshire. Some travelled overseas to Canada, the USA and New Zealand.

Families and connections

The social and business networks of families were as important in the past as nowadays. It is therefore not surprising that there was a fair amount of intermarriage of children in Oxfordshire cooper families. The selection of apprentices was commonly based on blood ties, neighbours or known connections. Migration was also influenced by these networks. Tracing a given Oxfordshire surname may require a good deal of working sideways to investigate social history to find those connections.

Keeping it in the family

There is a large group of Oxfordshire men who are documented as coopers but for whom there is little or no documentation of their apprenticeship. Researching their family history, they appear to have trained with a father, uncle or older brother and most stayed to work in the same village or town or one close by once they were qualified. In these families, if a couple had several sons and the father was a cooper then one or two sons would be trained to take over the business and the rest apprenticed in other trades – so spreading the risk to the family of business changes and allowing each son to make a decent living. Childless coopers or those with few sons (or none who appeared to want to take over), would take on their nephews and cousins, or an apprentice who eventually became part of the family through marriage.

A village community example

Figure 78. Spring Street, Chipping Norton.

In the Tite (Tight) End area of Chipping Norton (now Spring Street) lived a dynasty of coopers. The Matthews family began with William Matthews who had at least three sons. William junior was an agricultural labourer but Robert (*c.*1798–1868) and Henry (*c.*1807–1857) were coopers and probably trained with their father. Henry in turn had two sons who became coopers – Charles James (*c.*1837–1920) and William (1832–1914). In the fourth generation Charles James had two sons who followed in the trade – Walter (b. 1871) and William (b. 1876) – who most likely trained with their own father.

Robert (1798) married only late in life and did not appear to have children. He took on Robert Denyer, born locally from a Sussex immigrant family, as an apprentice. Denyer was still working for him in 1851, but left for Castle Cary in Somerset on the death of his own father. Robert Matthews also trained up his two nephews, Charles James and William, sons of his brother Henry. Towards the end of his career Robert took on another apprentice, William Powers junior, son of another cooper, from Deddington. It appears that William returned to Deddington to work though. Robert's nephew William Matthews had moved to Newark in Nottinghamshire to work as a journeyman cooper by 1861, then on to Mortlake in Surrey, Canterbury in Kent and eventually Reading, where he died. That left Charles James and his two sons as family members to carry on the Chipping Norton business. The younger (William, 1876) worked in the gloving industry for a time and returned to coopering in his later life, but his father Charles James and brother Walter (1871) worked in the family business through to the twentieth century. By the turn of the century young Walter had moved to work in Kidderminster in Worcestershire, eventually changing occupation, becoming an engineer in the car industry in Rugby, abandoning his work as a cooper. His father Charles James and brother William, on returning to the business, were the only ones left in Chipping Norton.

Just down the road in Middle Row lived John Eaton who could well have worked with the Matthews family. He was a contemporary of Robert Matthews, born c.1795 in Standlake, from another coopering family, probably trained by his father John in Standlake before moving as a young man to Chipping Norton. John had several sons in Chipping Norton but only one, Daniel (born c.1836), was trained to be a cooper. However, although John worked all his life as a cooper in Chipping Norton, his son Daniel moved as a young man to work in Burton upon Trent where he died relatively young in 1880.

The third family of coopers in Chipping Norton, also living in Tite End, had the surname Phillips. Coopers called Phillips operated in London, Worcestershire and several locations in Oxfordshire. This family goes further back and may have been earlier coopers in Chipping Norton. Brothers James (born c.1736) and Haddon (1740) Phillips, sons of John and Elizabeth, may have trained with their uncle James to become coopers. Haddon moved to Broadway, in Worcestershire, and trained other apprentices there, seemingly keeping up connections with his Chipping Norton family. His son Richard may have come back to work in Chipping Norton as there was a cooper of the right age whose wife and newborn son died in 1804. Thomas Phillips, born in 1803, worked for a time in Tite End but died in the 1840s, leaving his children to be cared for by their grandparents and none seemed to become coopers.

So from at least the mid eighteenth century through to the end of the nineteenth century, there were coopers in Tite End in Chipping Norton with the surnames Matthews, Denyer, Eaton, Powers and Phillips.

Migratory pull

The coopers of Oxfordshire also showed several examples of a pioneer family member who moved to Oxford, London or another large conurbation who then 'pulled' other family members with him. Robert Bland who worked in Oxford in the 1590s took on Robert Wilson of Kettlewell in Yorkshire and Marmaduke Brooke of Tiddington, on the Oxfordshire/Buckinghamshire border (although people with this name came from Yorkshire). Giles Edenbrough, who was a cooper in Bicester in the mid eighteenth century but whose family appear based in Aynho in Northamptonshire, took on several apprentices who had connections to Aynho, such as Richard Lambert in 1726 and Thomas Westley in 1735. Tobias Carr was in Oxford as a cooper in the 1660s. Carr is not an Oxfordshire surname. In 1725 a Toby Carr of Hinckley, Leicestershire, was taken on as an apprentice wheelwright to James Gardner in Oxford, hinting at a geographical surname trail to follow. Several Oxfordshire cooper surnames appear in London, such as Hiatt, Barfoot, Munday, Toovey, Franklin and Tidmarsh; once one cooper from a family was based in London then others sent their sons there to learn the trade and gain better prospects – often continuing for several generations. It is not surprising, therefore, that some traditional Oxfordshire surnames gradually vanish from the county and appear elsewhere.

Marriages

The example from Chipping Norton, above, shows how many families of coopers may have lived and worked closely together.

Apprentices were forbidden to marry during their training and this group showed a consistent pattern of marrying only a few years after their term had been completed, which may help those researching Oxfordshire tradespeople.

Another interesting pattern emerges when looking at who coopers or their sons and daughters married. There were several instances of a cooper's daughter marrying into other cooper families and also marrying the family apprentices! For example, John Boot, born 1753, apprentice to William Goldby of Mollington, married William's daughter Mary. Other connections (possibly marital) are hinted at from witnesses to wills, administrations and

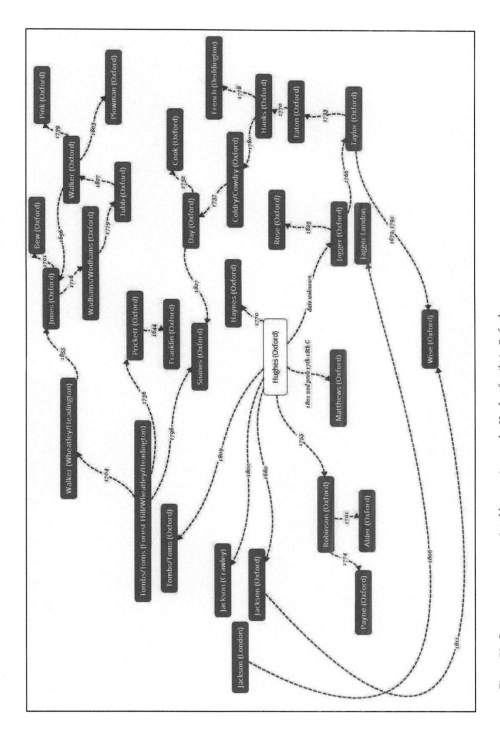

Figure 79. Cooper surnames associated by marriage to the Hughes family in Oxford.

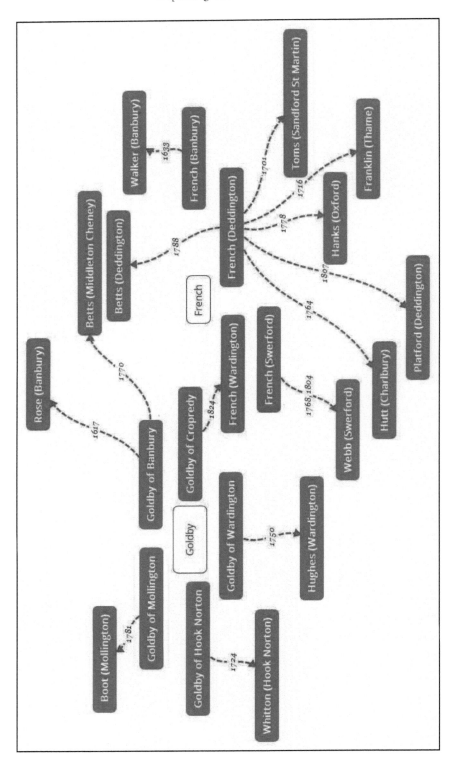

Figure 80. Cooper surnames associated by marriage to the Goldby and French families in the Banbury area.

inventories, such as John Deavon acting as a witness in 1741 in the will of Thomas Pratt of Henley, both coopers.

From some initial cooper-related marriages, connections to the wider family show a network of associated cooper surnames in Oxfordshire. Two simplified examples are shown here (Figure 79), based on the Hughes family of Oxford and the Goldby and French families of the Banbury area. Tracing these interconnections to known cooper families reveals a strong social network within this trade community. They also show how quickly one surname within an area can be connected to many others.

The Hughes family had been in Oxford for a long time, at least since the mid sixteenth century. Over time in this study there were fifteen coopers found in the family. They were largely concentrated in the parish of St Thomas and many lived on St Thomas' Street where the Lion Brewery/Morrell's Brewing Company was based. Their neighbours included the Jagger family of coopers (who had children with middle names of Hughes) and the Jackson family of coopers. One branch of the Jackson and Jagger families married in Marylebone and then moved to Oxford. There were several other interconnected families of coopering surnames in Oxford as can be seen from the diagram (Figure 79). (There are many others which have been omitted for clarity.)

The Goldby family were spread across several parishes in the Banbury area and connected directly and indirectly to the French family of Deddington. These families in the diagram (Figure 80) then connect further to those coopering surnames in Chipping Norton, Charlbury, Bicester and Oxford as well as other locations in the county.

Other social connections

Another benefit from exploring a whole community is the discovery of a consistent link outside the main research trail. For example, several families of coopers were Quakers. Joshua Webb, baptised as the son of Richard and Mary at Swalcliffe in 1800 was registered in the Banbury Quaker records, as were all his siblings. He eventually migrated to Michigan in the USA, taking his wider family with him. The French family of Hook Norton were also Quakers. There were members of the Franklin family in Witney and in London who were Quakers. Richard Tidmarsh whose family originated from Adlestrop near Stow-on-the-Wold had his marriage recorded in a London Quaker meeting in 1709. He worked as both a cooper and tobacconist. The Bland and Turner families, amongst others, were from Oxfordshire families in the Ratcliff area of London. Gideon Turner married Mary Hiatt (both Oxfordshire names) in Stepney. Charles Bland was recorded there too. The deaths of William and Daniel Bland of the parish of Mildred Bread St were reported in the Quaker meeting of Ratcliff and Barking; both died in 1741 – William aged twenty-eight and Daniel aged forty-two. Finding this type of connection opens doors to explore other records to trace a family and may lead to migratory information that can be traced through their religious affiliation.

Maintaining future business

Figure 81. Worker with barrels, Clinch's Brewery, Witney about 1939.

Not all of the apprentices who trained as coopers ended up in that profession. Several of the sons of yeoman appeared to revert to being landowning farmers themselves, perhaps after inheriting money or land. It may always have been the aim to have a back-up profession as a cooper just in case. A classic example is William Tuckwell from Signet near Burford who trained in London in the 1780s but returned to Signet, dying as a farmer in 1804. Others moved into allied trades such as carpenter/joiner, wine merchant, brewer or innkeeper. John Platford became a brewer in Hull by 1834. Thomas Maxey of Wallingford was apprenticed to his father John in 1666 but most likely became a joiner. John Clarke of Witney (b. 1826) made a dramatic change to a piano tuner and musician! In the nineteenth century, Thomas Baughan of Woodstock went to London and worked as a baker but eventually returned to being a cooper. In some cases young men trained as coopers and moved into other businesses but returned to become a cooper when their father died. Some worked as coopers until they became older, but it was a hard physical job and perhaps not surprising that in later life several became grocers or public officials (such as William Noad of Faringdon who became a registrar of births, marriages and deaths).

Businesses did not just die when the cooper died. Often his wife would take over and keep on one of their sons or an apprentice or two, probably both for the income and to fulfil obligations to complete apprenticeships. An example is Mary Staples who managed the business of her husband Robert in Thame. Others include Elizabeth Hazell, a confectioner in Bicester, who managed the coopering business of her son William on the death of her husband, and Oxford residents Charlotte Bowell, Sarah Plowman, and Susanna Taylor (widow of Joseph and mother to Agabus, also a cooper). Sarah Warren of London took on several apprentices including Charles and Bernard Butcher of Goring in the eighteenth century. Interestingly, most of the masters tended to take on apprentices within five to ten years before their death, so even if they did not train apprentices regularly (as a few, such as Robert Rogerson did in the 1550s in Oxford, or bigger businesses such as major brewers would have done), skilled coopers tended to prepare a succession plan. Sadly, the business of being a master cooper is now a trade of the past.

Key messages

What does this mean for family historians tracing their Oxfordshire ancestors?

- Tracing people through trade documentation can be very valuable, especially if it was a less common trade. There were several intermarriages, movements of people to core business areas of the country for a given trade and evidence of 'keeping it in the family' in terms of training up young people. People of all levels of society may have been apprentices in skilled trades.
- London was an important city for the people of Oxfordshire who were in a trade. If ancestors are missing they may well have gone to London or be trading between London and an Oxfordshire location.
- Apprentices frequently stayed in their place of training rather than return home once qualified.
- Many tradespeople would train up a child or relative to take over the business, but where that was not an option, coopers (and probably others) took on apprentices as they neared the end of their working lives, often within five to ten years of their death.
- Just because an apprentice trained in a specific trade, it did not mean that he continued in that trade.
- Women managed businesses that involved heavy manual work, often after the death of their husbands.
- Specific trades will be congregated where there is work – for coopers this means ports, and inland locations with breweries or bulk packaging requirements.
- By looking at a whole trade community other connections can be made – as in the case of a strong Quaker community within coopering families of Oxfordshire.
- Community forms an important part in choice of marriage partner, selection of apprentices and workplace location. It is not what you know, but who you know.

Ten

Oxfordshire DNA

Richard Merry and Sue Honoré

Introduction

Is there such a thing as Oxfordshire DNA? Probably not so much now as people become more mobile and genotypes become more mixed regionally, but traces of the DNA from families that lived in the county for long periods may be retained in their descendants for about five to eight generations in autosomal DNA before it gets broken up and unrecognisable, unless they continue to live within an area that has also retained its Oxfordshire DNA characteristics. However, there will be remnants of a localised gene pool shared regionally with nearby counties, as demonstrated by the People of the British Isles Project initiated in 2004.[1] The population genetics aspect of this project was able to distinguish some British 'tribal' groupings dating from the fifth century or earlier and additional detail has since been shown within the former Anglo-Saxon region by commercial development.[2] As might be expected, these results also show affinities with the genetic make-up of western European and Scandinavian communities.

The situation is much better for (male) Y-DNA which is usually associated with surnames, and male lines can be traced over very long periods of time using both short tandem repeat (STR) or single nucleotide polymorphism (SNP) approaches. Provided a family continues to produce male children to perpetuate the line, these tests can add a great deal to family studies. When combined with good family histories – an essential companion – the movements of families can often be traced and confirmed over long periods. Mitochondrial DNA (mtDNA), which is inherited through direct female lines, changes little over time and for most people is only informative over long periods (millennia) or forensically.

In 2013, the Oxfordshire DNA Project was established (through FamilyTreeDNA and the Oxfordshire Family History Society) with an initial aim to collect Y-DNA 'fingerprints' for the surnames of Oxfordshire families. In December 2020 the project had about 450 members. Subsequently, a 'companion' surname project was also begun to try and accumulate family history information to tie in with the DNA material. Autosomal DNA (atDNA) is also of great interest to the project because it helps confirm relationships among the Oxfordshire families. It is usual that people with Oxfordshire ancestry are able to list ancestors with several recognisable Oxfordshire surnames. This may have been possible because of the county's long history as a stable, largely agricultural community, as was also usually the situation in neighbouring counties. It should be kept in mind that, along with known family histories and evidence that people came to the county from diverse places (see Chapter 5), the gene pool probably had many centuries of relative stability until perhaps the mid to late 1800s. The effect of the presence of people from elsewhere attending the University of Oxford on the Oxfordshire gene pool is not known.

This chapter summarises some initial conclusions from the DNA information of various kinds contributed by about 450 people with Oxfordshire connections, although some project members made some or all of their DNA information unavailable. Matching of DNA of all three types used here depends on related people also having DNA tested. The lack of DNA matches is not uncommon for Y-DNA and mtDNA, but extremely unlikely for atDNA. Our conclusions are preliminary because the sample size is still small.

Y-DNA matching

STR matching for these male groups was not straightforward as the level of testing was not uniform and varied from 12 (rarely) to 111 markers. About a hundred individuals did not match anyone with the same surname, forty matched with one other of the same surname, fourteen with two others, and the remainder with up to twenty. To obtain a Y-DNA fingerprint for a surname using STR markers, two to several Y-DNA matches is desirable and best obtained with more distant cousins. Not matching with another person with the same surname is not unusual and the individual may match with no other or other different surnames depending on the number of markers tested – some with low-level testing can match with more than fifty other surnames. In some instances 'non-normal' familial events, such as adoption, illegitimacy, use of an alias or other reason for a surname change, may be the reason for matching a different surname. Very detailed Y-DNA SNP testing may be necessary in some instances.

So far about 165 Y-DNA STR 'fingerprints' have been obtained for individual surnames with an Oxfordshire history, but most have only a single result.

Y-DNA types among males with Oxfordshire male ancestry

Among the membership of the DNA project at the end of 2020, a total of 223 (about 50% of the total membership) males had Y-DNA test results that were associated with their Oxfordshire (or close by) male-line ancestry. More information is available for some surnames under the British Isles (by county) DNA project, but this was not used here. Where information is available and the person tested has Oxfordshire male-line ancestry, it is possible to allocate them to broad haplogroups on the main Y-DNA 'trees' that may stretch back in origin for tens of thousands of years. A haplogroup is a group of people in the population who genetically share a common ancestor on the paternal or maternal lines and inherit SNPs that define the group. Haplogroups are assigned letters of the alphabet, and refinements consist of additional number and letter combinations.[3]

For males with Oxfordshire descent, simplified haplogroups are presented in Figures 82 to 84. As would be expected from European genetic studies, the most common male grouping is haplogroup R with 151 members. This group (R1a and R1b) is thought to have originated in south-west Russia relatively recently. Haplogroup R1a (R-M420) is more commonly found in eastern Europe and R1b (R-M269) in the West. R1b is commonly associated with 'Celtic' types. Those belonging to R-M269 (97) have not had sufficiently detailed testing to be allocated to a subgroup. Haplogroup I is subdivided into two main groups, I1 (defined by the SNP M253) and I2 (defined by the SNP M223), I1 being more common among males with Oxfordshire ancestry. Haplogroup I1 is usually associated with Scandinavian origins in Britain and I2 with Germanic origins. At least six other haplogroups have been found amongst our Oxfordshire male lines (Table 22), mainly haplogroup J (9) and G (4) of a total of 18 individuals. Haplogroups J, G and T are often found in the Middle East, haplogroup E in north Africa, N in Finland/north Russia and L in South Asia.

More information on the European frequency, distribution and origins of the main haplogroups can be found at https://www.eupedia.com/genetics/index.shtml. As more information is accumulated and ancient DNA recovered with an archaeological context, the origins of these DNA groups and their travels are being updated and detailed information that is more than a few years old may be unreliable, although general pictures are not likely to change a great deal.

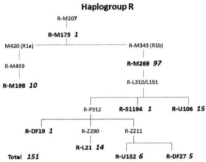

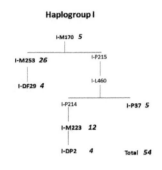

Figure 82. Simplified Y-DNA grouping of haplogroup R men with Oxfordshire ancestry. The haplogroups recorded are shown in bold and the number of individuals in each in bolded italics.

Figure 83. Simplified Y-DNA grouping of haplogroup I men with Oxfordshire ancestry. I-M253 is commonly known as haplogroup I1 and I-M223 as haplogroup I2. The haplogroups recorded are shown in bold and the number of individuals in each in bolded italics.

Haplogroup	E	G	J	L	N	T	Total
Total	2	4	9	1	1	1	18

Table 22. Other haplogroups represented among Oxfordshire Y-DNA.

Although total numbers for Oxfordshire are not large, about 210, the distribution among the Y-DNA haplogroups appears to be quite close to the average for England as a whole (data for comparison can be found at https://www.eupedia.com/genetics/britain_ireland_dna.shtml#origins). About 67% of the Oxfordshire males reported here belong to haplogroup R1b and about 10% each to haplogroups I1 and I2, 5% to R1 and 4% to J2.

Within the Oxfordshire DNA Project, the Y-DNA haplogroup distribution of the earliest known paternal ancestors is shown on the maps below.

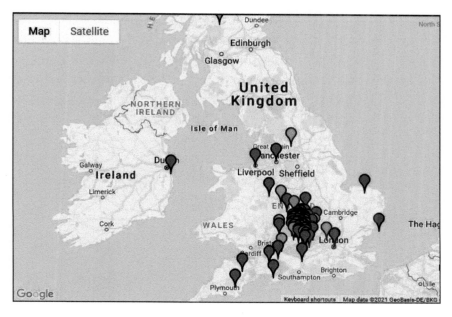

Figure 84. The distribution of earliest known paternal ancestor for males in the Oxfordshire DNA Project, shown (a) for the UK and Ireland and (b) in close-up for the Oxfordshire area. Grey indicates the 'R' haplogroup; blue is 'I'; green is 'G', orange is 'E' and white is unknown. Images produced by FamilyTreeDNA (at https://www.familytreedna.com/public/Oxfordshire?iframe=ymap) using maps by Google and printed with permission.

Mitochondrial DNA

Mitochondrial DNA (mtDNA) defines our maternal lines as it is only passed from mothers to their children. There are many copies of it in each cell, but not in red blood cells. Because the strands of mtDNA contain only about 16,500 base pairs and most of this is in genes that are required for essential functions, there is limited scope for variation as it is highly conserved and mutations are very infrequent, usually occurring over periods of millennia. In addition, fewer people undergo full sequence mtDNA testing as few find it useful in family history. For most, direct female lines are often difficult to follow over more than a few centuries due to the surname changes at marriage, unlike most males.

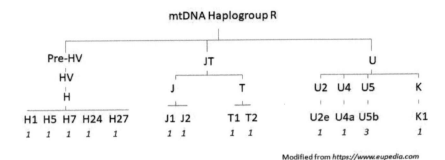

Figure 85. The mitochondrial DNA haplogroups of female lines identified as Oxfordshire, with numbers in italics. Note that mtDNA haplogroup R is not related in any way to the Y-DNA haplogroup of the same designation (see Figure 82).

In the Oxfordshire DNA Project, only a small number of people who have mtDNA information have been able to clearly indicate a female line associated with the county. Only fifteen mtDNA results were indicated as 'Oxfordshire' (Figure 85). As might be expected from data for the broader English population,[4] haplogroups H, U and J are represented. A further seven mtDNA results were indicated for project members whose female line had been traced to nearby counties. These were all haplogroup H (H1 *4*; H3 *1*; H4 *1*; H11 *1*). About 45% of people from western Europe can expect to belong to haplogroup H, 16% haplogroup U, 12% haplogroup J and about 8% each for haplogroups T and K.

Autosomal DNA

Autosomal DNA (atDNA) is by far the most common type of DNA test undertaken. Information is provided by about 700,000 SNPs from selected sites on the 22 pairs of autosomal chromosomes, one of each pair from each parent, and not the X or Y chromosomes. As our DNA is mostly identical, these SNP sites have been chosen to try to be useful in indicating variation among broader populations and serve to enable matching with other individuals – closely related people have more DNA in common with each other than do distantly related people. Due to the randomness of inheritance, a person may 'lose' the identifiable DNA from an ancestor from as few as four generations ago, and almost certainly by eight generations, but retain DNA information that is related to the general gene pools of ancestors that may give clues to geographic origins. For most family historians atDNA is most useful for helping identify 'cousins' related over the past eight generations or so. As with the other types of DNA discussed, successful matching with cousins depends on other people having also undertaken DNA testing.

We have attempted to investigate the 'relatedness' of people who have joined the Oxfordshire DNA Project by looking for matches among the group members. The results for 297 usable atDNA results from members show that two people each match ten others among the members, but most have DNA in common with another one to six DNA 'cousins'. These matches may be reasonably substantial in DNA terms (more than 20 centiMorgans). Those with many matches may include family groups with increased DNA testing for family research purposes. A large number have no matches despite having a good Oxfordshire ancestry. This may mean that the broader family has not had other cousins who have DNA tested and joined the project or that the main ancestor identifiable in a family tree left the county many generations ago, long enough for the atDNA trail to be broken up into small segments that are no longer identifiable, though Y-DNA testing may confirm a direct male connection. For example, instances are known where fifth cousins have been confirmed by Y-DNA matching, but not by atDNA, while another mutual fifth cousin has retained enough atDNA to suggest being a third or fourth cousin. This variation is the result of the randomness that occurs in inheritance and explains why siblings who are not identical twins don't look the same. Although atDNA may suggest that two people are distant cousins, say more than a fourth cousin, the reality is that at these distances of separation apparent DNA indicators of being cousins may arise just due to chance and family historians may spend time trying to document a relationship that may not exist due to chance inheritance of identical DNA segments, or a relationship that is the result of an undocumented situation.

No. of atDNA matches	10	9	8	7	6	5
No. of project members	2	2	3	7	17	13
No. of atDNA matches	4	3	2	1	0	Total
No. of project members	28	41	60	58	66	297

Table 23. The number of Oxfordshire DNA Project members who have 0–10 autosomal DNA matches in common with other members of the project.

Autosomal DNA is often used to estimate the 'ethnicity' or 'admixture' of people. This is attempted by comparing the DNA with that of 'control' populations of people who can show that they have (or are presumed to have) originated in specific geographical regions. Although the capability of this approach has improved as the quality of control populations has improved, many people are not happy with their suggested origins. This may be because the control data is still not good enough or because there is something unknown in the ancestry of the person tested, though this can usually be pursued by investigating previously unknown cousins. Others are quite satisfied. The estimates tend to work better if there is some ethnic contrast in recent generations. People who expect to see evidence of a Hungarian 4x great-grandfather may be disappointed, but they should not despair as they may find cousins who have retained the DNA that shows the ethnicity. It is probable that these estimates will continue to improve slowly in time.

Usable 'ethnicity' (sometimes called 'admixture') estimates were available for about 230 members of the Oxfordshire DNA Project. Autosomal DNA that may indicate ancestry that is from Oxfordshire, or from counties close by, has not been identified and may become more difficult to find due to increasing mobility within families. Most project members are mixtures with some of their ancestry from outside the county, as would be expected. About 12% show no British ethnicity but the *average* project member is 52% British, 16% Irish, 15% central European (this for some reason includes SE England and roughly from France to Denmark and western Poland to Austria), 12% Scandinavia, about 1% each from northern Mediterranean countries and relatively tiny amounts from other regions. Of course, no single project member has this specific make-up. There is always likely to be some overlap of ethnicity that makes these estimates confusing for some people. The apparent loss of British ethnicity for some members is likely due to the project member and some ancestors having resided elsewhere in other probably former colonial communities for some generations, if it means anything. However, it would be interesting if the technology improves sufficiently to suggest that Oxfordshire people might carry some DNA that is identified with the county.

Conclusion

The Oxfordshire DNA Project has provided some insight into relatedness of people with connections to the county. Many members find that DNA testing confirms a likely relationship with others in the project. Detail of Y-DNA (direct male line) and mitochondrial DNA (direct female line) testing suggests that they likely fall into groupings that are similar to those known for the wider English community. DNA fingerprints are being confirmed for Oxfordshire surnames. The discovery and confirming of DNA relationships of several kinds is likely to be of increased value to people with Oxfordshire ancestry. However, to be of greater value it is important that the number of people in the project is significantly increased and this may take some years to achieve.

Notes

1. University of Oxford. *People of the British Isles.* https://www.peopleofthebritishisles.org.
2. Leslie, Stephen, *et al.* 2015. The fine-scale genetic structure of the British population. *Nature.* 519. pp. 309–314.
3. International Society of Genetic Genealogy. 2020. *Haplogroup.* https://isogg.org/wiki/Haplogroup.
4. Eupedia. 2021. *European prehistory, anthropology & genetics.* https://www.eupedia.com/genetics/index.shtml.

Eleven

Surnames of Roman Catholics in Oxfordshire

Tony Hadland

NB: In this chapter 'Catholic' means 'Roman Catholic'. No offence is intended to anyone not of the Roman persuasion who considers themselves to be Catholic.

Survival strategy

Figure 86. Drawing of a priest with monks and worshippers outside a monastery.

Despite draconian legislation intended to suppress it, Roman Catholicism survived in a small way in England from the Elizabethan era until the early nineteenth century largely because of a strategy evolved in 1586. It was devised at the Thameside home of Richard Bold, former Sheriff of Lancashire, a few miles over the Oxfordshire–Buckinghamshire border at Harleyford, near Marlow.

Under the Harleyford plan, Catholic chaplains were based in the homes of sympathetic gentry and administered the Catholic sacraments to the household and local Catholics. This necessitated the construction of secret hiding places known as priest holes. The most famous builder of such hides was Nicholas Owen of Oxford, who died under torture in 1606. Within Oxfordshire and former north Berkshire, the Stonors of Stonor and the Eystons of East Hendred are classic examples of families who kept 'country house Catholicism' alive.

Relations between Catholics and Protestants

It is noteworthy that Oxfordshire Catholics did not live separate lives from the rest of society. Most were fully integrated in all respects other than the practice of their banned religion. Moreover, the boundaries between Catholicism and Anglicanism were more permeable than is often believed. Mixed marriages were quite common and many Catholics sometimes conformed to the Church of England. Occasional conformity could be for social reasons, such as the churching of women who had recently given birth. Alternatively it might be for pragmatic legal reasons: evading fines, prison or worse; to document legitimacy in the absence of civil registration; or because it was a strict requirement of the law, as under the 1753 Hardwicke Marriage Act.

People sometimes converted from one denomination to another (and sometimes back again). A Catholic might become an Anglican for reasons of genuine religious conviction or simply to avoid fines, imprisonment, the loss of inheritance or dowry, and to gain social and professional advancement. More rarely an Anglican might convert to Catholicism. Conversion could take place in either direction as a result of marriage or because of pressure from an employer. All Catholics had Protestant relatives – sometimes even siblings or parents. That most Puritan of poets, John Milton, had an Oxfordshire Catholic grandfather, a father who converted from Catholicism to Anglicanism and a brother who converted from Anglicanism to Catholicism.

Recusants, church papists and sympathisers

Catholics fell into various categories that affected the likelihood of them being detected by the authorities and consequently mentioned in documentation.

Anyone who refused to attend Anglican services was categorised by the state as a 'recusant' (from the Latin verb *recusare*, to refuse). The vast majority of recusants were Catholics and the terms are almost, but not quite, synonymous (just as the terms 'Nonconformist' or 'dissenter' are almost, but not quite, synonymous with non-Anglican Protestantism).

Then there were the 'church papists', usually the male heads of gentry households, who to avoid the penalties of the law outwardly conformed to Anglicanism while maintaining a Catholic household. Church papistry was much more common than traditional histories have suggested.

A third category comprised ostensibly Anglican families who nonetheless had strong Catholic leanings, and who would probably have become formally Catholic had the penalties been less severe. The Winchcombe family of Bucklebury, Berkshire falls into this category. In the seventeenth century, several of their daughters married into Catholic families, such as the Eystons of East Hendred and the Hildesleys of Littlestoke.

Church governance

In the seventeenth century, England and Wales were divided by the Catholic church into four missionary districts, each administered by a clandestine bishop known as a Vicar Apostolic. Oxfordshire, being north of the Thames, was in the Midland district; Berkshire, south of the river, was in the London district. The present Catholic dioceses are subdivisions of the four missionary districts: the Thames still forms an ecclesiastical boundary that disregards subsequent county boundary changes. Thus Oxfordshire and Caversham (now Berkshire) are in the RC Archdiocese of Birmingham; whereas old Berkshire, including the Vale of White Horse and those parts of south Oxfordshire south of the Thames, are in the RC Diocese of Portsmouth, and were for a while in the RC Diocese of Southwark.

The Vicars Apostolic only had authority over 'secular' clergy: that is, those who were not 'regular' clergy, regulated by a rule such as that of St Benedict (Benedictines), St Francis (Franciscans), St Dominic (Dominicans) or St Ignatius Loyola (Jesuits, members of the Society of Jesus). Each of the regular orders had its own administrative structure which was sometimes in conflict with that of the Vicars Apostolic: clandestine Catholic chaplains might be secular or regular clergy. In Oxfordshire the Jesuits were particularly active and a number of missions were run by them. As with the secular clergy, the Jesuits placed Berkshire and Oxfordshire in separate districts. Some Oxfordshire families had a tradition of favouring a particular religious order to provide its chaplains.

Factors helping the survival of Catholicism

Harbouring a priest could incur the death penalty and merely being a priest constituted high treason. Nonetheless, the Harleyford strategy worked well in several parts of Oxfordshire, including former north Berkshire. Various factors contributed to this:

1. Recusancy among the gentry was relatively strong, especially in the south Oxfordshire Chilterns, along the Thames between Henley and Oxford, in the Vale of White Horse and in parts of north Oxfordshire.

2. Most Anglican gentry did not invoke anti-Catholic legislation against their recusant neighbours, who were not only their peers but also often their relatives, friends, acquaintances or business partners.

3. Much of the time the anti-Catholic legislation was not enforced rigorously, although it always hung over Catholics like the sword of Damocles.

4. Occasional anti-Catholic crackdowns by the civil authorities produced a steady supply of martyrs with local connections to provide spiritual inspiration. From the reign of Henry VIII to that of Charles II these martyrs included Sir Adrian Fortescue, the Jesuit intellectual Edmund Campion, the priest-hole builder Nicholas Owen, Thomas Belson, who guided clandestine priests, and the priests George Napper and Richard Prince.

5. The presence of the Stonor family, based at Stonor Park near Henley-on-Thames, provided a strong focus for respectable recusancy, generally untainted by connections with extremist plots against the Crown. The martyred Sir Adrian Fortescue was a kinsman of the Stonors and Edmund Campion's secret printing press was at Stonor. The first post-Reformation consecration of a Roman Catholic bishop in England took place at Stonor, illegally but with the acquiescence of the authorities.

Figure 87. Stonor Park showing the chapel on the right.

How many Catholics and clandestine chapels?

After two centuries of repression, at a time when country house Catholicism was at its lowest ebb and before the growth of urban Catholicism, there were still about 800 Catholics known to the authorities in the Anglican diocese of Oxford. This amounted to approximately 1% of the population.

The Catholic Relief Act of 1778 put a formal end to the prosecution of priests by informers and allowed Catholics legally to purchase and inherit land. Thirteen years later a second act reopened the professions to Catholics and permitted the legalisation of Catholic chapels. During the recusancy period there were about two dozen illegal Catholic domestic chapels in what is now Oxfordshire, though not all operated simultaneously. Four of these chapels are still in use: at Hendred House, Mapledurham House, Milton Manor and Stonor Park.

Major centres of Catholicism in 1767

The government's 1767 Returns of Papists was one of several censuses of Catholics, long before a similar level of detail was sought for the population as a whole. Although the entries follow the official instruction not to record names, in most cases, the age, sex, rank, occupation and length of residence is given. Family relationships are also usually listed. It is therefore sometimes possible to deduce who certain individuals were by correlating the returns with other data. In any case, the entries provide a fascinating snapshot of Catholic demographics at a particular point in time.

The following brief summaries, based on the 1767 returns, highlight the locations where Catholicism was at its strongest within what is now Oxfordshire. This was at a time when country house Catholicism was in decline but before the growth of urban Catholicism in the nineteenth century. Catholicism was still predominantly a rural religion, sustained by members of the nobility, gentry and yeomen who were prepared to support a Catholic chaplain. It is significant that the combined parishes of the city of Oxford reported only 3% of the county's Catholics.

Figure 88. St Ignatius, St Clement's, Oxford. Until 1875 this was the only Roman Catholic church in Oxford, built by a Jesuit priest, Charles Lesley, in 1795.

Brize Norton

The Greenwood family had a domestic chapel served by Benedictines. There were twenty-five Roman Catholics in the parish. Apart from the squire and his family, there were two labourers and their families, a priest with his own servant, an elderly flax spinner and an old wool spinner.

Buckland

The Throckmorton family were completing construction of Buckland House, which included a domestic chapel. There were forty-two Roman Catholics in the parish. The squire is listed with his wife, their children, another gentleman who was probably the chaplain, eight servants, and a bailiff with his wife and children. There were also a farmer, two shopkeepers and their children, a labourer's wife, a middle-aged spinster, a gardener with his wife and their children, a dressmaker, and an innkeeper and her adult daughter.

East Hendred

Roman Catholic Chapel. East Hendred.

Figure 89. East Hendred Roman Catholic chapel.

The rector, who compiled the return, noted that the senior member of the squire's family present at the time was an elderly widow 'of an ancient family, ever since Henry VI', the Eystons. There were thirty-two Roman Catholics in the parish. Another elderly gentlewoman was listed together with a middle-aged male (possibly the chaplain), three female servants, an old coachman, a butler, a gardener, and an elderly couple and their daughter who were described as a 'decayed branch of the aforesaid family'. There were also two labourers and their wives, a middle-aged woman and her two daughters, an old carpenter and her son, two elderly wool spinners and an old pauper.

Souldern and Somerton cluster, including Deddington, Fritwell, Godington, Hardwick and Tusmore

These more or less contiguous parishes in the north of the county had a combined Roman Catholic population of 170. The dominant Catholic gentry family here was Fermor: they had a chapel at Tusmore and another at Somerton. Tusmore's Catholics merely comprised a servant and his family. Somerton had two farmers, a servant, two labourers, a carpenter, a tripe man, a lime burner, their respective wives and children and various spinsters and widows.

The Day family had a chapel with a resident priest at Hardwick Manor Farm that served a farmer, a gardener, a weaver and their families. The Cox family had a chapel at Souldern House which served a congregation of fourteen including a gentleman, two servants, and a tallow chandler and his family.

The Catholics at Deddington were mostly craftspeople and their families: a draper, a wheelwright, two coopers, a weaver, a pipe maker and a labourer. At Fritwell a gentleman and two servants lived alongside a wheelwright and a maltster and their families. Godington's Catholics were four graziers and a farrier and their families.

Kiddington and Heythrop cluster, including Chipping Norton, Enstone and the Tews

This cluster of parishes lies only a few miles west of the Souldern and Tusmore cluster and was home to 181 Catholics. The Browne (later Browne-Mostyn) family had a chapel at Kiddington whose Catholic population comprised a joiner, a carpenter, two masons, a labourer, a dressmaker, a shopkeeper, the families of all the aforementioned and three servants.

Figure 90. Heythrop House, home to the Talbot family, in an 1850 drawing.

At Heythrop the dominant Roman Catholic family was Talbot, which included the Earl and Countess of Shrewsbury. They had a resident chaplain whose congregation included a steward, two coachmen, nine servants, a butcher and his wife and sons, and a labourer and his extended family.

Chipping Norton was home to a maltster and his extended family, and a labourer, his wife, sons and daughters. Enstone had three resident gentlemen and their wives, children and servants. There were also two carpenters and their extended families. At the Tews were a farmer and his family, a labourer and his family, two other labourers' wives and children, and a widow.

Stonor cluster, including Britwell, Haseley, Newington, Pishill, Pyrton and Watlington

The Stonor family of Stonor Park dominated this cluster which had a total Catholic population of 136. Mass was celebrated in the Stonors' medieval domestic chapel, as it is to this day. Stonor Park was part of Pyrton parish which had more Catholics than any other in Oxfordshire. They included the squire, his wife, son, priest and thirteen servants. There were three farmers, two with wives and one with children. There were also a shopkeeper with a wife and children, a bricklayer and his wife and son, seven labourers, three with wives and children, three widows, and half a dozen other adult women.

A Catholic branch of the Simeon family held the manor at Britwell Prior, a detached part of Newington parish. In 1767 the Simeon household included the baronet, his chaplain and thirteen other Catholics; and there were eight other Catholics nearby in Britwell Salome.

Hazeley Court, home of the Wolfe family, had a chapel and eleven Catholics. They included a priest, servant, housekeeper, cook, farmer's wife and a coachman and his children. Pishill had only four Catholics: a gamekeeper and his family. Watlington had eighteen Catholics including a farmer and a publican with their families, two joiners, a cobbler, three lace makers, a milliner and a dressmaker.

Thameside: Mapledurham and Dorchester

Figure 91. Mapledurham: church exterior from the south-east showing the Catholic south chapel.

The Thames was the major route between Oxford and London. At various times there were Catholic houses on or near the river, particularly on the Oxfordshire bank: at Shiplake, Caversham, Littlestoke, Sandford and Iffley. By

1767 there were still two Catholic residences close to the river: Mapledurham House, home of the Blount family near Reading; and the Davey family home at Overy, a hamlet near Dorchester. Between them they had a Catholic population of forty-eight.

Mapledurham's gentry comprised two male Blounts a generation apart and the much older widow of another: they had a priest and thirteen servants. There was also a flax dresser, a carter, a labourer, a rope maker, various wives, a widow, and an alms-house woman. Nearby Whitchurch parish included lands across the Thames in Berkshire that formed part of the Catholic Hyde family's estate. (The boundaries of three parishes came together within the walls of Hyde Hall, which is now known as Purley Hall.) In 1767 Whitchurch had nine Catholics: a maltster and his family, a cordwainer's wife and children, and the wife of a ferryman.

The Catholic survival around Dorchester was primarily due to the loyalty of several yeoman families. Chief among these was the Davey family, who had a domestic chapel at Overy. Catholics in Dorchester included a gentlewoman, two farmers, two labourers, various wives and children, a servant, a carpenter's wife and daughter, a maltster's wife and a pauper.

Waterperry

This was the home of the Curson family whose domestic chapel was served primarily by Jesuits. There were thirty-two Catholics in the parish in 1767 but the information provided is scant. Apart from the Cursons they were mostly carpenters, labourers, servants and their families. This mission was the predecessor of Oxford's grandest Catholic place of worship, the Oratory Church of St Aloysius in Woodstock Road.

How does this relate to surnames?

Although the 1767 Returns of Papists deliberately omitted surnames, the above summaries are useful in focusing geographically and demographically on where surnames of Catholics may most readily be found. As Table 24 shows, there are records of named Catholics in almost all Oxfordshire locations, but in many places Catholics were recorded rarely and in very small numbers. In other areas, particularly those places mentioned in the summaries above, Catholics were present in significant numbers over relatively long periods of time (in the cases of the Eystons and Stonors, from before the Reformation until the present day.)

Table 24 links identified surnames of people thought to have been Catholics (including convicted recusants and suspected recusants and church papists) to specific Oxfordshire locations and approximate timespans. It also provides the dates of the earliest surviving sacramental registers and gives the number of any Catholics cited at that location by the 1767 Returns of Papists.

Figure 92. Two sections of the monument to the Fettiplace family at Swinbrook. The family originated in south Oxfordshire but a branch moved to Swinbrook.

Location	Surnames (non-exhaustive list)	Centuries	Earliest registers	Catholics in 1767	Notes
Abingdon, RC church of St Mary and St Edmund	Bowyer	Mid 19th to 21st	1856		Formerly Berks
Abingdon, St Helen and St Nicholas		Late 18th		4	Formerly Berks
Adderbury	Bustard, Cheriton, Joyner, Kinstone, More, Turner	Late 16th, 17th		2	
Adwell	Betham	Late 16th			
Ambrosden	Churchill, Denton, Mildmay	Late 16th to mid 17th			
Ascott-under-Wychwood	Ashfield, Croke, Fountaine, Kenyon, Sanders, Wollye	Early to mid 17th			
Assendon	Harbourie, Hicks, Stonor	16th			
Asthall	Deverell, Headlam, Kenyon	16th			
Aston Rowant	Belson, Buckland, English, Ewster, Gurney, Pigott, Randall, Tempest, Touchebourn, Tuthbury, Ward	Late 16th to mid 17th		1	Thomas Belson martyred 1589 at Oxford

Place	Surnames	Date range	Year	No.	Notes
Bampton, Including Aston, Cote and Haddon	Allen, Azzopardi, Bedall, Carey (Lady Falkland), Chapman, Colley, Hoord, James, Moore, Talbot (Earl of Shrewsbury), Wise, Yate	Late 16th to late 19th	1856	8	Domestic chapel (Earl of Shrewsbury) briefly at Bampton Castle 1856–7
Banbury	Bowen, Brent, de Poly, Dolman, Fox, Souter, Tandy	Late 18th to 21st	1832	7	RC church of St John succeeded Overthorpe
Barford St Michael and St John	Bourne, Haines, Joyner, Roberts	Late 16th			
Bartons, Steeple, Middle and Westcott	Collingridge, Constable, Corney, Green, Poulton, Sheldon, Smith, Todman	17th and 18th			Domestic chapel (Sheldon family) at Barton Abbey (formerly Sesswell's Barton Manor)
Begbroke	Stokes, Robinson	Late 19th to end 20th			Servite priory
Benson	Freeman	Early 17th			
Bicester	Blount, Boydon, Bryan, Butler, Denton, Glossop, Hart, Jackson, Moore, North, Peake, Sheldon, Stanley, Sweeney, Tenchio	Late 16th to late 17th, mid 19th to 21st	1902	4	Mass in cottage in Sheep Street from 1869; school chapel from 1883; 1902 convent chapel became RC parish church in 1920
Binfield Heath	Bishop, Carter, Langford, Money	Mid 17th			
Bix	Bishop	Mid 17th		5	

Parish	Surnames	Date			Notes
Bladon	Meades	Late 16th			
Bletchingdon	Braithwaite, Cox, Crowdson, Drayton, Elston, Foxe, Grimshaw, Langford, Poure, Smyth, Tailor, Writhington	Late 16th, early 17th, late 18th		1	
Bloxham	Counser, Danvers, Gable, Gillett	Late 16th, late 18th		4	
Bodicote	Bradford	Late 16th			
Brightwell Baldwin	Adams, Bisley, Cooke, Cowdrey, Fawkner, Ford, Gardner, Goode, Hedson, Martin, Ovye, Prince, Reve, Scattergood, Simeon	Late 16th, 17th			
Brightwell-cum-Sotwell		Late 18th		5	Formerly Berks
Britwell Prior (part of Newington)	Alder, Blount, Brown, Bruning, Campbell, Cope, Davey, Day, Edwards, Glaspole, Gosfort, Guerin, Harrison, Hobbs, Kimble, Kington, Kily, Lane, Marsh, Milward, Padwick, Parslew, Quartermaine, Richardson, Scoles, Simeon, Suderie, Tate, Taylor, Weetman, Weld, Weldon, Wiggins, Wingate	18th, early 19th	1731	15	Domestic chapel (Simeon later Weld family) at Britwell House (now Britwell Salome House); convent 1799 to 1813
Britwell Salome	Hambleton, Oglethorpe, Simeon	Late 16th, early 19th		8	

	Surnames	Dates		Number	Notes
Brize Norton	Allen, Bond, Bryerley, Davies, Greenwood, Kenyon, Messinger, Povy, Rathborne, Tempest, Twillye, Warmoll, Woodward, Yate	17th to early 19th		25	Domestic chapel (Greenwood family), closed 1769
Broadwell	Bailie, Cruse, Hopton, Nevell, Plott, Thompson, Trinder, Wilks	Late 16th, early 17th		4	
Broughton		Late 18th		1	
Broughton Poggs		Late 18th		1	
Buckland	Abraham, Acton, Archer, Ayers, Baker, Batchelor, Benson, Berington, Bishop, Brewer, Bridgeman, Budd, Burt, Butler, Bye, Carrascosa, Chair, Coffin, Cole, Constable, Corbett, Coverdale, Cox, Daly, Davey, Dearlove, Dennison, Dew, Draper, Fear, Farrel, Frogley, Gardner, Giles, Godwin, Gosling, Green, Haynes, Hewer, Hind, Hornat, Howson, Humphrys, Hyde, Jerdin, Johnson, Lamburn, Lapworth, Leary, Lindsay, Little, Martin, McCarthy, Mills, Morin, Morley, Musgrove, O'Brien, O'Neil, Partridge, Pierce, Pinnock, Rankin, Richardson, Rock, Shewry, Shorey, Simpson, Slade, Styche, Thorpe, Throckmorton, Waine, Ward, Watts, Wayman, Wenman, Westbury, Wheeler, Whitaker, Whiting, Wiggins, Williams, Yate	Late 16th to early 21st	1753	42	Formerly Berks; domestic chapel succeeded by St George's RC church from 1848

	Surnames	Date			Notes
Bucknell	Arden, Ashe, Ewer/Eure, Mayle, Stanshion, Walker, Warner	Early to mid 17th			
Burcot	Chirell, Day, Ford, Molyns, More, Nutt, Philpott(s), Tull	Late 16th to mid 17th			
Burford		Late 18th		4	
Cassington	Arden, Boones, Clarke, Emelyn, Gill, Greenway, Hawkins, Heyward, Jucklyn, Rainolds, Smyth, Townsend	Early 17th, late 18th			
Caversham	Alder, Alexander (aka Milward), Browne, Dalmas, Delavell, Forbert, Grey, Grimsditch, Haskew, Klomp, Newport, Patrick, Sheldon, Wilson	Late 16th to mid 17th, late 19th to 21st	18	1	Now in Berks; parish of Our Lady and St Anne founded as a mission in 1896
Chadlington	Butcher, Fox, Rowton	Late 16th			
Chalgrove	Chambers, Comber, Winchcombe	Early to mid 17th			
Charlbury	Baskerfeld, Beverley, Bourne, Brayne, Burnett, Clements, Emsworth, Fitzhughes, Fowler, Hatton, Lake, Raleigh, Snape, Tempest, Tenant, Tippinge, Trevis	Late 16th to late 18th, mid 20th to 21st			Former Primitive Methodist chapel became RC church of St Teresa of Lisieux in 1930
Chastleton	Annesley, Catesby, Jennings, Osbaston, Sheldon, Throckmorton	Late 16th, 17th			

Place	Surnames	Date	Number	Notes
Checkendon, see also Littlestoke	Astoll, Clarke, Doughty, Ebington, Hildesley, Tompson, Wintershul	Early to mid 17th		
Chesterton	Bourne, Davys (alias Price), Maund	Late 16th to mid 17th		
Childrey		Late 18th	1	Formerly Berks
Chinnor	Fieschi, Gravenor, Harper, Hawten, Higges, Penn	Late 16th to early 17th, late 18th	1	
Chipping Norton	Abbot, Bowdon, Eele, Fanning, Gage, Gatley, Heffernan, Mitchell, Sole, Talbot, Throckmorton	Early 17th, mid 19th to 21st	13	RC church of the Holy Trinity opened 1836; succeeded Heythrop
Churchill	Horne	Early 17th		
Clanfield	Yate	Early 18th		
Claydon	Raleigh	Mid 17th		
Clifton Hampden	Carter, Gamon, Hartley, Lake, Langley, Mosden Philpott, Prince, Sanders, Sheckelman, Tuchinder, Tull, Weston, White, Woolfe	17th		
Cogges	Sleep	Early 17th		
Cokethorpe	East, Heywood, Sanders	Late 16th to early 17th		

Place	Surnames	Date			Notes
Coombe	Alder	Late 16th			
Cottisford	Arden, Fermor, Johnson, Rowlands, Walker	Late 16th			
Cowley	Badger, Collins, Darby, Francklyn, Napper/Napier, Spencer, Woodward	Late 16th to mid 17th, late 18th		1	Safe house for Catholics at Temple Cowley
Crowmarsh Gifford	Archer, Biggs, Cheney, Cumber, Hildesley, Hulse, Joyner, Martin, Sussex, White, Williamson	Late 16th to early 17th, late 18th		1	
Cuddesdon	Archdale, Child, Horseman, Slyman, Stampe, Webb	Late 16th, early 17th			
Culham	Checkleman/Shekelman, Greenwood, Rainolds, Stringer, Young	Early 17th to early 18th			
Curbridge	Tempest	Early 17th			
Cuxham	Bourne, Butler, Laye	Late 16th to early 17th			
Deddington	Appletree, Blinco, Bustard, Coxe, Edmonds, Hall, Manning, Naylor, Pope, Sheppard, Smith, Walkett, Wilcock, Woolfe, Yate	Late 16th, 17th, late 18th	1772 in Hardwick	23	

Place	Surnames	Dates	Year	Number	Notes
Dorchester, see also Overy	Bannister, Barry, Beauforest, Coldrell, Davey, Day, Green, Ibbotson, Lewes, Manning, Mason, Nary, Newsham, Prince, Smith, Stringer	Late 16th to 21st	1849	19	RC church of St Birinus opened 1849; succeeded Overy
Drayton (probably Drayton St Leonard)	Tailor, Spencer, Werott	Early 17th, late 18th		1	
Drayton, near Abingdon	Southcott	Mid to late 18th		10	Formerly Berks
Ducklington	East, Haywood	Late 16th, 17th			
East Hendred	Appleton, Archer, Barrett, Bond, Bosher, Casey, Castle, Chambers, Champ, Chare, Collins, Constable, Ellaways, Elloway, Eyston, Godfrey, Hatto, Hunt, Lapworth, Lyston, Penniken, Pike, Quinch, Rouse, Sessions, Sherwood, Sheard, Shewry, Smith, Stibbs, Surman, Winchcombe, Wise	Late 16th to 21st	1786	32	Formerly Berks; domestic chapel at hundred House (still in use in 2020); RC church of St Mary from 1865
Elsfield	Holton	Late 16th?			
Emmington	Franklin	Mid 17th			
Enstone	Ashfield, Astrey, Bishop, Munck, Stanbridge	Late 16th to mid 19th	1753, later entries in Radford	55	Succeeded by Radford

Place	Surnames	Date			Notes
Ewelme	Ashfield, Gifford, Merrer, Howard	Late 16th, late 18th		2	
Eye and Dunsden	Higges	Early 17th			
Eynsham	Annesley, Barncott, Bomiell, Butler, Day, Elmere, Gardiner, Gould, Howard, May, Owen, Prescott, Rainolds, Stacy, Stanley, Tenant, Weston, White, Williamson	Late 16th to mid 17th			
Filkins	Amyes	18th?			
Forest Hill	Badger, Brome, Edgerley, Horseman, Plater, Powell	Late 16th to early 17th			
Fringford		Late 18th		1	
Fritwell	Andorus, Badger, Collet, Collingridge, Cox, Fermor, Fleming, Garner, George, Hall, Hatton, Hoare, Horne, Jarvis, Longueville, Lovell, Perkins, Robins, Smith, Tyrrel, Watts, Wells, Weston, Willes	Early 17th, 18th	1772 in Hardwick	21	Domestic chapel (Longueville family); closed 1729
Fulbrook		Late 18th		2	
Fulwell	Allibarton, Collingridge, Morse	18th	1772 in Hardwick		
Garsington	Ford, Spencer	Late 16th			
Gatehampton	Howse	16th?			

Place	Surnames	Date	Year	No.	Notes
Godington	Allen, Brinklowe, Browne, Busby, Capper, Collingridge, Colyer, Davis, Fermor, Friday, Gerrard, Godbeheere, Hall, Hawkins, Jackson, Mercer, Paxton, Pigott, Taylor, Tomkins	Late 16th to mid 19th	1772 in Hardwick	31	Domestic chapel at Moat Farm (Collingridge family); dismantled 1900
Godstow	Curteys, Day, Holloway, Owen	Late 16th and early 17th			
Goring	Braybrooke, Etheridge, Hallitt, Higges, Howse, Morris, Paslowe, Smith, Thompson, Weston	Late 16th to early 17th, late 19th	1898?		RC Church of Our Lady and St John built 1898
Great and Little Tew	Talbot	Late 18th		26	
Hampton, Gay or Poyle	Moore	Late 16th?			
Hanborough	Babington, Kingston, Poure, Rookes or Rowle, Slowe, Styles, Welbecke	Early 17th			
Hardwick	Barber, Bathe, Broadway, Bullen, Cadwallader, Collingridge, Corbishley, Day, Elmes, Fermor, Freeman, Hatton, Hattwell, Heywood, Hodges, Keale or Keate, Mercer, Reynolds, Saers, Smith, Tomkin, Tooley, Whitaker, Wise	Late 16th to mid 19th	1772	32	Domestic chapel (Day family) at Hardwick Manor Farm; succeeded by Hethe; closely linked to the Tusmore mission

Haseley, Great and Little, including Latchford	Adams, Bradshaw, Cooper, Fawkner, George, Hampshire, Horseman, Huddleston, Hynton, Johnson, Kate, Lenthall, Leversage, Moore, Newe, Wolfe, Yonge	Late 16th, early 17th, 18th	Entries in Britwell and Waterperry	11	Domestic chapel at Haseley Court, Little Haseley (Huddleston and Wolfe families); closed c.1768
Headington	Smith	Early 17th, late 18th		2	
Henley-on-Thames	Bacchus, Brownlow-Doughty, D'Allard, Hampshire, Mannock, Scott Murray, Stephens, Stonor, Thimlethorpe, Walshe	Late 16th to 21st	1884	10	Missions 1811–14 and 1864–68; temporary chapel from 1894; RC Church of the Sacred Heart opened 1935
Hethe	Bonner, Broadway, Clark, Collingridge, Dolman, Durcan, Fermor, Grant, McGuire, North, Patroli, Robson, Stapleton, Sweeney, Taylor	Mid 18th to 21st	1772 in Hardwick	10	Succeeded Hardwick and Tusmore; RC Church of the Holy Trinity from 1839
Heyford Bridge		Late 18th		1	

Heythrop	Armstrong, Ashfield, Bates, Beck, Bishop, Black, Bricknell, Brothers, Carthwight, Castle, Cleft, Clements, Clough, Corgen, Davies, Evans, Finch, French, Gillin, Green, Heffernan, Holloway, Hopkins, Ilsley, Johnson, Jordan, Kendal, Leslie, Lindsay, Lindsey, Louch, Mathews, Maycock, Osbaston, Parker, Parry, Phillips, Roper, Sheffield, Smelt, Smith, Somner, Spicer, Stanbridge, Stephens, Strong, Talbot, Timms, Tomkins, Tredwell, Wharton, Whittingham, Wilkes	Early 17th to mid 19th	1729	32	Domestic chapel (Talbot, Earl of Shrewsbury), closed 1859; no continuity with later Jesuit college
Holton	Astrey, Brome, Coxe, George, Stacy, Stamp, Wise	Late 16th, early 17th		5	
Holwell, near Burford	Cruse, Trinder, Wright	Mid 17th to early 18th			
Hook Norton	Dymoke, Nayle, Tasker, Wickham	Late 16th to mid 17th			
Horspath	Hinton, Joyner	Late 16th, mid 17th			
Horton	Sulley	17th?			
Howbery	Hildesley	Late 16th			

Place	Surnames	Dates		Number	Notes
Idbury	Berry, Cassey, Day, Digger, Fisher, Fleming, Fortescue, Freeres, Gainsford, Giles, Grey, Harris, Loggan, Morgan, Rainsford, Rock, Stanbridge, Turville, Wincott, Yonge	Late 16th to mid 19th		6	Domestic chapel (Gainsford, Loggan, Fortescue, Turville families); closed 1830s
Iffley	Atkyns, Badger, James, Johnson, Lewis, Martyn, Pitts, Powell, Sutton	Late 16th and early 17th			
Ipsden	Bates, Buckeridge, Hatton, Higgs, Jevans, Vachell	Late 16th to early 17th			
Islip	Bond, Hatton, Maynard, Plastod	Late 16th?			
Kelmscott	Thompson	Late 16th?			
Kencott	Frances, Yate	Late 16th, early 17th, late 18th		1	

Place	Surnames				Notes
Kiddington	Allen, Atkinson, Babington, Bateman, Battinison, Beames, Bowden, Brewer, Browne, Browne-Mostyn, Butler, Clary, Clements, Collingridge, Cook, Davys, Dillon, Evans, Gardner, Gibson, Greene, Griffin, Harris, Headlam, Howes, Jackson, Lee, Lyster, Meades, Memory, Morgan, Mud, Nash, Newman, Nicols, Parker, Potter, Queyneo, Rate, Reeve, Rock, Sherwood, Slowe, Smith, Smithers, Spereman, Stephens, Stiles, Styche, Tuttman, West, Weston, Wheeler, Willoughby, Willson, Winter, Woodward, Yoxon	Late 16th to mid 19th	1772	10	Domestic chapel (Browne later Browne-Mostyn family); succeeded by Hethe
Kidlington	Chamberlayne, Dewe, Gadbury, Hudson, Smith	Late 16th to late 18th			
Kingham	Gilks, Hadland	Late 16th			
Kirtlington	Arden, Baker, Ballarde, Ballowe, Barrett, Benson, Boyer, Braybrooke, Browne, Chamberlaine, Clifford, Day, Hamond, Hawley, Haywood, Hedges, Hill, Hore, Martyn, Napper, Owen, Prince, Rayer, Reinolds, Saunders, Sellinger, Slowe, Smith, Tempest, Tredwell, Walker, Woodward	Late 16th, early 17th			

Launton	Braybrooke, Ewer, Wissleton	Late 16th, early 17th		
Ledwell, in Sandford St Martin parish	Appletree, Birche, Smith	17th		
Lew, in Bampton parish	Wise	17th?		
Little Milton (Milton Parva)	Astrey, Molyns	Early 17th		
Littlestoke	Bacon, Hildesley, Wintershul	17th and early 18th		Now in South Stoke parish but earlier in Checkendon; Hildesley has many variant spellings
Long Wittenham		Late 18th	5	Formerly Berks
Lower Heyford	Carter, Norton, Paulinge	Late 16th		
Lyford (Berks until 1974)	Yate	Late 16th to early 18th		Fr Edmund Campion arrested here 1581 and subsequently martyred at Tyburn

Place	Surnames	Date			Notes
Mapledurham	Appleton, Archer, Bisley, Blount, Bosio, Bright, Brothwart, Burford, Clerk, Collis, Cooke, Cooper, Cowslade, Croydon, de la Croix, Eyston, Fellows, Geddis, Goldfinch, Hatton, Hoan, Holey, Ilsley, Isdel, Kimber, Lefevre, Lewington, Lillis, Madew, Martin, Morley, Needham, Parsler, Perkins, Poscott, Prince, Smith, Stoker, Stone, Switzer, Walker, Winstanley	17th to 21st	1710	29	Domestic chapel at Mapledurham House (Blount family, still in use by their successors, the Eyston family)
Marcham		Late 18th		5	Formerly Berks
Marsh Baldwin		Late 18th		1	
Marston	Bene, Brome, Ewin	Late 16th, late 18th		1	
Medley, south of Port Meadow, Oxford	Merrick	Late 16th			
Middle Aston	Calvert	Early 18th			
Middleton Stoney		Late 18th		1	
Milton, Great		Late 18th		2	
Milton, near Abingdon	Barrett	Late 18th to 21st		6	Formerly Berks; domestic chapel at Milton Manor; still in use by Barrett-Mockler family

Place	Surnames	Period							
Minster Lovell	Ewer or Ewen, Hatton, Kerwood, Morgan, Pearson, Tempest, Williamson	Early and mid 17th							
Mixbury	Arden, Greene, Pates	Late 16th, early 17th, late 18th	7						
Mongewell	Dancastle, Drewe, Keyne, Molyns, Spicer, Willis	Early 17th							
Nether Worton and Over Worton	Arden, Babington, Butler, Cheese, Clarke, Hastlett, Haule, Mayne, Penn, Rainolds, Wethman	mid 18th							
Nettlebed	Hambleton, Oglethorpe, Simeon	Late 16th, early 18th		1					
Newnham Murren	Crouch, Gamon, Hellier, Higges, Hildesley, Hyde, Molyns, Prince, Smith, Stampe, Stonor	Late 16th, early 17th							
Noke	Day, Fermor, Franklin, Hall, Hatton, Heycock, Hierons, Palmer, Plowden, Winchcombe	Late 16th to early 18th							
North Aston	Brooke, Fermor	Mid 17th							
North Leigh	Barefoot, Pollard	Late 16th							

Place	Surnames	Period	Date	Number	Notes
North Stoke	Crouch, Curson, Gibbes, Greene, Hildesley, Lawrence, Stonor	Late 16th, 17th, late 18th		2	
Northmoor	Butler, Hearles, Moore, Orpwood	Late 16th			
North Moreton		Late 18th		1	Formerly Berks
Nuneham Courtenay	Bisley, Hawkins, Hunt, Maye, Minors, Pollard, Prince, Wheeler, Yateman	Mid to late 17th, late 18th			
Oddington	Coxe, Fisher, Foxe, Ironmonger, Poure, Sellinger, Walkett	Late 16th and early 17th			
Overthorpe	Batchelor, Betts, Eyre, Fox, Gardner, Griffin, Grimshaw, Hatley, Jennings, Miller, Moreby, Perry, Sole	Early 19th	1798		In Northants but close to Banbury; succeeded Warkworth in 1806; succeeded by RC Church of St John, Banbury in 1838
Overy, hamlet adjoining Dorchester	Clinch, Collingridge, Davey, Gosford, Haskey, Milman, Philadelphia, Prince, Scoles, Stafford (alias Cassidy), Taylor, Thoumin des Valpons, Wells	18th to mid 19th	1753, in Waterperry and later in Oxford, St Ignatius		Domestic chapel at so-called Overy Manor; succeeded by Dorchester

Place	Surnames	Dates	Registers	No.	Notes
Oxford, All Saints	Denton, Dudley, Friar, Gefferies, Godbeheare, Green, Harrison, Hazlewood, Hencock, Hitchmore, Johnson, Moore, Philipps, Smith, White	Late 16th, early 17th, late 18th		3	
Oxford, Holywell	Brome, Darser, Harding, Joyner, Kimber, Napper/Napier, Neville, Pitts, Rucliffe, Thorpe	17th, 18th		1	Domestic chapel at Holywell Manor (Napper and Neville families); Revd George Napper martyred at Oxford 1610
Oxford, nonspecific	Allen, Atkinson, Banks, Copperthwaite, Loreinge	Late 16th, early 17th			
Oxford, RC chapel of St Ignatius	Bernard, Blackett, Brigham, Chadwick, Clarkson, Clifford, Cole, Comberbach, Conolly, Copus, Corry, Cruse, Curson, Davey, Douglas, Dwyer, Eaves, Evans, Gosford, Guilby, Hanley, Hastings, Hay, Hicky, Hopkins, Hothersall, Jarrett, Leslie, MacDonnell, Machenry, Mulhern, Nary, Newsham, O'Connell, O'Connor, Platt, Prince, Rock, Salamoni, Savage, Sewall, Smallwood, Smith, Talbot, Tallant, Tricquet	Late 18th to early 20th	1793, early entries with Waterperry		Succeeded Waterperry; chapel of ease for St Aloysius from 1875 until closed in 1911; succeeded by Oxford SS Edmund & Frideswide, Iffley Road.

Place	Surnames	Date		Number	Notes
Oxford, RC church of St Aloysius, now Oxford Oratory	Ariss, Barefoot, Barnard, Bateman, Berry, Bettriss, Bishop, Box, Bradley, Budd, Chambers, Champion, Cleaver, Connolly, Conroy, Cowley, Cox, Crapper, Crover, Daly, Davies, De Paravicini, Dixon, Edmunds, Forshaw, Gahagan, Ganter, Gessing, Goodall, Gorton, Griffin, Harrington, Hart, Heath, Heller, Hill, Hinton, Holloway, Izzard, King, Landers, Lee, Lloyd, Lyons, MacCarthy, Mannion, McFie, McKenna, Mitchell, Moore, Norton, Nutt, O'Brien, Perrie, Powell, Pratley, Rennison, Reynolds, Roberts, Robinson, Seeley, Sharp, Shipley, Simpson, Smith, Stowell, Taunt, Telfer, Tritton, Varney, Vaulters, Verchild, Walker, Warland, Warley, Wilkins, Wilkinson, Wizzard, Young	Late 19th to 21st	1875, registers begin earlier in St Ignatius		Succeeded St Ignatius
Oxford, St Aldate	Copperthwaite, Crew(e), Drayton, Henslowe, Ivery, Jewell, More, Morse, Noke, Tredwell	Late 16th			
Oxford, St Clement	Atkins, Browne, C(r)ooke, Clarke, Franklyn, Powell, Wise	Late 16th, late 18th		12	Not to be confused with the later RC chapel of St Ignatius at St Clement's

Oxford, St Ebbe	Comber, Founch, Mosse, Peerse, Wallingford, Wrenche	Late 16th, late 18th	1
Oxford, St Giles	Atkinson, Aylworth, Greenwood, Hall, Hatton, Stallocke, Standishe	Late 16th	
Oxford, St Martin	Blieth, Bowne, Huet, Jones, Willson, Wright	Late 16th	
Oxford, St Mary	Bourne, Davies, Joyner (alias Lyde), Lapworth, Wright	Late 16th	
Oxford, St Mary Magdalen	Barber, Barnes, Dudley, Filby, Holley, Huett, Lloyd, Polson, Transham/Stansham, Welbecke	Late 16th, late 18th	2
Oxford, St Michael	Dudley, Fearne, Graye, Lake, Marbecke, West, Weston, Williams	Late 16th, late 18th	4
Oxford, St Nicholas, formerly St Thomas	Atwood, Barlowe, Clerke, Day, Dexey, Dudley, Greenwood, Gunnell, Hazelgrove, Hollye, Humfry, James, Jenks, Mericke, Missen, Moore, Osbaston, Powell, Sheprey, Shrimpton, Weston	Late 16th	
Oxford, St Peter in the East	Badger, Chettle, Kale, Musgrave, Yates	Late 16th, early 17th	

Place	Surnames	Period			Notes
Oxford, St Peter le Bailey	Babington, Butler, Eaton, Ellemere, Foster, Hatton, Hewett, Howard, Mansell, Mosse, Owen, Pitts, Saule, Sergeant, Sheprey, Smith, Stacy, Tredwell, Wantige, Welbecke, Weston	Late 16th, early 17th			Priest-hole builder Nicholas Owen tortured to death in the Tower of London 1606
Piddington	Dynham, Fulwood, Hickford, Molyns, Vynes, Welch	Early 17th			
Pishill	Stonor	Late 18th		4	Advowson held by the Stonor family
Pusey		Late 18th		1	Formerly Berks
Pyrton	Clark, Follett, Ford, Harbury, Haskey, Higges, Hobstrowe, Rainolds, Simeon, Stonor	Late 16th, 17th, late 18th		82	
Radford, Enstone	Bowdon, Browne-Mostyn, Clements, Fitzgerald, Gannon, Heffernan, Lester/Lister, Nash, O'Grady, Rock, Sweeney, Taylor, Thompson, Turner, Winter, Witham	Mid 19th to mid 20th	1841		1841 Succeeded Enstone, Heythrop and Kiddington
Rotherfield Greys	Haldenby, Hobbes, Kennedy, Meade, Sarney, Ward, Wells	Late 16th, late 17th, 18th		1	

Place	Surnames	Date			Notes
Rotherfield Peppard	Biggs, Bourne, Cowper, Croft, Curson, Curtis, Deane, East, Fawconbridge, Gould, Hildesley, Pitts, Rewly, Stonor	Late 16th to early 18th			Blount's Court was a Stonor residence
Sandford St Martin, near Deddington	Appletree, Birch, Brickville/Bucknill, Smith	Late 17th to mid 18th?			Possibility of confusion in recusancy records between the Sandfords
Sandford-on-Thames	Betham, Brown, Collingwood, Craft, Digweed, Gold, Higges, Powell, Rainolds, Sharpe, Walson, White, Wilkinson, Winter, Yateman	17th, 18th	Entries in Waterperry	3	Domestic chapel (Powell family) adjoining manor house, sold 1760
Sarsden	Burnett	Late 17th, late 18th		1	
Shillingford	Bartholomew, Bisley, Hobbes	Late 17th			
Shilton	Allen, Stevens	Late 16th, early 17th			
Shiplake	Baylie, Blunsden, Carter, Englefield, Evans, Higgins, Plowden, Rainolds, Wilkinson	Late 16th to late 17th			Shiplake Court was home of the Plowden family
Shipton-under-Wychwood	Parsons, Yate	Late 16th, late 18th		2	
Shipton-on-Cherwell	Ley, Passiter	Late 16th			

Shirburn	Baglande, Chamberlain, Fortescue, Gage, Scoles, Tayler	Late 16th to early 19th		6	Presumed domestic chapel at Shirburn Castle
Shorthampton	Ashfield, Hoskins or Hodgekins, Howell, Morgan, Raleigh	Early 17th			
Shutford		Late 18th		2	
Somerton	Allwood, Anstree, Ansty, Bayley, Becke, Bolter, Bond, Brookes, Browne, Buller, Cadwallader, Callaway, Capper, Clerk, Clifford, Collett, Collingridge, Davies, Day, Dew, East, Fermor, Ford, Fox, Goslinge, Grove, Hall, Halleburton, Hardwicke, Hatton, Hawtree, Hedges, Hildesley, Hoar, Horn, Jennings, Knight, Lapington or Leppington, Messie, Mynne, Nichols, Philips, Quyntyn, Rand, Read, Rice, Roe, Rogers, Saunders, Servant, Smith, Stanbridge, Stinton, Taylor, Tempest, Thonger, Todkill, Tompkins, Tuckett, Ward, Williamson, Wood	Late 16th to late 18th		42	Merged with Hethe

Place	Surnames	Date		Number	Notes
Souldern	Bennett, Coster, Cox, Dolman, Draper, Fletcher, Glossop, Hall, Horne, Hyatt, Kilby, Lovell, McCarten, Morris, Neal, Painter, Penn, Poore, Reynolds, Robson, Smith, Stapleton, Stutsbury, Taylor, Tompkins, Volett, Weedon	Late 16th to mid 20th	1870, earlier entries in Hethe or Hardwick	14	Domestic chapel at Souldern House (Kilby, Cox, Dolman, Stapleton families) until 1781; chapel of St Joseph. Succeeded Heythrop in 1869
South Leigh	Byrde, Coleman, Holloway, Jones, Mayne, Moore, Prince, Reeve, Sara, Skinner	Late 16th, early 17th			
South Moreton		Late 18th		1	Formerly Berks
South Newington, near Deddington	Appletree, Fitzherbert, Shakerley, Shirley, Throckmorton	Late 16th to late 18th		6	
South Stoke	Albury, Braybrooke, Bunsham, Collin, Cooke, Coxsie, Curson, Ford, Hance, James, Owen, Prince, Smith, Wollascott, Yates	Late 16th, early 17th			
Spelsbury	Ingram, Poure, Raleigh	Early 17th			
Standlake	Beaumond, Belcher, Benion, Bourne, East, Fawkner, Hyde, Lord, Snappe, Streete (alias Bruer), Yate	Late 16th, early 17th, late 18th		3	
Stanford in the Vale		Late 18th		1	Formerly Berks
Stanford Place, near Faringdon (Berks until 1974)	Eyston	Mid 19th to early 20th	Entries in Buckland		Domestic chapel (Eyston family)

Stanton Harcourt	Barnard, Brewer, Buttle, Gage, Harcourt, Parker, Pope, Roberts, Wolfe	Late 16th to mid 17th		
Stanton St John	Ainslow, Benford, Bennett, Edmonds, Harris, Lovelace, Milton, Pitts, Rooke, Stacye, Staples	Late 16th to late 18th	1	
Steeple Aston	Atkinson	Late 16th		
Stoke Lyne, near Bicester	Ewers, Goddard, Kitchyn, Willis	Late 17th to late 19th	5	
Stokenchurch	Davis, Davye, Pigott	Late 17th late 18th	1	
Stonesfield	Maunsell, Owen	Late 16th		

Place	Surnames				Notes
Stonor Park	Barnes, Beech, Birks, Blondel, Bowden, Campbell, Campion, Cluer, Collingridge, Comberbach, Cook, Cox, Davey, Dobell, Dolman, Duxbury, Eyre, Field, Franklin, Fressar, Frewen, Garret, Gildart, Golding, Graneau, Greenaway, Hamblin, Hannington, Harrington, Haskey, Heath, Hine, Hollis, Holmes, James, Keates, Kembal, Kimberley, Kimble, King, Laner, Langford, Langton, MacDowal, Mannington, Martin, McLeary, Morley, Mortuaire, Nary, Norcote, Payne, Persons, Poole, Powel, Rolles, Scoles, Scot, Sherlock, Simpson, Stone, Stonor, Strickland, Suchard, Sumner, Tagg, Thompson, Ullathorne, Webb, Wesh, White, Williams, Wise	Late 16th to 21st	1758		Domestic chapel of the Holy Trinity (Stonor family) still in use
Stratton Audley	Hales, Southcote	Mid to late 18th	1772 in Hardwick	4	
Sutton Courtenay	Wollascott	18th		2	Formerly Berks
Swalcliffe	Hunt, Wickham	Late 16th, late 18th		3	

Place	Surnames	Dates	Number	Notes
Swyncombe	Ashfield, Deane, Dormer, Fettiplace, Fortescue, Harding, Hussey, Plasden, Rooke(s), Stevens	Late 16th and 17th		
Taynton	Ardge, Bray, Read, Tempest	Late 16th, early 17th, late 18th	11	
Tetsworth	Phillips	18th		
Thame and North Weston	Chanderelle, Clerke, Collingridge, Despons, Etheridge, Gardenett, Green, Greenwood, Haslett, le Bihan, Mayne, Owen, Seymour, Stones, Vaillant de Joyeuse	Late 16th to early 17th		
Thame Park	Bertie, Hothersall, Stafford, Wenman	Late 16th to early 17th, mid 18th to early 19th	5	Domestic chapel (Wenman family)
Toot Baldon	Pollard, Spencer, Young	Late 16th to mid 17th		

Place	Surnames	Period	Year	Number	Notes
Tusmore	Adams, Barran, Barrow, Bennett, Bishop, Booth, Brooke, Burgess, Butler, Callaway, Clarkson, Clay, Claydon, Clifford, Collingridge, Collis, Corbishley, Curtis, Davies, Denning, Earl, Essery, Fairbairn, Fermor, Fitzherbert, French, Gardener, Gibbs, Gillibrand, Grant, Green, Hadley, Hatton, Hatwell, Hawkes, Hewins, Hill, Hilliar, Hitchman, Holmes, Horne, Howell, Howes, Hyat, Jackson, Jarvis, Jennings, Johnson, Jones, Jopp, Justice, Kemble, Kempley, Knibbs, Le Grand, Marchant, McHenry, Mead, Newton, Page, Parcell, Paxton, Phillips, Platford, Potter, Price, Rate, Robson, Rogers, Rose, Smith, Taylor, Turill, Tyrrel, Walmesley, Waring, Webster, West, White, Wilkins, Wintringham, Wise	Early 17th to early 19th	1788	7	Domestic chapel (Fermor family to 1810); absorbed on Somerton; centred on Hardwick from 1810 to 1828; succeeded by Hethe
Wallingford, St Mary and All Saints		Late 18th		8	Formerly Berks
Warborough	Bisley, Bull, Coles, Hobbes, Holle, James (alias Phelpes) Janes or Jones, Leach (alias Bulie), Martin, Martin (alias Bartholomew), Moulder, Porter, Webbe	Late 16th to mid 17th			

Place	Surnames	Date	Year	Number	Notes
Wardington	Allibone	Mid 17th			
Warkworth	Barrett, Bedingfield, Butler, Cassidy (aka Stafford), Challoner, Eyre, Gardiner, Gother, Hall, Hersent, Holman, Jephs, Judd, Kemble, Mulhern, Onslow, Rider, Taverner (alias Banister), Taylor, Yates	17th to early 19th	1772 in Hardwick		In Northants but part of an Oxfordshire mission; domestic chapel (Holman and Eyre families); succeeded by Overthorpe
Waterperry	Barnwell, Bartlet, Brinkhurst, Brooke, Butler, Closette, Collins, Coxe, Curson, Cusack, Geary, Harding, Hoskins, Hothersall, Jenkins, Leslie, Nelson, Pole, Roper (Teynham), Spencer, Stanley, Taylor, Westby, Woods, Woodward, Young	17th and 18th	1700	32	Domestic chapel at Waterperry Manor (Curson family); succeeded by Oxford St Ignatius
Watlington	Altam, Barker, Bennett, Benwell, Callis, Dobinson, Ford, Hoptrowe, Horne, Horner, Jefferies, Jenks, Johnson, King, Lloyd, Lovejoy, Shepherd, Simeon, Stonor, Welbeck	Late 16th to 21st		18	
Watlington Park	Stonor	Mid 18th			Domestic chapel of Bishop Stonor
Wendlebury	Aprice (alias Davy), Berkely/Beckley, Bourne, Carter, Eden, Hitche, Jackson, Kitchinge, Oven, Paxton, Penn, Smith (alias Hadden)	Late 16th, early 17th			

Place	Surnames	Dates		Count	Notes
Westcott Barton		Late 18th		2	
Weston-on-the-Green	Greene, Poure	Early 17th			
Westwell, near Burford	Trinder	18th			
Wheatley	Archdale, Goldwier, Horseman, Stratford	Late 16th, early 17th, late 18th		2	
Whitchurch	Bennett, Howse, Hyde, North, Stone	Early 17th, late 18th		9	
Witney, including Crawley	Cuffe, Dekins, Hampshire, Jones, Ostler, Tempest, Wenman, Whiting	Late 16th to early 17th, late 18th, mid 19th to 21st	Entries in Oxford then Buckland	12	Present church of Our Lady and St Hugh completed 1975
Wolvercote	Adkins/Atkins, Bell, Betterton, Bullyn, Cheriton, Fitzhughes, Goodyer, Hatton, Jynke, Lewis, Messenger, Owen, Rainolds, Stratford, Wead	Late 16th, early 17th			
Wood Eaton		Late 18th		2	
Woodstock	Babington, Dingley, Leslie	Early 17th, late 18th		1	

Wroxton Abbey	Helle, Higginson, Legendre, North, Riche, Rieter, Van den Berg, White	Late 16th, late 19th
Yarnton	Fowler, Goad, Spencer (Althorp)	17th

Table 24. Records of Catholics in Oxfordshire.

Bibliography

British History Online. *A history of the county of Berkshire* (4 vols). https://www.british-history.ac.uk/search/series/vch—berks

British History Online. A history of the county of Oxfordshire (19 vols). https://www.british-history.ac.uk/search/series/vch—oxon.

Catholic Family History Society. 2001. *The bishops' register of confirmations in the London district of the Catholic Church in England, 1826–1837 and 1843.* West Wickham: Catholic Family History Society.

Davidson, Alan. 1970. *Roman Catholicism in Oxfordshire from the late Elizabethan period to the Civil War (c.1580–c.1640).* D. Phil. Thesis. University of Bristol.

Estcourt, Edgar E. and John Orlebar Payne. 1885. *The English Catholic nonjurors of 1715.* London: Burns & Oates.

Gandy, Michael. 1993. *Catholic missions and registers, 1700–1880, Volume 1: London and the Home Counties.* Whetstone: Gandy.

Gandy, Michael. 1993. *Catholic missions and registers, 1700–1880, Volume 2: The Midlands and East Anglia.* Whetstone: Gandy.

Kelly, Bernard W. 1907. *Historical notes on English Catholic missions.* London: Kegan Paul, Trench, Truebner & Co.

Registers of the RC church of St Aloysius, Oxford and the RC missions at Buckland and East Hendred.

Stapleton, Mrs Bryan. 1906. *A History of the Post-Reformation Catholic Missions in Oxfordshire – with an account of the families connected with them.* London: Henry Frowde.

Worrall, E. S., ed. 1989. *Returns of Papists, 1767. Dioceses of England and Wales except Chester. Volume 2.* [S.l.]: Catholic Record Society.

Twelve

Methodists in Oxfordshire

Charles Eldridge and Sue Honoré

Introduction

Nonconformity had existed in Oxfordshire in various forms from the fourteenth century, but became more common from the eighteenth century onwards. Early Nonconformist chapels and churches were supported by all levels of society but appealed especially to labourers, the poor and the illiterate, for whom there was little comfort or understanding in their parish church. John and Charles Wesley were both ordained ministers in the Church of England and encouraged their followers to attend their parish churches, but their views and ideals met with opposition from Oxford University and other clergy within Oxford who closed their churches to them, encouraging the development of Methodism.

Figure 93. John Wesley from Alfred Beesley's extra illustrated copy of his History of Banbury, Vol. 11, p. 58.

During his fifty-two-year ministry (1739–1791), John Wesley would travel up and down England, covering on average thirteen miles a day, and delivering more than two sermons; many of these sermons were in the open air and to hostile recipients. He was especially effective in London, Cornwall and Yorkshire, as well as the industrial centres of Bristol, Manchester, Newcastle upon Tyne and Birmingham. Methodism was very much a religion of the poor and had a great deal to do with a revolution in English religion which was as radical in its effect as the Industrial Revolution itself.

Where possible, John Wesley relied on his preaching to support the creation of local house meetings that would become viable Methodist societies before the creation of custom-built chapels, which were usually financed locally.

Methodist ministers would deliver sermons across geographical 'circuits'; circuit plans were developed from the early nineteenth century, with preachers rotating through the various chapels and meeting places within a circuit. Many of the circuits covering Oxfordshire crossed county boundaries. Those circuits relative to modern-day Oxfordshire include: Banbury, Chipping Norton and Stow, Oxford, Vale of Aylesbury, Wantage and Abingdon, and Witney. Each circuit would include all of the surrounding villages where there was a Methodist presence.

Figure 94. John Wesley's pulpit placed outside the Lincoln College buildings, Oxford. John Wesley was an undergraduate here when he preached his first sermon at the Church of St James, in the nearby village of South Leigh.

Oxford city drove the early impetus of Methodism in the county, with a society from at least 1748, becoming head of a circuit by 1765.[1] There was no permanent chapel, with sermons given in private houses and gardens and in other available buildings such as the New Road Presbyterian Chapel and, by the 1780s, a building at 32–34 New Inn Hall Street leased from Brasenose College. It is probable that most of the congregation were sympathisers rather than formal members, as most inhabitants of Oxford depended on a living from the university which still opposed Methodism. In 1815, largely on the initiative of John Pike (a prominent member for many years) the local society undertook to build their own chapel, just down the road, which was opened in 1818. The new chapel stimulated an increase in membership although, as in other locations in the county, evening attendance was much higher (600 in Oxford in 1851) than in the morning (380), bolstered by those who attended local Church of England churches in the morning and Wesleyan chapel later in the day.

Following John Wesley's death in 1791, the Wesleyan movement broke away from the Church of England and then suffered from several different divisions, the most significant being the Primitive Methodists who arrived in Oxfordshire in 1824.

In general, Primitive Methodism reached geographically where the Wesleyans had not, as seen in the difference between the locations of their meeting houses (Figure 95).

The Primitive Methodism movement originated in the Potteries, where an open-air camp meeting was held at Mow Cop in 1807, and quickly spread across the Midlands. It was aimed at working-class communities; miners, mill hands, farm labourers and workers in developing factory towns. In rural areas such as Oxfordshire, Primitive Methodists often came into conflict with the local landowners and the Anglican clergy, who saw them as a threat to the established order.

Primitive Methodists wanted a return to an earlier, purer form of Methodism. They aimed to give people a sense of self-worth and a desire for self-improvement. Chapels provided education and an opportunity to develop skills in public speaking and leadership. Primitive Methodism provided a way of life based on moral values, helping to raise families out of poverty.

By the 1851 religious census, forty-two Primitive Methodist congregations had formed in Oxfordshire with only eight being in towns. Many were in hamlets or villages where there were no Church of England churches or Wesleyan chapels. However, seventeen of the forty-two would disappear by 1883 and only nineteen would remain open continuously until 1915. In general, the communities in towns would survive whilst the rural communities would decline in line with general depopulation of the countryside.

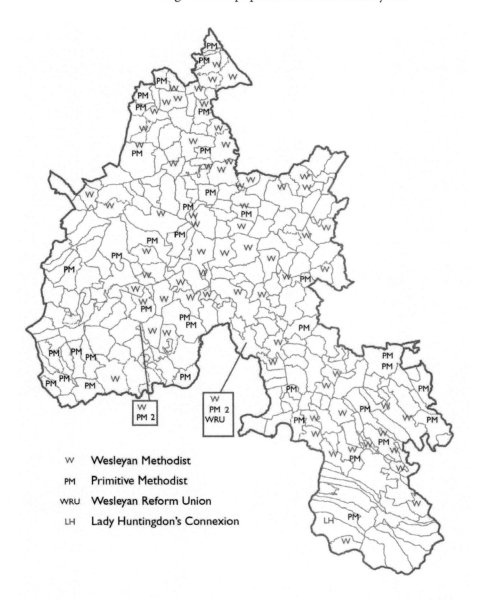

Figure 95. Methodist places of worship in Oxfordshire, 1851.[2]

What drove the development of Methodism in Oxfordshire?

There were a number of reasons that Methodism grew rapidly in the late eighteenth and nineteenth centuries in Oxfordshire. The following elements of social history may help explain the lives of ancestors in the county.

Charisma

In order to encourage people to join any movement, persuasive and knowledgeable speakers are needed. Certainly the charisma of people such as Charles Wesley was influential in Oxfordshire and throughout the country, appealing to those who felt disenfranchised by the Established Church.

Wesleyan itinerant preachers visiting Witney in 1762 and 1763 met with some success, and when John Wesley preached there in 1767 he found a congregation 'both large and deeply attentive.'[3]

Decline of the appeal of the Church of England

At the same time as Methodism grew, the Established Church was failing to meet the needs of new industrial areas and suffered from widespread absenteeism, particularly in poorer rural areas. The physical fabric of the buildings had often deteriorated and the connection between many of the vicars and their congregations was not as strong as in the past. Communication channels had also opened up, with improved transport generally, including the coming of the railways, leading eventually to widespread newspaper syndication, which allowed more people to have knowledge of what was happening elsewhere in the country and the world.

Figure 96. First Wesleyan Meeting House, Calthorpe Lane, Banbury.

Not only that, but in parts of Oxfordshire, especially around the Banbury area, there had been a long history of Nonconformism and dissent, which meant that a movement away from the Established Church was not a big step. In Banbury James Ward (a dyer) and Leonard Ledbrook (a grazier) built the first meeting house in Calthorpe Lane, which was opened in 1791. By the 1851 census, the dissenting churches in Banbury were attracting more people than the parish church. The Wesleyans were by far the strongest of the individual denominations. Dissenters usually had a majority on the borough council; they possessed their own charitable and educational organisations, and won victories over the Established Church on such matters as church rates. The ease with which money was raised to build a new chapel in 1863 indicates the wealth of the Methodist community at the time.

Preaching and networking

Once some members of a family became involved in Methodism, their influence encouraged other relatives and neighbours to join. Methodist strongholds also attracted immigrants. There were plenty of opportunities for discussion, and the system of circuits – which were often geographically large – meant that preachers travelled many miles each week, meeting different communities, and thus providing chances for the conversion of new members.

Methodists were perhaps far more equality-driven than the Established Church. There were many more women including female preachers and younger people involved in positions of influence than in the Church of England. Crucial to the development of Methodism were the efforts of Ann and Edward Bolton, children of a Witney baker and Independent, whose conversion suggests a dynamic appeal to the younger generation. Ann became a lifelong confidante of Wesley, along with several other women, whilst Ann and Edward, a Finstock farmer and a respected local preacher, were instrumental in securing the first Witney meeting house in 1769. Teenagers were often drawn into the community and later became preachers, such as fatherless Charles Wyatt of Brize Norton (1845–1898), Joseph Knipe of Ducklington (1839–1908) and John Neville, a farm lad of Minster Lovell (1839–1919), who all rose in the Primitive Methodist circuit.[4]

WASHING UP THE TEA-THINGS
WESLEYAN SUNDAY SCHOOL TREAT

Figure 97. Washing up after an Oxfordshire Methodist picnic, probably from the Oxford circuit 1903–11.

The movement had a strong social aspect. Methodists invited 'sinners' and those who were distressed or outsiders to their homes and to Methodist picnics. Methodism relied heavily on raising funds within the community and, through that approach, developed a community of people willing to join together, not only for worship but also for mutual support. From these social networks marriage partners could be found, resulting in several strong dynasties growing from Methodism in Oxfordshire, such as the Early family of Witney, the Danburys (of Bladon) and Nixes (of Oxford).

Workplace influence

Although the movement may have appealed to the working classes initially, partially due to its strong educational offerings, over the nineteenth century it drew in many middle-class traders and employers as well as wealthier landowners. In Witney by the 1790s, Wesleyan adherents included many leading manufacturers and tradesmen, among them the master blanket-weavers Jeremiah Biggers, Thomas Early and James Marriott, and the glove manufacturer William Pritchett. These employers led by example and encouraged their workers to convert. Some, it may be said, may have done so to retain their jobs, but the men in power had a persuasive influence on workers.

Figure 98. Charles Early (seated) and his two sons, Charles William and James, both company directors of Charles Early & Co.

Figure 99. The blue plaque commemorating the Early family's contribution to the Witney blanket-making industry.

Strong financial support was provided by William Mewburn, a self-made Yorkshire businessman, who came to live at Wickham Park near Banbury in 1865. He became circuit steward, responsible for the spiritual wellbeing of the churches and circuit administration, in 1867. He gave a tenth of his income to charity, and much of this went to Wesleyan causes. He was generous in opening Wickham Park and its grounds for Wesleyan social occasions.

In other cases, people in the same trade or type of employment may have encouraged others in their networks to join, particularly in the larger towns. A large proportion of Banbury's businessmen and professionals were also members of the Methodist congregation. Among them were John Vanner, a London businessman; William Edmunds, the brewer; Banbury's borough accountant, a solicitor, a woollen draper, a butcher, and the two partners in a large High Street grocery business. In Witney, shopkeepers Caleb Viner and Richard Harbud, ironmonger Samuel Lea and the shoemaker Joseph Dutton were leading lights.

External influx of people

As towns such as Banbury and Witney grew and people migrated in from elsewhere, they brought Methodism with them, particularly from northern counties, London and Wales. Regular travel for business or to visit families outside Oxfordshire also helped to grow Oxfordshire's Methodist reach.

In 1831 the first Methodist chapel was built in Little Milton. One of the leading Methodists was Thomas Perkins, a Little Milton grocer from London, and the chapel trustees included another grocer and a labourer of Little Milton, two Great Milton farmers, and tradesmen and labourers from other parishes, including Drayton, Chalgrove and Watlington. The chapel had a congregation of about thirty, who were taught by a shoemaker and a visiting preacher.

Summary

Methodism drew in people who felt they needed a change from the Established Church, seeking something which better represented their needs and which fostered a strong sense of community. It was also very much a word-of-mouth conversion for many, through their relatives, friends and neighbours and employment networks.

It was largely driven by local needs and varied in strength, the branch of Methodism and membership size in different locations over time, eventually with a merging together of Methodist branches in the twentieth century.

For those researching their families in Oxfordshire, Methodist records may be useful for labourers in particular in the late eighteenth century and first half of the nineteenth century. Rural villages which were part of a large parish unsupported by the Established Church and middle-class traders and wealthy business owners in the mid to late nineteenth century were likely to be Methodists. If Methodist ancestors are found, then looking over a wider area of Oxfordshire and beyond for other relatives may be useful, given circuit size and the nature of the spread of influence of the religion.

Case studies

Three case studies help to illuminate the discussion. Firstly, a statistical review of baptisms of Methodists from 1803 to 1874, mainly in the Wesleyan and Primitive Methodist communities in the Banbury and Witney circuits, but also with smaller contributions from Faringdon, Wantage and Wallingford.[5] The second case study looks at the influx of a Chartist community into Minster Lovell, and the third reviews what happened in the village of Epwell.

Case study 1: Baptisms and Methodist surnames

This analysis looked at Methodist baptism records in the Oxfordshire Family History Society parish record set. It is somewhat limited because the records do not cover all years or all places. By targeting people of childbearing age, it examines a subset of the full population, but covers those most likely to be in work and to be mobile.

A total of 789 surnames (grouped into variant spellings) were recorded. Given that the maximum period covered was seventy years, and in many cases much less than that, this is a remarkably large number of individual surnames.

Approximately two-thirds of the names might be regarded as generic for the UK or 'non-Oxfordshire'. Although it does not mean that the individual Methodist families came from their ancient surname origins, they are quite likely to have migrated to Oxfordshire from elsewhere, even if it took many generations to get from the ancient surname location to Oxfordshire. Unsurprisingly, in the Methodist community there were a large number of Welsh names, such as Bevan, Evans, Jones, Lloyd, Owen, Davi(e)s, Griffiths, Hughes, Morgan, Powell, Price and Thomas. There were, less expectedly, several Scottish names such as Macdonald, McDougal, McCauley and Stuart/Stewart.

A large percentage had surname origins in the north of England, such as Armett, Armstrong, Brocklehurst, Brummit, Douphrate, Inns and Pickering. There were some from eastern counties (e.g. Aylswood, Clare, Clee, Julian, Lammas, Speed), the Midlands (Giggers, Grissold/Griswold, Goff, Loxley, Ludlow, Shaddock), the West Country (Gessey, Hornabrook), the south (Cleaver, Dyke, Lampitt, Paradise, Parslow, Wimbush) and others from counties surrounding Oxfordshire (Bumpus, Clapton, Minty, Quennell).[6]

During transcription it was noted that several new surnames were added every year, indicating that Methodism was growing strongly in the nineteenth century in Oxfordshire.

There were a total of 519 names in Witney and 385 in Banbury. Each location had two Methodist chapels – Primitive Methodist and Wesleyan. The two Methodist chapels shared 23% of their surnames in Witney and 18% in Banbury. Overall, 69% of the surnames were in one chapel only. Names were therefore localised geographically and religiously.

The overall total number of surnames was 789 and, of those, 66% were found in Witney and 49% in Banbury. Looking at the names found in one place but not the other, 50% were found only in Witney, 34% only in Banbury and 16% shared across both locations. This does indicate that, relatively speaking, there are a large number of unique names. This reinforces the idea that the Methodist population came from many different localised families (see Figure 100).

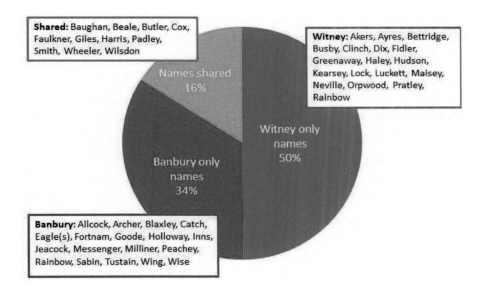

Figure 100. Some of the Methodist names in Witney and Banbury.

There were more individual surname families in this Oxfordshire Methodist population than in other comparable Oxfordshire groups of a similar size analysed in other chapters of this book. Therefore, Methodists were a diverse group, often with localised names, with Primitive Methodists and Wesleyans largely separated in terms of surname.

Occupations

Occupations were not recorded for the whole period of the records and, in general, stopped when the 1836 Births and Deaths Registration Act came into place. Mostly the occupations cover a short period from 1810 to 1837.

Reinforcing the view that Methodism appealed to the working classes, both Wesleyan and Primitive Methodists showed 'labourer' as by far the most common occupation over this period. However, it is interesting that the Primitive Methodists consisted of a much higher proportion of labourers (Banbury 64%, Witney 72%) than the Wesleyans (Banbury 21%, Witney 25%). As a comparison, in the 1851 census labourers made up about 16.5% of the occupations in Witney. More Primitive Methodists came from the general labouring classes although both groups attracted a very high percentage of labourers relative to the overall population.

Both Banbury and Witney were market towns and a high number of skilled workers and shopkeepers would be expected. As each town had its specialist trades (blanket manufacturing and weaving, including plush weaving in the Banbury area), it is not surprising that they feature highly in Methodist congregations. Figures showed that 12% of Wesleyan Methodist baptisms had fathers in the textile industry; the number was 15% in Witney. The Primitive Methodist figures were 3% of Witney and negligible for Banbury. The textile trades were therefore more associated with Wesleyans. In both towns and both chapels, tailors, millers and shoemakers or cordwainers were common, as well as masons and stonecutters. Carpenters and blacksmiths were more numerous in Primitive Methodist baptisms, and grocers and other shopkeepers with the Wesleyans. There were more people of higher status (gentlemen, men of independent means, yeomen) in the Wesleyan congregation in both Banbury and Witney.

Summary

This evidence supports the fact that both branches of Methodism attracted labourers as the largest occupation group. There was more of a tendency for middle-class participants amongst Wesleyans. The spread of Methodism was reflected in the wider connections that individuals made through the Methodist networks and circuits. Many new surnames continued to be added to Methodist registers as the denomination grew in the nineteenth century, and these surnames reflect names from a large part of the British Isles.

Case study 2: Charterville, Minster Lovell

Feargus O'Connor, a determined leader of the Chartist movement, skilled orator and MP, believed that poor families should be given the opportunity to move out of crowded city slums, become self-sufficient, and gain greater opportunities to vote. His National Land Company was formed in 1845/6 to achieve this aim. He advertised for subscriptions to this company through his own newspaper, the *Northern Star*, which cleverly listed by locality the subscribers who had contributed in the hope of 'winning' a plot of land. His notices were syndicated in other local newspapers including *Jackson's Oxford Journal*. He then toured the country buying up suitable sites at auction – Heronsgate near Rickmansworth, then several in Worcestershire and one eventually named Charterville in Minster Lovell, Oxfordshire, which was built in 1848/9.

There was little Nonconformity in the village prior to the nineteenth century, but the Oxford Diocese returns of 1854 record more than 200 'Dissenters' on the new estate,[7] when the total village population was 450 (up from 300 a few years before the estate was built). The local curate alleged that the 'O'Connor cottages ... formed another parish almost, the generality of the occupants being bigoted Dissenters'.[8] Temporary buildings were used initially, but the existing Wesleyan chapel was built in 1858 and a Primitive Methodist chapel in 1893. The latter closed in 1964 and all Methodists now use the main Wesleyan building.

Figure 101. A cottage in the Charterville development in Minster Lovell a hundred years after it was built.

There were seventy-seven plots of two, three and four acres offered at Charterville. The original allottees came mainly from Lancashire (Ashton-under-Lyne and Manchester) and Yorkshire (Leeds and Bradford), strongholds of Nonconformism and Chartism. However, fifteen never took up the offer and their plots were transferred to others. There was also some swapping and changing, so about eighty names remained.[9] The two-acre plots were not popular, being almost impossible to use for sustaining a family. Of those who migrated and can be traced, 23% were from Lancashire and 14% from Yorkshire. They also came from other northern counties such as Cheshire, Derbyshire, Nottinghamshire and Northumberland, with another cluster from London and Kent. An additional group were closer – from Gloucestershire, Warwickshire and Northamptonshire. There was a relatively large group from the Pershore area of Worcestershire, near to where early Chartist settlements already existed. So this group of geographically dispersed people descended en masse on an Oxfordshire village, bringing their largely Nonconformist religious beliefs with them.

The surnames that arrived were also not common in Oxfordshire. Those from Yorkshire or Lancashire included Lockwood, Littlewood, Dyson, Kirk, Seed, Rothery, Brierley and Denton; from Kent there was Stallwood and Willis; Worcestershire brought Howse, Horsefall, Wheeler, Conn/Cown, Price and O'Leary. Wearing, De Bank, Minty, Bowl, Robinson and Stratford came from Gloucestershire. These incoming surnames may have been the first instance in Oxfordshire in some cases but, if not, they may have been the first of a new branch of a given surname in the county (for example Howse and Wheeler) and, although some did not stay, some of these names may have started new family lines in Oxfordshire.

Conditions were difficult and the new smallholders were often city folk unused to the way of life. Within two to three years about two-thirds of the families had left. Initially many men tried to go home in order to make a living to supplement their earnings, and several wives such as those of the Bower, Chandler and Littlewood families, were left behind to manage the Charterville property. By the time of the 1851 census about half of the houses were empty. There then followed a formal reorganisation and consolidation of plots, with a strong influx of local buyers: over 55% with a traceable origin came from Oxfordshire and another 12% from local counties, with some investors from London renting out plots. There was an ongoing influx from Pershore, possibly because the land was good for growing fruit trees. Potatoes were the only other successful mass crop, despite blight attacking a few times in the second half of the century. Many of the new owners used the land as a supplementary income, earning most of their money as mill workers in nearby Worsham or Crawley or as farm labourers. The strong religious community which had been founded by the incomers continued with the locals and even drew in other residents from the remaining parts of the parish to join the Methodist community. More surnames common in Oxfordshire such as Basson/Baston, Timms, Drinkwater, Mourbey, Gardner, Batts and Busby were now in Charterville. By 1861 it was rare to find any of the original allottees or their families.

Of the survivors, James Beattie moved in and out but died in 1865 in Minster Lovell; John Bennett was still present in 1871; Thomas Holland, although he spent time in in Oxford Gaol and the workhouse, died in Minster Lovell in 1883 and James Price (formerly of Pershore) died in Minster Lovell in 1869. George Townley had a heart attack in 1848 soon after moving to Charterville, but left his children to be adopted in the village.

There was also continuity through the Pershore connection. William Howse, an agricultural labourer born in Hinton-on-the-Green, Worcestershire, married and moved to Minster Lovell where he had children for a decade from 1819. By 1831 he had moved to Pershore but returned to take over a Charterville plot by 1851. His second wife died there in 1852 and he moved to London. He may have been a key influencer of migration from the Pershore area and he may have had local ancestry, with the Howse family in Minster Lovell going back to the early sixteenth century.

Figure 102. Lily Jael Wheeler, granddaughter of Walter Edward and Jael Wheeler from Worcestershire. Lily's father died at an early age during harvesting, leaving the family to manage through early employment of the children in glovemaking and working in Witney blanket factories. She is pictured with her two children, Peter and Donald.

Patrick O'Leary, an Irish accountant from Kidderminster whose family worked in the carpet industry, and Samuel Stone, a cheese factor born in Somerset but married and resident in Pershore in 1841, were original Charterville allottees. Stone's wife Martha was sister to Walter Wheeler, a shoemaker, who also brought his family from nearby Peopleton to Charterville to own land by 1852. Walter also acted as a part-time Baptist preacher and a tax collector in Minster Lovell and owned twenty-seven acres of land by 1861. Samuel Stone had acquired five cottages and twenty acres by 1852, so was a major landowner and, although he was back in Pershore by 1862, his estate still owned the Charterville property in 1873. Walter Wheeler was the last original Pershore landowner to leave Charterville after his wife died in 1871. His son, Walter Edward Wheeler, married Hannah Green, a Minster Lovell woman, and died in Minster Lovell in 1883. Some of his descendants were still in the area near the turn of the twentieth century.

So, despite a rapid turnover of residents, Charterville started a new Methodist community in a very short space of time from 1848, which was continued via some original residents of the estate, the drawing in of locals who were already Methodists or recently converted, as well as ongoing immigration to the community from outside Oxfordshire.

Case study 3: Epwell

Figure 103. Cottages in Epwell.

Epwell was mainly an agricultural village included in the parish of Swalcliffe but, like all Oxfordshire villages which were reliant on farming, it declined in the latter half of the nineteenth century. Enclosure in the late eighteenth century had reduced the number of profitable farms as well as opportunities for employment. Plush weaving had moved into factories, and stone quarrying, although stable, did not provide widespread employment.

The vicars at Swalcliffe, responsible for Epwell, helped to create a difficult environment. John Caswell (1761–1808) was seen as rather casual in his approach and tried to avoid travelling to Epwell to preach. He was succeeded by John Stevens (1808–1837) who struggled with the financial aspects of managing a poor parish and throughout his time managed to alienate many of his parishioners, especially as he became older. The welfare of his parishioners was unsupported, particularly as he often paid so little for curates that only the less competent were employed. Attendance at church dropped considerably during his time. Methodist preachers from over the border in Warwickshire started coming to the village from 1814. There had also been a precedent for Nonconformism with Quakers and Anabaptists being strong in the area since the late seventeenth century.[10] The seeds of dissent had been sown and, despite the fact that the next incumbent (Edward Payne; 1837–86), did much to improve the ministry, in the more neglected villages such as Epwell, Methodism took over. The religious survey of 1851 showed Epwell's population at 330 but the Primitive Methodist chapel, which had been erected in 1830, had a congregation of 129 compared to the main church of 32.

Notes

1. Wesley, John, and Henry D. Rack. 2011. *The Methodist societies: the minutes of Conference. Works of John Wesley.* Nashville (Tenn.): Abingdon Press. pp. 224, 317.

2. Tiller, Kate and Giles Darkes, eds. 2010. *An historical atlas of Oxfordshire.* Oxfordshire Record Society. Vol. 67.

3. *Dictionary of Methodism in Britain and Ireland.* John Wesley's journal August 1767. http://dmbi.online.

4. *Primitive Methodist Magazine.* https://www.myprimitivemethodists.org.uk/.

5. Oxfordshire Family History Society Parish Records – Baptisms. Data extracted: Banbury Wesleyan 1805–1874 (summer); Banbury Primitive Methodist 1840–1873; Faringdon Primitive Methodist 1834–1837; Wallingford Primitive Methodist 1833–1837; Witney Primitive Methodist 1843–1874 (summer); Witney Wesleyan 1803–1874 (summer). The figures count number of baptisms (not number of families) for any child born in the county of Oxfordshire from the named circuit.

6. Reaney, Percy H. and R. M. Wilson. 2005. *A dictionary of English surnames.* Oxford: Oxford University Press; and original research for this project.

7. 'Carterton, Minster Lovell & Environs' in Colvin, Christina *et al.* 2006. *A history of the county of Oxford: Volume 15, Bampton Hundred (Part Three),* ed. Simon Townley. London: Victoria County History. *British History Online.* http://www.british–history. ac.uk/vch/oxon/vol15.

8. 'Carterton, Minster Lovell & Environs' in Colvin, Christina *et al.* 2006. *A history of the county of Oxford: Volume 15, Bampton Hundred (Part Three),* ed. Simon Townley. London: Victoria County History. *British History Online.* http://www.british–history. ac.uk/vch/oxon/vol15.

9. Hadfield, Alice Mary. 1970. *The Chartist Land Company.* Newton Abbot: David & Charles. https://archive.org/details/chartistlandcomp0000hadf; The *Northern Star;*

'Carterton, Minster Lovell & Environs' in Colvin, Christina *et al.* 2006. *A history of the county of Oxford: Volume 15, Bampton Hundred (Part Three)*, ed. Simon Townley. London: Victoria County History. *British History Online.* http://www.british–history. ac.uk/vch/oxon/vol15; and original research by Sue Honoré.

10. Colvin, Christina *et al.* 1972. *A history of the county of Oxford: Volume 10, Banbury Hundred*, ed. Alan Crossley. London: Victoria County History. *British History Online.* http://www.british–history.ac.uk/vch/oxon/vol10.

Thirteen

Quakers in Oxfordshire

Christopher Farrand

Background

Figure 104. The sign to the Quaker Meeting House in Wallingford.

The Quaker movement developed out of the religious ferment of the period of the seventeenth-century Civil War. Quakerism represented a radical rejection of the outward forms of Christianity and the institutions of the religious establishment – the rituals, liturgy and sacraments as well as the authority of the clergy. Quakers saw these aspects as standing in the way of a spiritual understanding of the Gospels. Unlike Puritans, who believed that the Bible was the source of all religious authority, Quakers (or Friends, as they preferred to call themselves) looked to the Spirit of Christ which spoke directly to the heart. As George Fox put it, 'Christ has come to teach his people himself'. The scriptures could only be understood in the same spirit in which they had been brought forth. Arising from their rejection of the clergy, Quakers refused to pay tithes and other church rates. In keeping with Jesus' injunction to 'swear not at all', they refused to swear oaths.

Believing also in the equality of all men and women before God, they refused to bow or doff their hats to their social superiors, what they referred to as 'hat honour', or use honorifics. They addressed everyone in the second person singular – 'thee', 'thou' – rather than the formal 'you', what they referred to as 'plain speech'. Contrary to the common view at that time, Quakers also believed in the spiritual equality of men and women, and many women actively participated in spreading the Quaker message. These views earned Quakers the active hostility of the clergy as well as the political establishment, both during the Commonwealth/Protectorate as well as after the Restoration.

Oxfordshire Quakers

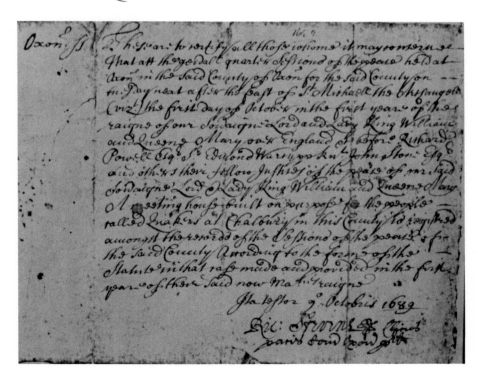

Figure 105. A licence for Quakers to hold meetings in Charlbury dated October 1689.

From its beginnings in the north of England in 1652, the Quaker movement quickly expanded southward. The first 'First Publishers of the Truth', as the earliest Quaker missionaries were referred to, appeared in Oxfordshire in 1654. In that year John Audland and John Camm, of Westmorland, who would soon play prominent roles in the growth of Quakerism in Bristol, arrived at Banbury to spread the Quaker message. They were followed by their wives, Anne Audland and Mabel Camm. Anne Audland would be arrested for blasphemy for calling the local priest a false prophet. Other Friends, Elizabeth Fletcher and Elizabeth Leavens, also from Westmorland, arrived at Oxford, where they would be harshly met – abused by the Oxford students, whipped, and gaoled in the Bocardo Prison. They would be followed to prison that year by John Audland, John Camm, Richard Hubberthorne, Humphrey Smith and William Simpson.

Friends quickly gained a foothold in Banbury, where, despite intense persecution, they received support from some prominent figures such as woollen draper Edward Vivers, Bray Doyly and innkeeper James Wagstaff, whose tavern was the first Quaker meeting place. A number of small preparative meetings soon sprung up around Banbury; at Adderbury, Hook Norton, Shutford, Sibford and South Newington. Banbury would remain the principal centre for Friends in Oxfordshire for many years. Other meetings were soon established along the western edge of the county at Chipping Norton, Charlbury, Burford and Witney. A meeting was first established at Oxford at the home of Richard Betteris, a surgeon, near the church of St Peter-le-Bailey. Friends in Oxford, however, were faced with the aggressive opposition of university officials. One Oxford Friend, Thomas Loe, would travel in the ministry to Ireland. William Penn credited him for his convincement, recalling the words Loe had spoken during a visit to the Penn home in Macroom: 'There is a faith that overcomes the world, and there is a faith that is overcome by the world ...'. Other meetings sprung up in the southern part of the county around Warborough and Henley-on-Thames.

Figure 106. The meeting house in Charlbury with graves for the Clary, Bowly, Albright and Spendlove families in the foreground.

Persecution and punishment

Friends were submitted to the active persecution by civil and religious authorities for forty-five years until the Toleration Act of 1689, and even then persecution did not completely disappear. During this period 262 individual Friends (220 men and 42 women) are known to have suffered persecution, often repeatedly. The penalties included imprisonment, fines, distraint of goods, excommunication, *praemunire,*[1] eviction and beatings.

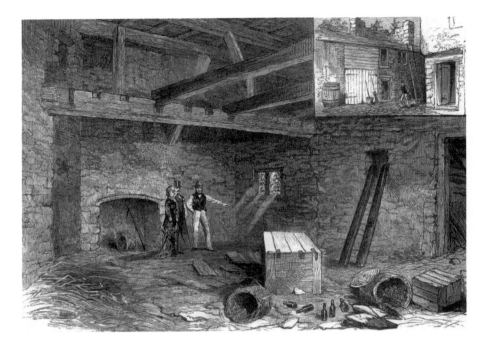

Figure 107. The Bocardo or Old Prison at Oxford.

During this forty-five-year period, there were 232 instances of imprisonment. These ranged from overnight to ten years. The Friend suffering the lengthiest stay was William Pettifer of Burford, who received a ten-year sentence and a sentence of *praemunire*, the confiscation of all his property, for unlawful assembly in 1662. Thomas Minchin of Burford spent eight years and six months in Oxford Gaol under a writ of *excommunicato capiendo* for not attending church.[2] Henry Phillips of Banbury also spent eight years and six months in prison for refusing the Oath of Allegiance. Three other Oxfordshire men, James Wagstaff of Banbury, James Carpenter and Paul Newman, were each imprisoned for eight years and six months while visiting Warwick, also for refusing to take the Oath of Allegiance. George Weston of Stansfield [*sic*] was gaoled for eight years under a writ of *excommunicato capiendo* for 'religious non-conformity'.[3] Giles Tidmarsh of Chipping Norton spent seven years under a writ of *excommunicato capiendo* for refusing to contribute to the cost of repairs to the church. Richard Wright of Henley served six years and six months in prison for refusing to have his child baptised. Thomas Reeves, of Great Tew, would die in Oxford Gaol after six years and six months under a writ of *excommunicato capiendo*. Many others served for shorter periods.

Thomas Reeves would not be the only Friend to die while in prison; others included William Cole, Thomas Deane and William Staple Cole, of Charlbury, for refusing to pay tithes or take the Oath of Allegiance, and Deane and Staple, both of Hook Norton, for refusing to pay tithes. Four other Friends, Elizabeth Fletcher, Richard Clinton of Shutford, Alexander Harris of Milton-under-Wychwood, and Robert Willett of Burford, would die shortly after their release, their health having been broken in prison.

During this period, there were at least 198 instances of Friends being fined or imprisoned for holding unlawful meetings. There were also seventy-three cases of Friends refusing to pay tithes. As Friends usually refused to pay fines this led to the distraint of goods, of which there are at least 154 cases. These were often occasions for priests and tithe farmers to take the property of Friends. The parish priest at Widdington [sic] seized sheep, corn, hay and peas valued at £100 from George Tomkins of Milcombe in payment for tithes.[4] Bray Doyly of Adderbury had five cows and fifty-two sheep, valued at £32, seized in payment of a fine for attending a meeting for worship. Benjamin Ward of Tadmarton had forty-two sheep valued at £20 seized for a demand for £3 in tithes. Some even had their property seized for tithes while being held in prison for other reasons.

In some cases, priests took their revenge against Quakers by having landlords evict their tenants. In 1675, Richard Holliman, a miller at Cuxham, left the Established Church following his convincement as a Quaker. As a result, he was evicted with his large family by his landlord Justice Gregory at the urging of the parish priest who declared him a heretic.

There were four instances between 1660 and 1663 where Oxfordshire Friends were sentenced to *praemunire*, the surrender of all their goods and property to the King. This affected Thomas Goodyear, William Pettifer, Henry Phillips and Benjamin Staples.

Besides the five Friends imprisoned under a writ of *excommunicato capiendo*, nine others were excommunicated but not gaoled during this period. The most interesting case is that of Francis Dring of Brize Norton, whose father was the vicar. Following his son's excommunication, the vicar reportedly was no longer able to bring himself to preach from the pulpit and died soon afterwards.

Friends were often arrested without charges. Officials would then require them to swear the Oath of Allegiance, which they knew Friends would not do as they opposed oaths of any kind as contrary to truth. In at least eighty-six cases, Friends were imprisoned, fined or both through the use of this practice.

Many Friends were subjected to multiple instances of persecution. Edward Vivers of Banbury was imprisoned or fined at least nine times, including for refusing to pay tithes or pay for repairs to the church, for unlawful assembly, for praying in public and for refusing the Oath of Allegiance. Edward Drinkwater of Gagingwell, near Enstone, suffered eight times, as did George Tomkins of Milcombe. Benjamin Staples of Chadlington suffered seven times and Bray Doyly of Adderbury, John Long of Neithrop, Nathaniel Ball of North Newtown, John Shackerly of Oxford, Thomas Minchin of Burford, and Thomas Nichols of Oxford, six times each.

The persecution of Friends could impact others as well. In January 1684/5, Banbury officials seized the property of John Haynes as a fine for his 'exhortation' during the funeral of a Friend. When the officials attempted to enlist the assistance of bystanders in removing Haynes' goods from his home, these 'poor men' refused. One of them, Nathaniel Reason, was gaoled for his refusal. By the end of the seventeenth century, the zeal for persecution had cooled down.

Quakers in the Oxfordshire community

Figure 108. Two illustrations from Memories of Banbury by Marjory Lester, painted by the author and showing the outside (a) and interior (b) of the Meeting House in Banbury.

From very early on, each Quaker meeting maintained its own registers, recording births, marriages and deaths. Quarterly meetings often maintained duplicate registers. Until the Act for Marriages of 1836, Quakers, along with Jews, were the only religious organisations to conduct their own marriages. All others were required to be married by Anglican clergy. In the early 1700s, there were some forty different surnames found in the Banbury Meeting's register – these include Wagstaff, Potter, Haynes, Long, Tredbrook, Stow, Ball, Gulliver, Hill, Gilkes, Wills, Parks, French and Lamb.

With the end of persecution, Friends became respectable, if odd, members of the community. Because of their refusal to swear oaths, Quakers were barred from attending university or entering the professions, serving on juries or in Parliament.[5] Consequently, Quakers found their principal professional outlet in business and industry. Over the next two centuries, many played leading roles in business and in their communities. From the Banbury Meeting the Gilkes family, starting with Thomas Gilkes (1675–1757) of Sibford, was associated with clockmaking. Other Quaker clockmakers in the county included Thomas' sons Thomas Jr. (1704–1772), also of Sibford, John (1707–c.1790) of Shipston-on-Stour and Richard (1715–1787) of Adderbury. John Fardon (1700–1744), an apprentice of Thomas Gilkes Sr., set up in Deddington while William Green, an apprentice of Thomas Jr., set up at Milton-under-Wychwood. Others include John Wells of Shipston, Richard Gilkes (1767–1855) of Sibford Gower, Thomas Gilkes (1736–1799) of Charlbury, Ezra Enoch (1799–1860) and John Enock (1834–1883) of Sibford Gower, John May (1726–1800) of Witney and Edward May (1732–1805) of Henley-on-Thames.[6] Chipping Norton was home to a number of Quaker watchmakers, including William Atkins (c.1738–1823), John Gilkes (c.1774–1861) and Charles Price Simms (1820–1910). Related by marriage to the May family of watchmakers were the Flexney brothers, John and Daniel of Witney. At first they continued their father's business as fullers, but progressed to being clothiers, trading in the fast-expanding business of blanketmaking. They were both prominent in the Witney Meeting and helped finance the construction of a Meeting House there. They had depots in London, and both of Daniel's sons eventually moved there. The elder son, also Daniel, both visited and traded in Pennsylvania.

In the mid 1800s, Joseph Ashby Gillett (1795–1853) founded Gillett's Bank in Banbury and would serve as clerk of Banbury Meeting. His son Charles would begin the development of Neithrop into a planned community. In 1919, the bank was sold to Barclays, another bank with Quaker origins.

A number of Banbury Friends left literary works. Alfred Beesley wrote a history of Banbury. Banbury-born Thomas Wagstaff (1724–1802) compiled a collection of biographical sketches of Friends and their dying words in a book called *Piety Promoted.*[7] William Charles Braithwaite (1862–1922), the son of prominent minister Joseph Bevan Braithwaite (1818–1905) and Martha Gillett, daughter of Joseph Ashby Gillett, played an important role towards the end of the nineteenth century in reforming the Religious Society of Friends. His religious views contrasted with those held by his strongly evangelical father. William Charles Braithwaite was among a group of younger Friends seeking to rediscover the lives of early Friends. He was the author of several major histories of Quakerism, including *The Beginnings of Quakerism*[8] and *The Second Period of Quakerism*.[9] He lived in Banbury from 1896 until his death in 1922.

James Cadbury (1802–1888), a grocer and wine merchant of the Birmingham family, also lived in Banbury. A leader of the temperance movement in Banbury, he wrote *A New History of Banbury* in 1855.[10] The Huntley family of Sibford Ferris would migrate to Reading, where Sibford-born Thomas Huntley (1807–1853) would become one of the founders of the biscuit company Huntley & Palmers. Other Banbury Quaker family names during the eighteenth and nineteenth centuries include Brown, Cross, Harlock, Head, Lamb, Midwinter, Plester, Reynolds, Rutter, Tyler and Wells. By 1851, Banbury Meeting recorded, during the religious census of that year, an attendance of sixty Friends at morning meeting and thirty-nine in the evening. Sibford recorded 120.

Figure 109. The Friends' School at Sibford Ferris.

In 1841, at Sibford Ferris, the Quarterly Meeting founded Sibford School in Walford Manor. The school, which began with twenty-six boys and twenty-two girls, was a working school, originally designed for the children of disowned Friends – Friends who married out to non-Quakers, but wished to maintain links with the Society. Later the school would admit the children of active Friends as well. The school still exists today as a Friends school.

While Banbury was the principal of the three Quarterly Meetings in Oxfordshire, the other two were at Witney (which included Burford, Charlbury, Chipping Norton and, eventually, Oxford) and Warborough, which also included Henley-on-Thames. These were considerably smaller meetings. Warborough Meeting would eventually merge with Reading Meeting. In 1851, Charlbury had the largest attendance in Witney Quarterly Meeting with thirty-nine in the morning and twenty-seven in the evening. The other meetings had an attendance of roughly a dozen each. Prominent names in the Witney district in the eighteenth and nineteenth centuries were Brayshaw, Garnett, Long, May, Rutter, Smith and Tyler at Witney, Huntley at Burford, Albright, Dell, Gilkes and Sessions at Charlbury, and Atkins, Fardon, Gilkes, Green and Simms at Chipping Norton. By 1851, Warborough had only twelve attenders. Besides the Huntleys, other Oxfordshire families found their way to Reading, including the Whitings and Rutters of Witney, and the Fardons, originally from North Newington.

Today there are Quaker meetings at Banbury, Sibford, Charlbury, Witney, Burford, Abingdon, Headington, Oxford, Wallingford, Faringdon and Wantage.

Notes

1. *The Statute of Praemunire* (16 Ric 2 c 5) was an Act of Parliament enacted in 1392. It was originally designed to limit the powers of the Pope in England. It was revived during the Restoration period to use against Friends. 'The person found guilty was to be put out of the King's protection, his estate forfeited to the crown, and he was imprisoned during life or at the royal pleasure. The simplicity and severity of a *praemunire* quickly recommended it, and the rust weapon forged for use against the pretensions of Rome was turned against the harmless Quakers'. (Braithwaite, William C. 1919. *The second period of Quakerism*. London: Macmillan, p. 14.)

2. *The Writ De Excommunicato Capiendo Act 1562* (5 Eliz 1 c 23): A *writ de excommunicato capiendo* (Latin for 'taking one who is excommunicated') commanded the sheriff to arrest a person who was excommunicated, and imprison him till he should become reconciled to the church. (Wikipedia)

3. Besse, Joseph. 1753. *A collection of the sufferings of the people called Quakers*. London: Luke Hinde.

4. Besse, Joseph, op. cit.

5. It was not until the repeal of the Test Acts in 1828 that Quakers could serve in Parliament. The Quakers and Moravians Act of 1833 allowed Quakers to serve on juries. The repeal of the University Test Acts in 1871 finally opened up university education to Quakers.

6. See Marshall, Tim. 2013. *The Quaker clockmakers of north Oxfordshire*. Ashbourne: Mayfield Books.

7. Tomkins, John. 1812. *Piety promoted, in a collection of dying sayings of many of the people called Quakers*. London: W. Phillips. https://archive.org/details/pietypromotedinc00tomk.

8. Braithwaite, William C. 1912. *The beginnings of Quakerism*. London: Macmillan.

9. Braithwaite, William C. 1919. *The second period of Quakerism*. London: Macmillan.

10. Cadbury, James. 1855. *A new history of Banbury, before and after a Maine liquor law*. London: W. Tweedie. http://books.google.com/books?id=9VxZAAAAcAAJ.

Fourteen

Implications for Family Historians

Jessica Feinstein

What are the implications of the research undertaken for this book? If you have traced your ancestors back to Oxfordshire, or if you have an interest in Oxfordshire families, villages, or surnames, the suggestions throughout the book will point you to new avenues to explore, and introduce some new perspectives that help to shed light on the lives of your ancestors and the decisions that they made. The notes at the end of each chapter can all be pursued to take your knowledge further, and it is worth familiarising yourself with relevant websites (such as British History Online)[1] as well as checking your local library's reference collection to see the books they have available.

Much of this advice will also be relevant for those whose ancestors came from elsewhere, for example learning about more unusual records, collaborating with others through surname projects such as those registered with the Guild of One-Name Studies[2] and DNA projects,[3] and making the most of what family history societies and specialists have to offer in terms of expertise, resources, and shared interests.

If you are trying to determine whether the name you are researching is an Oxfordshire surname, Chapter 1 offers some ways to help you decide. You will need to work out, for example, how long the surname has been present in the county, using a range of records such as wills, civil registration, tax documents, early rolls, muster rolls, censuses and parish registers. This chapter also highlights the fact that our ancestors were not confined to one county: they could and did move to neighbouring counties or further afield. Collaborating with others by joining or setting up a surname project or a DNA project is a way to make progress with your research, learn from experts, and also help those who will be interested in these surnames in the future.

As can be seen from Chapter 2, the surname you are interested in may appear in the records spelled in many different ways, some of which you may not have expected. This is particularly the case for earlier records, so allow for flexibility in your searching, and take the time to learn how to search the relevant databases, e.g. by using wildcards, soundex and phonetic spellings. Keep your own list of the different spellings that you have come across.

It is helpful to know when the family you are interested in first appeared in the Oxfordshire records. Following the surname through the records can help with understanding where they may have migrated from, where they lived, whether they moved around within the county, and how long they stayed. As Chapter 3 suggests, it is well worth making a study of the name you are researching, including variant spellings, and following the branches of daughters as well as sons. It is also important to consider the occupations carried out by family members, and how they affected the decisions that families made to move within the county or to leave it altogether. Reading accounts of local and social history will provide context for what happened to your family, and why.

Chapter 4 highlights the reasons for migration, and the underlying social networks that may explain why your family moved around. There are many family history records that can help you here, such as wills, manorial documents, and online migration records, so it is important to discover what is available and how the records can be accessed. A good tip is to plot the movements of your family on a map, and to learn about the history and geography of that area, combined with your own knowledge of your family's occupations and fortunes over time. Widen your study to include family networks, as well as friends, neighbours, employers and business associates. These can all provide reasons why your ancestors moved. If your ancestors vanished from the county at some point, consider the possibility that they moved elsewhere, and don't restrict your search too much. They might have gone to a big city, over the border to Scotland, or across the sea to another continent that offered better opportunities.

If you are researching a family whose surname is the same as the name of a place, Chapter 5 explains that one shouldn't assume that the family came from that place. There are other reasons why that surname may have been chosen. Again, careful research into the records is needed, and it is worth joining the relevant surname projects.

Other sources of surnames, particularly before they became hereditary, are discussed in Chapter 6, helping you to work out whether your name of interest is locative (e.g. Stonehouse), describing a relationship (e.g. Simmons), occupational (e.g. Miller), status-related (e.g. Freeman), or a nickname (e.g. Gaunt). Learning more about the history and geography of the area where your ancestors lived, and studying the local trades and wider economy, will greatly increase your understanding of the wider context as you follow your family back through time in the records.

Chapter 7 highlights more sources of family information that you might be able to find if your ancestors owned or worked in a shop or business in Oxfordshire, such as advertising materials of various kinds, trade directories and maps, surveys, photographs, and even the products themselves in some cases. This kind of material is invaluable for adding to your appreciation of your ancestors' lives, and adding colour to your family history.

Chapter 8 helps us to understand what was happening as we follow our ancestors through the census records, using the wider context to explain why their occupations may have changed. It also shows how the same surnames can often be found carrying out the same occupations, and this is another way to approach your family history.

Learning more about a trade that your ancestors followed is a valuable way of discovering new records and making sense of family connections and wider networks that affected some of the choices your family made. Chapter 9 illustrates this through the trade of coopers, but the suggestions also apply to other trades, for example thinking about how apprenticeships worked, where jobs would have been found, the involvement of family members, including children, and the community networks that would have been so important to your family members.

We hope that Chapter 10 will encourage you to take a DNA test if you haven't considered it before, and to join any relevant DNA projects. This will be a great contribution to future research, and may help you to gain an insight into whether and how different branches bearing your surname of interest are related to each other. Taking a DNA test can also help you to find relatives who might have more information, photographs, family stories or clues that can help you with your research.

Chapters 11, 12 and 13 provide a focus on the religions that our ancestors followed, giving us another way to approach our research and highlighting the different records available for Roman Catholics, Methodists and Quakers.

Yet again, these chapters highlight the importance of learning as much as possible about the wider context in which our ancestors lived so that we can understand the events that affected them, the pressures they were under, and the decisions that they made.

Notes

1. British History Online. https://www.british-history.ac.uk/.
2. Guild of One-Name Studies. https://one-name.org/.
3. See for example https://www.familytreedna.com/group-project-search and the Oxfordshire DNA Project at www.familytreedna.com/groups/Oxfordshire.

Figure 110. A postcard showing farm workers with their tools by a hay waggon and cart. From a collection of items of the Sims family who lived in Wallingford 1910–27 and Cowley from 1928.

Picture Credits

Unless otherwise stated all pictures were sourced from Picture Oxon, the online image archive of the Oxfordshire History Centre, with kind permission of the History Centre staff. They are © Oxfordshire History Centre, Oxfordshire County Council. These images are referenced by the Picture Oxon reference number (starting POX) and the collection from which they were sourced. Images labelled as VDM are produced by kind permission of the Vale & Downland Museum, Wantage, and the image from the Comrie collection is produced with permission of the photographer Julian Comrie. The Methodist map is produced with the permission of Kate Tiller and is the copyright of Oxfordshire Record Society and Kate Tiller. The Quaker paintings of Marjory Lester are produced with the kind permission of Charles Lester, her son. All other images list the photographer or image owner after the description and are the copyright of the individual photographer.

Picture Oxon can be found from the Oxfordshire History Centre website at: https://www.oxfordshire.gov.uk/residents/leisure-and-culture/history/oxfordshire-history-centre

Foreword
Oxford Spires, POX0003864, Malcolm Graham.

Introduction
Reeves ice cream (VDM), POX575688, Vale and Downland Museum.

Chapter 1: What is an Oxfordshire Surname?
Police group, POX0251019, Oxfordshire History Centre collection; St Giles Fair 1905, Richard Merry.

Chapter 2: Oxfordshire Surname Variants
Osiers working at Fisher Row, POX0112575, and Abel Beesley in punt at Fisher Row, POX0112577, both by Henry Taunt; Druce & Co, POX0061279, Centre for Oxfordshire Studies; Calcutt shop Eynsham, POX0115563, Henry Taunt.

Chapter 3: Oxfordshire Population
Corn Street, Witney, POX570077, Oxfordshire Museums Service.

Chapter 4: Migration in and around Oxfordshire
Clack family, POX0005618, Centre for Oxfordshire Studies; Pether builders including Locks, Minster Lovell Historical Society; Dumbleton village, Sue Honoré; Men shearing sheep, Minster Lovell Historical Society.

Chapter 5: Oxfordshire Surnames derived from Place Names
Bloxham fire engine, POX0562682, Malcolm Graham; Clanfield bus, Sue Honoré; Signs containing locative surnames in Oxfordshire, Sue & Jacques Honoré; Buckingham Street, POX562285, Malcolm Graham.

Chapter 6: Medieval Bynames and Surnames in Langtree Hundred and the Wychwoods
Mapledurham watermill, Kevin Poile; Old Smithy Baker family, POX0000503, Cowley; Barrett family in Wychwood Forest, POX0119181, Hall; Girl on donkey, POX0165346, Centre for Oxfordshire Studies; Gathering thatching straw, POX0144044, Henry Minn; Langley Farmhouse, POX0572703, Oxfordshire Museums Service; Chaundy gravestone, Sue Honoré.

Chapter 7: Advertising Family Businesses in Oxfordshire
Pratley motorcycle van, Michelle Hawke; James Archer Train, POX0081534, Centre for Oxfordshire Studies; Wiblin sausages, POX0081262, Centre for Oxfordshire Studies; Dodge brothers, POX0081539, Centre for Oxfordshire Studies; William Wilkinson's grocery shop, POX0163812, Centre for Oxfordshire Studies and June Whipp; Smart Faulkner shop, POX0600858,

Oxford City Council; Coxeter's shop, POX0107212, Oxfordshire County Libraries; Castle's shop (VDM), POX0575754, Vale and Downland Museum; Butler's shop, POX0600383, Oxford City Council Heritage; Baker's shop, POX0063721, Centre for Oxfordshire Studies; Scrivener's shop, POX0151042, Oxfordshire Museums Service; Lamprey and Son shop, POX0012264, Malcolm Graham; Harris horse and cart, POX0165345, Centre for Oxfordshire Studies; Fred Skuse van, POX0140783, Oxfordshire County Libraries; Bartlett Bros Witney, Aubrey Cummings; Upstone van, Nigel Upstone; Hobbs van, POX0159700, Oxfordshire Museums Service; Adams of Bladon, Bob & Vicki Ashby; White Lion Hotel, POX0081024, Banbury Library; Hitchman poster, POX0571641, Oxfordshire Museums Service; Cottrell's Bacon, POX0081609, Centre for Oxfordshire Studies; Oliver & Gurden cake wrapper, POX0067099, Centre for Oxfordshire Studies; Hitchman bottles, POX0570635, Oxfordshire Museums Service; Oxford Covered market, Charles Clark sausages, POX0101918, Taunt.

Chapter 8: Oxfordshire Village Life: Changes in the Nineteenth Century

Cattle in Bletchingdon, POX0184374, Packer; Chalgrove Manor, Kevin Poile; Tadmarton villages by cottage, POX0169522, Packer; Barnes Store Brize Norton, POX0118173, Henry Taunt; Charles Gillett, Yvonne Hiley; Hornsby traction engine (VDM), POX0576074, Vale and Downland Museum; Oxford narrowboats, POX0149880, Minn.

Chapter 9: Tracing Coopers in Oxfordshire

Pyne's sketches of coopers, POX0159813, Oxfordshire Museums Service; Morland coopers, POX0162354, Abingdon Museum; Spring Street in Chipping Norton, POX0570554, Oxfordshire Museums Service; Clinch's Brewery in Witney, POX0570329, Oxfordshire Museums Service.

Chapter 11: Surnames of Roman Catholics in Oxfordshire

Priest and monks at monastery, POX0065883, Minn; Stonor Park, POX0009592, Comrie; St. Ignatius, St. Clements, POX0108008, Taunt; East Hendred Roman Catholic chapel, POX0128143, Oxfordshire County Libraries; Heythrop House 1850, POX0076356, Prints & Drawings; Mapledurham chapel POX072607, Malcolm Graham; Fettiplace Monument (left and right side) at Swinbrook, Jacques Honoré.

Chapter 12: Methodists in Oxfordshire

John Wesley, POX0067255, Beesley; Wesley pulpit, POX0143341, Taunt; Methodist places of worship in Oxfordshire, 1851, reproduced from *An Historical Atlas of Oxfordshire* (2010), copyright Kate Tiller and Oxfordshire Record Society; Calthorp Lane, Banbury, POX0165144, Banbury Library; Methodist Picnic, Richard Merry; Early family portrait, POX0091325, Taunt; Charles Early blue plaque, Jacques Honoré; Charterville cottage, Aubrey Cummings; Lily Jael Wheeler, Helen Sutton; Epwell, POX0191770, Packer.

Chapter 13: Quakers in Oxfordshire

Quaker Meeting House sign, Sue Honoré; Permission to hold Quaker meetings, Charlbury 1689, POX0148348, Oxfordshire County Libraries; Meeting House at Charlbury with graves, POX0117610, Henry Taunt; Bocardo Prison, POX0078880, Prints & Drawings; Quaker Meeting House Banbury, POX0199870, Marjory Lester, Parish Packages; Inside Quaker Meeting House, POX0199871, Marjory Lester, Parish Packages; Sibford School, POX0196617, Packer. More on Marjory Lester can be found at www.stepping-back.co.uk.

Chapter 14: Implications for Family Historians

Farm workers with waggon, POX0560595, Oxfordshire Museums Service.

Index

Index entries that refer to a surname rather than an individual or a place name are listed in SMALL CAPS. *Please browse the list to find all possible spellings of your name of interest. (They are not cross-referenced.)*

BANK, DE, 244
BANKS, 214
BANNISTER, 203
BANTING, 12
Banwell Ratio, 3
Baptism records, viii, 2, 3, 5, 13, 14, 15, 16,
19, 25, 27, 28, 29, 30, 31, 33, 34, 35, 36,
37, 38, 50, 51, 52, 53, 56, 59, 60, 85, 135,
161, 240
BAR(E)FOOT, 32, 39, 168, 212, 215
BARBER, 205, 216
Barford St John, 197
Barford St Michael, 53, 74, 197
BARKER, 225
Barking, Essex, 172
BARLOW(E), 87, 158, 216
BARNARD, 215, 221
BARNCOTT, 204
Barnes Stores, 131
BARNES, 216, 222
Barnett family, 158
BARNWELL, 225
BARRAN, 224
Barrett family, 96
Barrett-Mockler family, 211
BARRETT, 203, 209, 211, 225
BARROW, 224
BARRY, 203
BARTHOLOMEW, 218, 224
BARTLET(T), 30, 37, 40, 225
Bartlett Brothers, 119, 121
Bartlett family, 137, 158
Bartlett, A. H., 138
Bartlett, C. N., 138
Bartlett, H. J., 138
Bartlett, H. S., 138
Bartlett, H., 138
Barton Abbey, 197
Barton-on-the-Heath, Warwickshire, 69
BARTON, 79
BASEL(E)Y, 14, 39
BASKERFELD, 200
BASSON, 245
BASTON, 54, 245
BATCHELOR, 48, 199, 213
BATEMAN, 209, 215
BATES, 207, 208

BATHE, 205
Batsford, Gloucestershire, 66
BATT(S), 19, 40, 245
BATTINISON, 209
BAUGHAN, 241
Baughan, Thomas, 173
BAUGHEN, 30
BAYLEY / BAYLIE, 218, 219
Bayley family, 139
BAYLIS, 163
Bazeley family, 152, 157
BEALE, 241
BEAMES, 209
BEAMSLEY, 27, 36, 87
Beattie, James, 245
BEAUFOREST, 203
BEAUMOND, 220
BECK(E), 207, 219
BECKINSALE, 30, 40, 86
BECKL(E)Y, 20, 225
BEDALL, 197
BEDDIN(G), 12
Bedfordshire, 82
BEDINGFIELD, 225
BEDWYN, 12
BEECH, 222
BEECHEY, 37, 40
BEESLEY, 14, 30, 54
Beesley, Abel, 13
Beesley, Alfred, 230, 257
Beesley's Rush Works, 14
Begbroke, 197
BEISLEY, 14
Belcher family, 158
BELCHER, 220
BELEBOUCHE, 95
BELL, 226
Bellson, Richard, 152
Belson family, 158
BELSON, 158, 196
Belson, Thomas, 187, 196
BENE, 211
BENFORD, 221
BENION, 220
BENNELL, 12
BENNETT, 163, 220, 221, 224, 225, 226
Bennett, John, 245